RADICAL BEHAVIORISM:
THE PHILOSOPHY
AND THE SCIENCE

RADICAL BEHAVIORISM:

THE PHILOSOPHY AND
THE SCIENCE

MECCA CHIESA

Authors Cooperative, Publishers
SARASOTA, FLORIDA

RADICAL BEHAVIORISM:
THE PHILOSOPHY AND THE SCIENCE
Copyright © 1994 by Mecca Chiesa

Library of Congress Catalog Card Number 93-73792
ISBN: 0-9623311-4-7

Authors Cooperative, Publishers
Sarasota, FL 34236
http://www.authorscooperative.com

Printed in the United States of America

To my parents
Catherine and Mario Chiesa

Preface

Psychology students consistently note the lack of unity in the discipline. Psychology seems a motley and chaotic collection of ideas, practices, and competing theoretical and explanatory systems. Putting together a picture of psychology and evaluating approaches and systems is a daunting task. A single theme, however, runs through psychology and through a psychologist's training—an emphasis on experimental methods as a means of tackling questions and making assertions about people and their behavior. Psychologists claim that their assertions are scientifically derived and thus reliable.

Like other psychology students, I was trained as an undergraduate in the concepts and methods of hypothesis testing and statistical analysis of data. And, like other psychology students, I was involved as a subject in some of the experiments that formed a part of our training in research methods. Something about those methods and the subsequent assertions we were asked to make troubled me, although at the time I could not articulate my discomfort. When we were instructed, on the basis of a significance test, to assert, "Event x affects behavior in this way," I protested that measures from some of the subjects in the group (often including my own) contradicted this assertion. How could I claim to have demonstrated a scientific fact when I could see in my own data that it did not hold, that it simply did not apply to some of the individuals involved in the experiment? Since no one else seemed troubled, I assumed I had misunderstood some crucial aspect of methods training and tried hard to ignore my reservations about the scientific status of psychological assertions.

Turning to evaluations and critiques of research methods in psychology did not help a great deal. They seemed more concerned with undermining the scientific approach, with arguing, for example, that science is not an appropriate method for understanding human conduct. Many attempted to develop alternatives to the scientific approach, but these alternatives seemed only to add to the confusing array of discourses and to multiply explanatory systems still further.

The distinctive philosophy of radical behaviorism offered a scientific alternative to the methods that dominate psychological texts and journals. Its critique of concepts and methods and its examination of psychology's practices helped give voice to my discomfort by directing me to consider some of the most fundamental of scientific issues. Rather than worrying about whether there were enough subjects in a group or if they had been randomly assigned, it directed me to philosophical issues underlying the statistical treatment of human conduct and the scientific logic and utility of using large numbers and group designs. It led me to question the formal restriction of hypothesis testing as a means of discovering regularities. It encouraged me to look at the kinds of theoretical constructs that psychologists use to explain behavior, to ask questions about the scientific status of those constructs, and thus to examine concepts such as causation and explanation in science. Radical behaviorism's coherence as a philosophical and scientific system helped clear up many of my confusions relating to scientific practices in psychology.

This book is my attempt to bring together and to articulate radical behaviorism's position on issues relating to how we ask questions about behavior and how it can be explained within a scientific framework. Some may disagree with my interpretation, others may find aspects of it helpful to their own understanding. Above all, I hope that this book will do for other students and practitioners of psychology what writing it has done for me: provide an integrative theme for evaluating the multiplicity of theoretical approaches in psychology today. As the practice of science establishes order out of chaos in the world, the theme of science provides a means for establishing order out of chaos in psychology.

It is my pleasure to acknowledge important contributions to the production of this book. Derek Blackman of the University of Wales, Cardiff, introduced me to radical behaviorism, guided and encouraged me through my doctoral studies, and has continued since then to give generously of his time by reading and commenting on parts of the manuscript. Without his consistent support and enthusiasm, it is doubtful that this project would have been completed, and I am sincerely grateful to him. Andrew Belsey introduced me to the fascinations of the philosophy of science and has helped to clarify many of the philosophical issues discussed in this book. Marc Richelle of the University of Liege, Belgium, offered encouraging and helpful comments on the doctoral thesis from which this book is derived. The influence of B. F. Skinner's scholarship will be evident throughout. In addition, the scholarly works of Phil Hineline, Vicki Lee, Jack Marr, Murray Sidman, and Laurence Smith contributed substantially to my appreciation of philosophical and scientific issues in radical behaviorism and psychology as a whole. I am additionally grateful to Murray Sidman for his enthusiasm for this project and for his patient and careful editing. My colleague, Sandy Hobbs of the University of Paisley, and Phil Elliott read and commented on several chapters, and I believe those chapters are now clearer as a result. Harry Chiesa gave time to proofread and Mike Harries, yet again, turned hideously clumsy sentences into recognizable English.

A shorter work extracting themes from the book can be found in the special edition of the *American Psychologist* devoted to B. F. Skinner's life and work (November, 1992).

On References

Many of B. F. Skinner's papers are now published in collected works. For example, *Cumulative Record: A Selection of Papers* (Skinner, 1972) contains papers dating back to 1931. So that the reader is able to place Skinner's work in a historical as well as philosophical context, the papers referred to in *Cumulative Record* are also given their original date and their original reference, although quotations and page numbers are taken from *Cumulative Record*. One example is Skinner (1950/1972), which refers to *Are Theories of Learning Necessary?* Quotations from this paper are taken from *Cumulative Record* and page numbers refer to that work. But the reader will also note that the paper was originally published in

1950 and will be able to place the arguments therein in their historical context, in relation to psychological debates of that time.

Other works, such as Ernst Mach's *The Science of Mechanics* and David Hume's *Enquiries*, carry the original date of publication for the same reason. In cases where a paper or other work is separated from its original publication date by only a few years, it has been deemed unnecessary to give the original publication date.

Contents

Contents

Contents

Chapter 1

Introduction

Profound changes have taken place throughout the philosophy of science since the turn of the century, when physics was thrown into turmoil by evidence that the principles of Newtonian science previously thought to be universal truths could not be applied to certain types of physical phenomena. The philosophers of the Vienna Circle (Logical Positivists) attempted a program of defining the limits of scientific explanation and eliminating metaphysics from such explanations. More lately, theorists like Kuhn (1962) and Lakatos (see Lakatos and Musgrave, 1970) have swept away popular notions of absolutes and ultimate truths in science by pointing out that even in the process of validating scientific knowledge there is a measure of arbitrary decision making. Since Kuhn and Lakatos, it is no longer feasible to argue that the world is just so because science claims it to be, and the possibility of pure observation (observation independent of theory, uninformed by background assumptions) has similarly dropped out of the mainstream of acceptable opinion (for example, see Hanson, 1958).

The development of the social sciences has helped generate new insights and critiques in the philosophy of science. Indeed, Thomas Kuhn acknowledged that his concept of the paradigm arose partly out of puzzlement over "the number and extent of the overt disagreements between social scientists about the nature of legitimate scientific problems and methods" (Kuhn, 1962, p. viii) when measured against the relative cohesion of the philosophical and methodological underpinnings of natural science. At the end of the 20th century, philosophers and scientists continue to debate the implications of new views of science, and of new views of nature given by contemporary science. The impact of such debates is neatly captured in the words of Steve Woolgar when he states: "One of the most remarkable features of modern thought is the extent to which ideas about science have changed" (Woolgar, 1988, p. 9).

Broadly speaking, this continuing debate is founded on the shift from certainty to uncertainty in science and in the philosophy of science. New findings in physics have demonstrated that principles once thought certain, the principles of Newtonian science which, it was thought, could be applied to all physical phenomena, no longer describe certain aspects of nature. The physical world no longer seems as straightforward and calculable as it once did. Similarly, new critiques in the philosophy of science and developments in the social study of science have undermined cherished notions of the everyday work of scientists proceeding in a logical, rational, and objective way. The behavior of scientists and the social organization of science are themselves now subjects for debate. The certainty of scientific knowledge that once characterized our thinking about science has given way under the weight of scientific evidence and philosophical argument to a recognition that scientific knowledge may be as much a product of human behavior as it is a description of the world "out there."

These new views of science and nature, and the implications of the loss of certainty in science and in the philosophy of science, have been especially considered over the past two decades. An illustrative set of titles, with authors ranging from science journalists to Nobel prizewinning chemists, indicates the breadth and depth of this new thinking: *The Tao of Physics* (Capra, 1975); *Mathematics: The Loss of Certainty* (Kline, 1980); *The Death of Nature: Women, Ecology, and the Scientific Revolution* (Merchant, 1982); *The Turning Point: Science, Society and the Rising Culture* (Capra, 1983); *Order out of Chaos: Man's new dialogue with nature* (Prigogine and Stengers, 1985); *Mathematics and the Search for Knowledge* (Kline, 1985); *The Cosmic Blueprint* (Davies, 1987); *Chaos: Making a new science* (Gleick, 1988); *A Brief History of Time* (Hawking, 1988); and *Does God Play Dice?* (Stewart, 1989). Several of these titles are published in popular paperback editions, indicating that they are not aimed solely at an academic audience. The scientific revolution of the early part of the 20th century has generated a philosophical literature that challenges our thinking to an extent that may be called a philosophical revolution at its end.

One aspect of science unaltered by the philosophical revolution is its prestige. Scientists and their work continue to be held in high regard, viewed with respect and consequently granted institutional and financial support to an extent unmatched by other disciplines. Furthermore, science is associated with ideas like reliability, with the notion that assertions are confidently made on the basis of evidence, that explanations given by scientists are not invented but firmly derived from observation and measurement of natural phenomena. It is widely felt that science is distinguishable from myth or personal opinion, that when scientists make claims about the world they do so not on the basis of cherished cultural assumptions or personal bias but on the basis of experiment or some other form of data manipulation. For this reason, disciplines other than physics, chemistry, biology, mechanics, and so on strive to develop rigorous methodology, to be able to claim reliability for their assertions and thus to claim some of the prestige associated with reliability.

Psychology and Science

Scientific psychology has likewise undergone profound changes in the course of the present century. As a scientific discipline, psychology is naturally concerned with the impact of broad philosophy of science debates as well as with its own internal debates over the nature of its subject matter and appropriate methods of investigation. Today, the discipline is as much concerned with philosophical questions as when it emerged from academic departments of philosophy into a discrete field of inquiry. Many areas of investigation that currently constitute psychology can be traced in the literature of philosophy and found to be carrying out a program that seeks answers to age-old questions on the nature of persons, their behavior, their relationship to the world of things and other people, the possibilities and limits of their own perceptual processes, their potential as humans, the relation of biology to culture, and so on.

There is no generally agreed definition of the broad term, Psychology. The discipline is best thought of as comprising a set of subdisciplines, each with its own view of the person, its own questions, and its own methods for tackling those questions. Where the discipline is given form, in introductory texts, it is usually organized around six major themes: Biological, Ethological, Behavioral, Cognitive, Psychodynamic, and Phenomenological. Further demarcation adds social psychology, neuropsychology, physiological psychology, developmental psychology, artificial intelligence, learning and memory, motivation and emotion, abnormal psychology, and others.

In the same way that the broad discipline has no generally agreed definition, each subdiscipline also may not agree on the precise nature of its subject matter or on a set of appropriate methods. There may even be overlap between two areas that seem separate. For example, a social psychologist may object to laboratory investigations on the grounds that the laboratory is itself a social setting and that field observation is the only logical and acceptable way of doing social psychology. Methodologically, this type of psychology overlaps with ethology, which is generally taken to be the study of other species in their own environments. Similarly, developmental psychology contains at least two distinct trends, cognition and social learning. Recently, social/cognitive developmental psychology has set about the task of unifying these two trends. The same overlapping and divergence can be found among many other subdisciplines in contemporary psychology. The broad discipline lacks a unified framework or set of principles that define the field and guide research. Beyond their everyday research, psychologists still debate the fundamentals and contest the overall framework. Vicki Lee noted that the lack of unity in psychology is more fundamental than a simple incompatibility between interpretations of particular experiments, "It has to do with what counts as the subject matter of psychology, with what questions we should ask about this subject matter, with how we should go about finding answers to these questions, with the status of existing psychological knowledge, and with whether psychology can be a science.

Introduction

Psychologists do not agree upon these basic matters" (Lee, 1988, pp. 2-3). Each subdiscipline garners its data using various techniques and measures those data against its own general framework or theory, with little generalization of principles from one theoretical approach to another. Perhaps the only unifying principle is a commitment to the practices of science (in the broadest sense of that word). Psychologists look to science for the means of settling philosophical questions and it is safe to say, therefore, that they pursue an empirical epistemology. The physical sciences have demonstrated their power to understand, explain, predict, and manipulate the world around us, and the hope is that their methods will prove equally powerful when applied to questions of human psychology. Bertrand Russell, among others, expressed this faith in the superior explanatory power of science over other methods of knowledge gathering: "I have no doubt that, insofar as philosophical knowledge is possible, it is by these methods (the methods of science) that it must be sought. I have also no doubt that, by these methods, many ancient problems are completely soluble" (Russell, 1946, p. 788).

Some, however, feel that psychology has gone too far in its commitment to science and that this commitment has been allowed to overshadow the real nature of its subject matter. Sigmund Koch, for example, argued, "Ever since its stipulation into existence as an independent science, psychology has been far more concerned with being a science than with courageous and self-determining confrontation of its historically significant subject matter. Its history has been largely a matter of emulating the methods, forms, symbols of the established sciences, especially physics" (Koch, 1961, p. 629). There are others who, while retaining their commitment to a scientific approach, recognize the modern philosophy of science position that science is not the straightforward, logical pursuit it was once thought to be. B. F. Skinner, for example, wrote, "If we are interested in perpetuating the practices responsible for the present corpus of scientific knowledge, we must keep in mind that some very important parts of the scientific process do not now lend themselves to mathematical, logical, or any other formal treatment. We do not know enough about human behavior to know how the scientist does what he does" (Skinner, 1959, pp. 360-361). Still others caution that psychology must keep abreast of new developments in the physical sciences in order not to model itself after a form of science that no longer exists. In his 1955 address to the American Psychological Association, the physicist Robert Oppenheimer warned, "The worst of all possible misunderstandings would be that psychology be influenced to model itself after a physics which is not there any more, which has been quite outdated" (Oppenheimer, 1956, p. 134).

Given psychology's commitment to science (again, in the broadest sense of that word) as a means of knowledge gathering, the breadth of debates and disputes that the commitment engenders, and the modern debate in the philosophy of science generated by the shift from certainty to uncertainty, it is no exaggeration to claim that philosophy of science issues are fundamental concerns for contemporary psychology. They are fundamental concerns also for a society relying on psychological assertions. Psychologists' expertise is drawn upon in a broad range of settings: in education, social work, industrial selection practices, and clinical situations where behavior has somehow "gone wrong," bringing distress to individuals, their families and friends, and to legal and medical institutions. As a scientific discipline, psychology must be concerned with current issues in the philosophy of science while continuing its internal debates over the nature of its subject matter and appropriate methods of investigation. A society that accords status and value to scientific assertions, that relies on claims made by psychologists in educational, social work, clinical settings, and so on, must also be concerned with the nature of science as it is practiced by psychologists and thus with the nature of psychology's scientific claims.

Radical Behaviorism: A Distinct Philosophy of Science

It has already been argued that psychology is best thought of as a set of subdisciplines, each of which garners data by various means and measures those data against its own general framework or theory. It has also been noted that there is little or no generalization of principles across theoretical approaches and that even within a subdiscipline there may be

Introduction

disagreement over the nature of the subject matter and the appropriateness of techniques. As such, the philosophy of science of the broad discipline and even that of many of the subdisciplines is difficult to characterize. Although a commitment to scientific method unites the subdisciplines, this does not mean that the commitment is to the same kind of science.

Perhaps the most coherent philosophy of science in psychology today is radical behaviorism, the philosophy that informs behavior analysis (or functional analysis, as it is also known). Norman Malcolm, for example, correctly described behaviorism as "essentially a *philosophical* doctrine" (Malcolm, 1964, p. 144), and Hillix and Marx declared it to be "the closest thing to a school or paradigm among all modern positions" (Hillix & Marx, 1974, p. 264). The definition given by Skinner himself describes behaviorism not only as a philosophical position, but specifically as a philosophy of science: "Behaviorism is not the scientific study of behavior but *a philosophy of science* concerned with the subject matter and methods of psychology" (Skinner, 1969, p. 221, emphasis added).

This philosophy of science (and the behavior analysis it informs) is distinct within psychology in two major respects. First, it is characterized by a degree of internal coherence unmatched by other subdisciplines. Its subject matter is carefully defined and generally agreed upon by researchers within the field. Its methods of data collection, analysis, and interpretation are also agreed upon to an extent not found in other areas, and it is this internal agreement among workers in the field which prompts Hillix and Marx to describe it as coming close to a "school" or "paradigm." Second, it is distinct from the contemporary mainstream of experimental psychology in that its historical influences have led to the development of a descriptive, observational, and integrative system of inductively derived principles, in contrast to the theory-driven, hypothetico-deductively derived, statistical principles of most branches of experimental psychology. Radical behaviorism and behavior analysis generate a coherent and distinctive explanatory system within the broad discipline of psychology.

B. F. Skinner consistently supported the view that a scientific understanding of human affairs would go a long way toward unravelling and finding solutions for the innumerable and complex social problems facing the modern world. It is arguable that, given the emphasis on scientific method throughout psychology generally, this view might be common to all psychologists. Yet radical behaviorism in general (and often B. F. Skinner in particular) has suffered some of the severest criticisms levelled against psychology. These criticisms have come from within and without the psychological community. Michael Binyon, profiling B. F. Skinner for *The Times Higher Education Supplement* some years ago, began his article by noting, "Perhaps no academic has suffered as much vituperation as B. F. Skinner, the eminent behaviorist. His books have been received with a hail of critical gunfire; his psychology has been called vacuous, irresponsible, unscientific, without a psyche; he himself has been called a fascist, a megalomaniac, a cold-hearted manipulator; and these accusations have come from distinguished figures: Noam Chomsky, Thomas Szasz, Carl Rogers, Rollo May, Stephen Spender, to name a few" (Binyon, 1977, p. 7). Skinner the person and behaviorism the philosophy evoke strong reaction from a broad range of scientists and philosophers, from complete works such as Mackenzie's (1977) *Behaviorism and the Limits of Scientific Method* to abrupt and dismissive comments from an alternative viewpoint such as Michael Eysenck's: "There is no doubt that contemporary research in the field of cognition represents a strong reaction against the facile approach of Behaviorism" (Eysenck, 1984, p. 20).

Skinner's name and his radical behaviorist philosophy have been cited in recent decades in relation to the modern philosophy of science debate concerning the "new world view" and its implications. Unfortunately, serious errors of interpretation within the debate lead to radical behaviorism and behavior analysis being linked to philosophical traditions that do not accurately describe them. Such errors of interpretation are frequent, and not restricted to this case. They are inherent dangers in every field of scholarship, wherever ideas are used selectively and passed on in condensed form. Participants in the debate have sometimes gone to secondary sources for their picture of radical behaviorism and have thus perpetuated errors already in the literature. Unless radical behaviorism is accurately represented, its proper place within the debate will not

Introduction

be understood and any commentary, critical or otherwise, will refer to an erroneously perceived position rather than a stated one.

Some of the notable misrepresentations of radical behaviorism within the broader psychological literature have been covered by Todd and Morris (1983), Cooke (1984), and Morris (1985). MacCorquodale (1969), Czubaroff (1988), and Sherrard (1988) have applied themselves specifically to the errors in Chomsky's (1959) influential and damaging review of Skinner's *Verbal Behavior* (Skinner, 1957). MacCorquodale, for example, describes Chomsky's review as "relentlessly negative" (MacCorquodale, 1969, p. 831) and notes that one of the crucial errors in the review is an interpretation that mistakenly places the Skinnerian system in the same tradition as Watson and Hull: "Unfortunately for his purposes, Chomsky did not grasp the difference between Skinnerian and Watsonian-Hullian behaviorism, and his criticisms, although stylistically effective, were mostly irrelevant to *Verbal Behavior*" (MacCorquodale, 1969, p. 841). Czubaroff and Sherrard focused on the style of Chomsky's review and suggested that his critique was motivated as much by concern "to gain professional attention and ascendency" (Czubaroff, 1988, p. 324) as by concern with scholarly disputation. Whatever else Chomsky's attack may have been, it was based on a mistaken interpretation of Skinner's underlying philosophy and consequently, it missed the theoretical mark.

Although philosophy of science issues form the core of radical behaviorism, this core has not been fully articulated in one place but is threaded throughout the work of B. F. Skinner and other writers who adopt the position. Perhaps the nearest to such a work is Laurence Smith's *Behaviorism and Logical Positivism: A Reassessment of the Alliance* (Smith, 1986), comparing the work of three behaviorists (or neobehaviorists, as Smith refers to them) to that of the logical positivists in order to test a claim made by Sigmund Koch (1961), Brian D. Mackenzie (1977), and Thomas H. Leahey (1980). The claim is that behaviorism and logical positivism are allied intellectual traditions and, as such, behaviorism must share the fate of logical positivism. Or as Smith recounts the claim, "the failure of one reflected on the viability of the other" (Smith, 1986, p. 13). The penultimate of ten chapters in this closely argued book is devoted to Skinner's philosophy of science and remains specific to the original research question—a reassessment of the alliance between behaviorism and logical positivism.

Although not venturing far beyond the bounds set by the original research question, Smith presents a well documented case against linking behaviorism too closely with logical positivism. His work should finally dispense with this often cited and erroneous reference. But Smith himself makes a link which, though it is common throughout such literature, may serve to perpetuate yet another error—the notion that a philosophical continuity is to be found among various strands of behaviorism. Although he clarifies some of the distinctions between different behavioral traditions in his chapter on Skinner's psychology of science, this approach is discussed in a work tracing strands of behaviorism through Tolman and Hull before reaching the Skinnerian stance. Any reader would be forgiven for assuming some kind of continuity in these approaches, but under close examination the Skinnerian position will show fundamental divergences from earlier behavioral positions. These divergences result in a wholly distinct view of the subject matter and lead to different sets of scientific questions. That this position comes under the behaviorist heading at all will eventually be shown to be an accident of history.

A broader treatment of the relation between the Skinnerian system and other approaches in contemporary psychology is given by Lee (1988). Lee argues that, contrary to popular interpretation, contemporary psychology is characterized by an underlying input-output formulation of behavior and that (again, contrary to popular interpretation) Skinner's radical behaviorism holds the promise of moving psychology beyond this mechanistic framework. Lee's work should also help dispense with erroneous interpretations of radical behaviorism, but there remains a need to distinguish this position from other behavioral trends and to articulate its philosophy of science in a single work so that its distinctiveness from other behavioral traditions, as well as from other areas of contemporary psychology, may be understood. Furthermore, clarifying Skinner's philosophy of science will help place radical behaviorism in its proper position in relation to the new-world-view debate, for dispensing with erroneous interpretations (as Smith and Lee have done) will allow participants in the debate a better understanding of radical behaviorism's relation to both the old and the new world view given by science. Finally, it will allow other readers to assess the scientific claims made by behavior analysts in their laboratory procedures and in the application of their science in the wide range of settings they share with other psychologists.

Recurring Errors: Behaviorism, Mechanism, Dualism

The first and most ubiquitous error to be tackled places radical behaviorism in the tradition of S-R or input-output psychology. This error assumes that the term Behaviorism refers to a unified approach whose various adherents subscribe to the same definition of the subject matter of psychology, to the same philosophy of science, to the same view of the behaving person, and to the same form of data interpretation. Skinner and radical behaviorism are frequently lumped together under the same heading as Pavlov, Watson, Tolman, Hull, Thorndike, Spence, Guthrie, and others, and subjected to the same critical analysis as these other figures as if they shared a common philosophical and theoretical heritage.

It has already been noted that Smith's (1986) inclusion of Skinner's philosophical position in a work tracing strands of behaviorism through Tolman and Hull may help to perpetuate the view that the Skinnerian system is continuous with these other behavioral trends (although Smith himself recognizes the distinctions). Mackenzie (1977), in *Behaviorism and the Limits of Scientific Method*, discusses the Skinnerian system along with other behavioral accounts and applies broadly the same critique to radical behaviorism as to other kinds of behaviorism. Mahoney (1989) also allied radical behaviorism to other behavioral traditions by describing Skinner as having had a "preoccupation with input-output functions" (Mahoney, 1989, p. 1373). In the same paper, Mahoney makes the connection more subtly by implying that a critique of Pavlovian conditioning also functions as a critique of Skinnerian psychology. He notes, "Respected scientists [have] challenged or revised radical behaviorist

11

accounts of learning" (Mahoney, 1989, p. 1374) and cites several papers as examples. By citing the paper, *Pavlovian conditioning: It's not what you think it is* (Rescorla, 1988) he implies that a challenge to Pavlovian accounts of learning must also be a challenge to Skinnerian accounts. Even the most superficial reading of Skinner's work illustrates that his system differs in important scientific and philosophical ways from Pavlov's, but Mahoney's assertion and subsequent reference imply the opposite.

The second error this book will repair is the charge that radical behaviorism provides a mechanistic account of human behavior and belongs to the old world view of Newtonian science. This charge comes from within the psychological literature and from participants in the debate concerning the implications of the new world view given by modern physics.

Skinnerian philosophy has been linked to the tradition of Newtonian science in several places and it is claimed that radical behaviorism belongs to a world view and a scientific practice that is now outdated. Mahoney (1989), for example, states, "The Newtonian ("billiard ball") form of determinism so stridently emulated by orthodox behaviorists was abandoned by most physical scientists in the decades following the 1927 Copenhagen Interpretation of Quantum Mechanics" (Mahoney, 1989, p. 1373). Mahoney first argues that radical behaviorism is committed to Newtonian causation, which allows him to assert that since this view of causation is anachronistic, radical behaviorism has "isolated itself from and [come] to lag behind changing perspectives on the nature and practice of optimal scientific inquiry" (Mahoney, 1989, p. 1373). If the Skinnerian system is indeed committed to causation in the Newtonian sense, then Mahoney's assertion may well be justified. Clarifying the form of causation advocated by radical behaviorism will, however, show that Mahoney's interpretation of its causal mode (Newtonian causation) is inaccurate, and his subsequent assertion that radical behaviorism "lags behind changing perspectives" is therefore also inaccurate.

Macleod (1970) also links Skinner's radical behaviorism to the Newtonian scientific tradition. Macleod's argument proceeds in the following way:

Introduction

Newtonian science was the inspiration for a group of philosophers "who were willing to play with the idea that the realm of natural law might encompass the phenomena of human mentality";

John Locke became the spokesperson for the "Newtonian conception of man" when he argued that it was possible to have a science of mind analogous to the science of physical nature. "This involved the assumption of *mental* elements analogous to physical particles, and the assumption that to explain anything complex is to break it down into its elements";

Locke's successors attempted to demonstrate "how all the complexities of human experience and behavior can be reduced to combinations of mental or behavioral elements" (Note that without warning the terms of this discussion are expanded from simply "human mentality" and "mental elements" to "all the complexities of human experience and behavior.");

The "Newtonian conception of mind" was elaborated in Britain by the British Associationists, in Germany by Wundt, Helmholtz, and others, in Russia by the Pavlovians, and in the United States by John B. Watson "and his friends" (1970, pp. 209, 210).

In tracing the influence of Newtonian science this way, and by expanding his terminology to include not only mental but also experiential and behavioral elements, Macleod manages to link Skinner to the concept of Newtonian science, concluding that, "The most brilliant contemporary representative of the Newtonian doctrine of man is in my opinion B. F. Skinner" (Macleod, 1970, p. 210). He implies, like Mahoney, that the Skinnerian philosophy of science is outmoded in relation to contemporary physics: "It is interesting to note that long after the physical sciences, prodded by Einstein and others, have given up the elementaristic explanation of physical nature, we still have psychologists who insist that a psychological explanation must involve the reduction of the complex to the simple" (Macleod, 1970, p. 210). Precisely what Macleod means by "elementaristic explanation" is not clear, but presumably it refers to his previous assertion that a science of mind concerned with "*mental* elements analogous to physical particles" was a goal for Locke and his successors. If this is the case, Macleod is claiming that behavior analytic accounts are analogous to accounts of physical phenomena couched in terms of interacting physical particles. Again, this claim will be shown to be erroneous.

Both Macleod and Mahoney charge radical behaviorism with "lagging behind" contemporary views of science and of clinging to anachronisms. This argument concerning new and old world views has been most thoroughly articulated by Merchant (1982) and Capra (1983), both of whom also relate radical behaviorism to the now outmoded Newtonian (mechanistic) world view.

They argue that Newtonian science drew primarily on the machine metaphor of natural phenomena, a model that overshadowed an older organic view of nature and derived its power from the success of seventeenth century industrialization. Merchant describes machines as "structural models for western ontology and epistemology" (Merchant, 1982) and elaborates thus:

> The imagery, iconography, and literary metaphor associated with machines extended the experiences of everyday life to the realm of the imagination, where machines became symbols for the ordering of life itself. Out of such symbolic universes evolve conceptual universes as new definitions of reality replace the old. As the machine and clock increased their symbolic power as root metaphors, in response to society's changing needs, wants, and purposes, the symbolic force of the organism declined in plausibility and the organic conceptual framework underwent a fundamental transformation. The images and symbols associated with the machines of

everyday life helped to mediate the transition between frameworks (p. 227).

Capra also argues that an older organic view of nature gave way under the influence of the machine metaphor, culminating in a world view he refers to as "The Newtonian World-Machine" (Capra, 1983, p. 37): "The notion of an organic, living, and spiritual universe was replaced by that of the world as a machine, and the world-machine became the dominant metaphor of the modern era. This development was brought about by revolutionary changes in physics and astronomy, culminating in the achievements of Copernicus, Galileo, and Newton" (Capra, 1983, p. 38). Newtonian science, it is argued, gave us a view of nature as a "great machine" operating in much the same way as the emerging industrial machines of that age. Modern physics, however, reasserts the organic metaphor, a metaphor that speaks of nature as an interrelated whole. Furthermore, modern physics challenges the notion of the scientist as objective observer, since the scientist, too, is involved in the interrelations of the subject matter. The mechanistic world view that has dominated the physical sciences (and the social sciences which, it is argued, take their cue from physical science), has passed its zenith and is giving way under the pressure of modern scientific data to an organic world view.

Merchant and Capra both relate Skinnerian philosophy to the old and dying mechanistic world view. Merchant argues, "Attempts to reduce human behavior to statistical probabilities and to condition it by such psychological techniques as those developed by B. F. Skinner are manifestations of the pervasiveness of the mechanistic mode of thought developed by the seventeenth-century scientists" (Merchant, 1982, p. 292). And of Skinner's approach, Capra states, "This, then, is Newtonian psychology par excellence, a psychology without consciousness that reduces all behavior to mechanistic sequences of conditioned responses and asserts that the only scientific understanding of human nature is one that remains within the framework of classical physics and biology....behaviorists still adhere to the mechanistic paradigm and

15

often defend it as the only scientific approach to psychology, thus clearly limiting science to the classical Newtonian framework" (Capra, 1983, p. 181).

Macleod, Merchant, and Capra call for the adoption of a new organic conception of nature to replace the Newtonian, mechanistic conception. Each interprets radical behaviorism as an example of an approach in psychology underpinned by the Newtonian world view. In calling for a new conception, a new underlying metaphor, the older model is cited as a root cause of many current abuses of people and of nature. The old metaphor must go, it is argued, and with it must go the sciences which adopt that metaphor, including radical behaviorism.

Again, it will be demonstrated here that interpretations of radical behaviorism which ally that philosophy to Newtonian science and to a mechanistic account of behavior are misplaced. They attribute historical influence to the wrong scientific tradition and altogether miss the distinction between Newtonian causation and the causal mode that is the basis of radical behaviorism. This error of interpretation adopts the previous error, that Behaviorism refers to a unified approach within psychology, and assumes that the mechanistic accounts given by other strands of behaviorism also characterize radical behaviorist accounts. Billiard ball causation is very much a part of modern psychology, but not of behavior analysis.

The third major error that will be repaired attributes historical influence to Descartes and implies that radical behaviorism accepts Cartesian mind/body duality but ignores the mind or consciousness aspect of that duality. This is linked to the first and second errors mentioned and relies on them being true. If radical behaviorism is philosophically compatible with other strands of behaviorism then it is dualistic since other behavioral traditions accept a mind/body separation as an initial assumption. Furthermore, if radical behaviorism belongs to a mechanistic world view and offers a mechanistic account of human behavior then it is Cartesian in the sense that Descartes is given as one of the major influences on mechanistic thinking.

Merchant and Capra cite both Descartes and Newton as the primary movers of mechanistic thinking in science and in the larger world view given by the old science, while Mahoney argues that Descartes "holds a revered place in the history of behaviorism" (Mahoney, 1989, p. 1373). According to Mahoney, it was Descartes who formalized the mind/body dualism of Greek philosophy, and it was his "mechanistic theory of bodily action" (Mahoney, 1989, p. 1373) and his anticipation of the reflex arc that "won him respect among 20th century behaviorists" (Mahoney, 1989, p. 1373). It is in this context that Mahoney refers to Skinner as being preoccupied with "input-output functions" (Mahoney, 1989, p. 1373).

When he asserts that Descartes "holds a revered place in the history of behaviorism," Mahoney refers to Rachlin's (1970) *Introduction to Modern Behaviorism* as a source. On examining this source, it turns out that Rachlin refers to Descartes and to his mechanical theory as a historical influence on the development of psychology *as a whole*. He argues that Descartes himself was as much influenced by the dominant theological interpretations in his time as modern psychology is influenced by dualistic thinking. Descartes undertook the study of behavior within the theological terms and assumptions of his own time, dividing behavior into voluntary and involuntary realms and thus resolving the problem of free will. Descartes' distinction survives in much of contemporary thinking about human behavior, and it is this point Rachlin emphasizes in his outline of the Cartesian influence on psychology when he notes, "The dualism of Descartes' psychology is the feature that is essential to our understanding of the history of psychology" (Rachlin, 1970, p. 7). Rachlin does not cite Descartes as an influence on the development of behaviorism specifically, but on the development of psychology as a whole. Descartes' mind/body dualism continues to inform much of contemporary psychology, but not Skinnerian psychology.

Other errors are to be clarified in this book. Skinner's position on objectivity, for example, on the relation between observer and observed, will become clear. The interrelation between scientist and subject matter and controlling variables of the behavior of scientists will be shown to be an important feature of the thinking of radical behaviorists, who do not separate observer/observed or knower/known in the traditional way. Scientific behavior, in the radical behaviorist formulation, is as much a product of contingencies of reinforcement, present and past, as other kinds of behavior. When Mahoney correctly states, "there is an increasing recognition that the knower/observer cannot be removed from either the process or the product of knowing" (Mahoney, 1989, p. 1374), he fails at the same time to note that this is in line with Skinner's own arguments and asserts instead that the doctrine of objectivism (in simple terms, the separation of observer from observed) "lies at the core of orthodox behaviorism" (Mahoney, 1989, p. 1374).

These errors will not be addressed in point-by-point fashion but more in the style of an illustration, an articulation of Skinner's philosophy of science that should free it to take its proper place in the new-world-view debate and in contemporary psychology. Once free of the persistent errors that characterize summaries and interpretations of radical behaviorism, the reader will be able better to judge its relation to old and new world views, to dualism and mechanistic thinking, to other strands of behaviorism, and to various branches of contemporary psychology.

Chapter 2 (*Ordinary Language and Science*) illustrates radical behaviorists' concern with the relations between ordinary, vernacular language and the behavior of scientists. Radical behaviorists view as unwise the practice of adopting ordinary language terms uncritically, since its conceptual systems, its syntax and grammar subtly influence the way psychologists view their subject matter. This chapter firmly establishes the principle that scientists are not immune from controlling influences to be found in the wider culture, the principle that the observer is subject to the same scientific laws as the observed.

Chapter 3 (*Science: Aims and Methods*) outlines the broadest distinction between behavior analytic methods and those which comprise the "methodological package" of much of contemporary experimental psychology. The psychological community demands adherence to a rigorous set of scientific procedures, promoting hypothetico-deduction as an indispensable part of those procedures. Radical behaviorism is characterized by a less formal and more inductive approach to science, one that easily dispenses with formal hypotheses and the testing of theoretical statements. Hypothetico-deduction and induction are contrasted, and it is argued that the method of hypothesis is indispensable only for certain types of theories. Speculative theories that explain natural phenomena by reducing them to fundamental mechanisms, that postulate hypothetical mediating entities, must rely on the method of hypothesis since the only way of throwing light on such theories is by deducing their observational consequences and testing for them. Radical behaviorism relies on induction; its theoretical system is data driven, derived from observation, and does not postulate entities beyond its data. As such, it does not agree with formal prescriptions which state that scientific questions cannot be answered without the method of hypothesis.

Chapter 4 (*Aims, Methods, and the Individual*) examines divergent views on variation and individuality. The statistical view considers variation to be an undesirable feature of psychological data and requires individuality to be suppressed in favor of the average. Inferences or generalizations drawn from statistical analysis refer to average effects of variables on average (or ideal) subjects. The biological view of variation and individuality underpins behavior analytic methods, where individuality is built into both the methods and the scientific generalizations that arise from experimentation. Behavior analysts respect and work with the fact that people and other organisms are unique. Striving to find order by developing experimental rather than statistical control of their subject matter, they attempt to trace and eliminate sources of variability rather than to silence it. They derive principles that constitute reliable background knowledge, generalizations that continue to hold true until contradictory evidence comes to light, unlike the body of knowledge derived from the statistical inference model that may be altered or modified by a change in procedure, a change in a merely conventional level of confidence.

Chapter 5 (*Concepts of Causation*) begins with an issue that may seem at first to be unrelated to the notion of causation. Examining the concept of the person as it is found in western culture, however, helps to illuminate how this concept feeds into causal thinking about the person in psychology, how it informs and guides research questions and encourages particular types of explanations. Attendant notions of self-agency relate to the principle of force in a popular conceptualization of causation. The view that human behavior is not amenable to causal description is discussed. Then, the chapter moves on to consider how the concept of causation in science has moved away from popular notions of cause as force, and causal relations as sequential chains, to functional relations and causal webs or networks. The substitution of function for cause is elaborated here. Mechanistic accounts of behavior are related in this chapter to the chain metaphor of causation. Radical behaviorism's causal mode is traced to the philosophy of Ernst Mach as well as to the Darwinian principle of selection on variation. It is argued that much of contemporary psychology neglects personal history because of a commitment to mechanistic, contiguous causation.

Chapter 6 (*Interpretive Techniques and Explanatory Theories*) deals with the concepts of description, explanation, and theory. Ernst Mach's influence on Skinner's philosophy of science is at its most evident here. A distinction between description and explanation is traced to Mach's dispute with theories invoking hypothetical constructs not contained in data, a dispute that took place in the 19th century and was known as the "atomic debate." As heuristics, such theories have a place in Mach's philosophy of science. They become problematic, however, when elevated to the status of explanation. Further, they belong to a view of natural phenomena that Mach consistently opposed: a world-as-machine view. Skinner was less amenable than Mach to hypothetical entities, but was as consistent as Mach in his opposition to mechanistic theories, theories that require links in a causal chain to mediate between functionally related events.

Chapter 7 (*Mechanistic Thinking in Psychology*) looks at selected systems in contemporary psychology to illustrate Mach's and Skinner's scientific and philosophical concerns about theoretical constructs not derived from data. Such constructs tend to divert attention from the phenomena they were invented to account for, with their structure and function becoming a focus of inquiry. Relying on the chain metaphor of causation, they encourage a mechanistic view of the subject matter— behaving organisms. This chapter illustrates the relevance to 20th century psychology of Mach's 19th century views on interpretation and causal modes in physics, and demonstrates that Skinner's concerns remain relevant to psychology today.

Chapter 8 (*Behaviorism and Radical Behaviorism*) compares the work of key figures cited as behaviorists in the psychological literature. This comparison demonstrates crucial differences between Skinner's scientific framework and those of Pavlov, Watson, Tolman, and Hull. In its earliest days, radical behaviorism moved beyond the mechanistic, mediational framework established by Tolman and Hull. Contemporary experimental psychology, however, continues to question and explain its subject matter according to this framework. In this sense, much of today's psychology is behavioral. Behaviorism marks a chapter in psychology's history rather than an essential methodological or philosophical unity; it is a historical rather than a philosophical marker. Its continued use as a label for one of psychology's "major approaches" obscures the fact that psychology still relies on an early behavioral input-output formulation, while radical behaviorism has moved beyond this formulation and relies on an integrative, relational framework.

Chapter 9 (*Concluding Remarks*) returns briefly to the new-world-view debate and points out similarities between the concerns of Capra and Skinner. Capra calls for the relational approach to be adopted by disciplines that have traditionally modelled themselves after physics, citing mechanistic science as a source of contemporary problems. He advocates turning to "ways of knowing" other than science as a means of dealing with these problems. Skinner argued that human behavior is the source of contemporary problems, including the behavior of people who use and abuse science. Science is our strength; it has led to the alleviation of much suffering, famine, and illness. Rather than turning away from science, its methods should be used to confront the source of the problem, human behavior. Mechanistic science, however, offers no way forward because the constructs with which it purports to explain behavior are internal, unobservable, and usually hypothetical. Such constructs cannot be used to effect change. A science concerned with how organisms interact with their environment, with functional relations between behavior and the context in which it occurs, provides practical means for analyzing and changing behavior. Examining science as it is practiced in psychology demonstrates that the relational framework of radical behaviorism offers possibilities for change unmatched by the mechanistic approach.

Chapter 2

Ordinary Language and Science

The relation between ordinary language and science requires special consideration in the behavioral sciences. Scientific disciplines identify a subject matter and describe relations and processes occurring among its constituents with their own language and terminology. Part of the work of scientists is to identify as precisely as possible the meaning of terms in order to facilitate communication within their discipline. Nature is divided and classified according to some system or order and studied under different headings: physics, chemistry, biology, mechanics, astronomy, and so on. In some fields, scientific language consists partly of a symbol system such as mathematics or the element and compound symbols of chemistry. In other fields, scientific terms are derived from our everyday language, with words carefully defined to avoid confusions about the part of nature or kind of process being discussed.

Much of everyday language is already considered to be descriptive of behavior. We come to the science of behavior already shaped by our verbal community to describe behavior in ordinary language terms that often lack the accuracy of definition characteristic of a scientific account. Ordinary verbal behavior precedes scientific verbal behavior, and ordinary language terms provide ready-made conceptual classifications that guide and direct the scientific investigation of behavior. Our everyday language contains prescientific assumptions and classifications that may or may not be useful for a scientific analysis of behavior.

An important part of the philosophy of science that is radical behaviorism is concerned with the relation between ordinary language terms that are considered to be descriptive of behavior and the way those terms influence the scientific study of behavior. Radical behaviorists view as unwise the practice of adopting ordinary language terms uncritically, arguing that those terms themselves can influence the behavior of scientists and may bring with them unnecessary problems. Words have been shown to exert a controlling influence on behavior in other fields of psychology, notably in the field of eyewitness testimony where, for example, Loftus and Palmer (1974) and Loftus et al. (1978) demonstrated that differential wording of questions about an incident often results in dissimilar verbal reports from subjects. People will recall incidents differently depending on subtle differences in the wording of questions about the incident. Analysis of the relation between ordinary language and science is an important part of radical behaviorism's overall philosophy of science. Once explicated, this analysis demonstrates that the behavior of the scientist is not exempt from controlling influences embedded within the larger culture. Scientists do not come to the study of behavior free from the assumptions and presuppositions of the surrounding culture but are in part guided by its conceptual classifications, some of which are to be found in the words we ordinarily use to describe behavior and in the grammatical patterns of ordinary language.

A simple illustration of the way confusions can arise when ordinary language terms are taken into behavioral science is found in the field of psychology dealing with the language of emotion. We describe ourselves or others in everyday situations as happy, disappointed, angry, guilt-ridden, surprised, aggressive, and so on, but when we try to define such terms for the purpose of scientific study we run into at least three problems.

First, it is virtually impossible to agree on a definition of these kinds of words. What are we describing when we use the words happy, disappointed, angry, and so on? Some measure of physiological arousal? Or is an emotion an experience that accompanies the arousal? Textbooks continue to juxtapose the major theories of James/Lange and Cannon/ Bard, which do not agree on whether emotion is definable as what we do at the time we say we feel joy or sorrow or anger, or whether it should be thought of as an accompaniment to our behavior at that time.

A second problem is topographical. One person smiles, laughs, and dances round the room after hearing good news, while another in similar circumstances sits quietly in a corner, hands folded, smiling. Both say they feel joyful, but which topography best indicates the feeling of joy? And is that feeling constituted in the same way for both people? How is a researcher to handle two such dissimilar performances described by the same word?

A third problem for the scientist trying to study emotion lies in differential responses to the same situation. One person may respond to an experimental setup in a quite different way than another, and the same is true of everyday settings. Following a minor car accident, one person jumps out of a car and shouts angrily at the other driver, while another calmly notes the details of the accident, expresses concern for the other driver, and concludes philosophically that these things simply happen sometimes.

How does the scientist cope with the facts that a) definitions cannot be agreed upon, b) when two people apply the same word to their feelings they are at the same time exhibiting remarkably dissimilar behavior, and c) in both experimental and everyday settings, people respond differently to the same situation? This is not to suggest that nothing useful or important has emerged from attempts to study emotion, but it illustrates difficulties that can be encountered when ordinary language words are taken into the realm of science with the assumption that they refer to entities that can be defined, categorized or quantified.

From its earliest days, radical behaviorism has dedicated itself to precision in terminology. Part of Skinner's doctoral dissertation examined the development of the concept of the reflex and demonstrated that in the course of its development it had acquired implications not given by data (for example, that behavior can be divided broadly into voluntary or involuntary classes and that reflexes are members of the involuntary class). At the same time, Skinner suggested to his Harvard department that he might more profitably spend his time carrying out "an operational analysis of half-a-dozen key terms from subjective psychology" (Skinner, 1945/1972b, p. 381) than preparing for a doctoral examination. His first major work, *The Behavior of Organisms* (Skinner, 1938), clearly defines the word behavior for the purpose of his experimental inquiries and elaborates some of the problems inherent in carrying over terms from ordinary language into the scientific domain. *The Operational*

Analysis of Psychological Terms (Skinner, 1945/1972b) is entirely concerned with this same problem and when he asked in another paper, *Are theories of learning necessary?* (1950/1972b), he was careful to specify what was meant by the word, theory, for the purpose of that argument. In *Schedules of Reinforcement* (1957), Ferster and Skinner clarified key terms in behavior analysis by providing a useful glossary.

Other workers in the field are equally concerned with terminological precision. A. C. Catania's *Learning*, now in its third edition (1992), carries etymological notes at the beginning of each chapter. In Catania's view: "Consistencies in vocabulary are essential to technical treatments, but the language must also grow and adapt to new findings and new perspectives. We must use our language of behavior with care, but perhaps we will be less likely to become rigid about it if we know something of its origins" (Catania, 1992, p. xiv). *The Behavior Analyst* publishes articles of general interest in the field of radical behaviorism and regularly contains a section, *On Terms*, wherein contributors attempt to clarify contexts appropriate to the use of key terms. Some examples are: *When we Speak of Knowing* (Hineline, 1983); *Stimulus Control Terminology* (Deitz & Mallone, 1985); *A Rule for the Use of the Term "Rule Governed Behavior"* (Brownstein & Shull, 1985); *Observer Drift: A Drifting Definition* (Smith, 1986); and *Misdescribing the Carneau: A Perplexing Plurality* (Gleeson & Lattal, 1987).

Skinner (1985) examined the *Report of the Research Briefing Panel on Cognitive Science and Artificial Intelligence* (Estes et al., 1983) and found that report lacking in definitions of key terms such as intelligence, mind, mental operations, imagination, reasoning, induction, understanding, thinking, and the like. He concluded by accusing cognitive scientists of "relaxing standards of definition and logical thinking and releasing a flood of speculation characteristic of metaphysics, literature, and daily intercourse, perhaps suitable enough for such purposes but inimical to science" (Skinner, 1985, p. 300). A later paper came to the same conclusion: that the words people use in describing how they feel or what they are thinking "are part of a living language that can be used without embarrassment by cognitive psychologists and behavior analysts alike in their daily lives. But these words cannot be used in their science!" (Skinner, 1989, p. 18).

It is clear that radical behaviorists take a keen interest in the relation between ordinary language and science. But their concerns are not confined to definitions and proper usage. Definitions may turn out to be the least of the problems inherent in taking ordinary language into science. The use of key terms can often be stipulated for the purpose of research or philosophical discussion, as when Skinner clearly defined his use of the terms behavior and theory for the purpose of his argument. Other problems in the relation between ordinary language and science are obscured by the ubiquity of language and buried so deeply within linguistic practices that only the most careful analysis can bring them to light. Radical behaviorists are concerned with the controlling influence of several features of ordinary language, features that guide the behavior of scientists toward views of their subject matter and toward forms of interpretation that are at odds with a scientific analysis. The remainder of this chapter will discuss three features of ordinary language that are problematic for scientific psychology.

The first problem is that along with ordinary language, we inherit conceptual systems involving ways of thinking about people and their behavior that are not based on scientific analysis and that encourage certain kinds of questions and theoretical interpretations of behavior not necessitated by scientific data. The second problem is inherent in the structure of Indo-European languages, specifically in the syntactic requirement of providing agents for actions. The third problem concerns the practice of accounting for action in different directional modes (either from person to behavior or from environment to behavior) depending on whether the account is of our own or of someone else's behavior, and depending on the extent to which people respond individually or collectively to environmental events. This problem specifically affects radical behaviorists because their accounts are structured in a directional mode that violates cultural practice. It will become clear that these three features of ordinary language exert a powerful controlling influence on the behavior of scientists.

Conceptual Systems and Ordinary Language

Radical behaviorism's concern with terminological precision and its rejection of uncritical acceptance or usage of the vernacular is essentially captured in an early passage of Skinner's: "The important objection to the vernacular in the description of behavior is that many of its terms imply conceptual schemes. I do not mean that a science of behavior is to dispense with a conceptual scheme but that it must not take over without careful consideration the schemes which underlie popular speech" (Skinner, 1938, p. 7). Words are the medium through which behavioral scientists express relations; they are the "calculus" of behavioral science (Hineline, 1980, p. 72). Unfortunately, this calculus was not developed specifically for its purpose in the same way as the calculus of physics, and is therefore not as clear-cut or unambiguous. This calculus has been inherited, taken out of the realms of everyday discourse and moved into the laboratory. Its terms guide the investigation of behavior, but also describe the products of those investigations. It is no surprise that confusions and inaccuracies arise from this dual functioning. Radical behaviorists, with their concern for scientific issues, have to be wary lest their calculus raise "the ghosts of dead systems" (Skinner, 1938, p. 5).

Mind in language. We inherit a conceptual system in the language of mind or mental life that suffuses everyday discourse. When we make a note to ourselves to remember something, we say we will bear it in mind; when we cannot remember something, we easily refer to having a mental block. If we have puzzled and worried over a problem, we will tell a friend "it has been on my mind"; we offer a person two or more alternatives and ask them to make up their mind. Instructing someone to be careful, we may say "mind how you go," and if we want to put someone at ease, we are trying to put their mind at rest or simply telling them "never mind." In everyday discourse, as Skinner said, these expressions are unproblematic and may be used comfortably by all kinds of psychologists. But if we move this term, mind, and its related conceptual system from our everyday discourse to the laboratory, then try to search for the mind we bear things in or the mind that is put at rest, or the mind we have had something on, we run into the logical problem of trying to submit to scientific analysis a term that has no physical or spatial referent.

Skinner offered a solution to this logical problem: "We can see how the word is used and what people seem to be saying when they use it" (Skinner, 1989, p. 17). In other words, when we examine *the language of mind*, we find that we can easily dispense with the concept of mind without dispensing with meaning. For example, the above phrases involving the concept of mind may be translated in the following ways:

MENTALISTIC STATEMENT	TRANSLATION
I will bear it in mind.	I will remember this in the future.
I have a mental block.	I cannot remember this.
It has been on my mind.	I have been thinking about this a great deal (a statement about behavior); This has been worrying me (a statement about feelings).
Make up your mind.	Make a decision; choose one of these options.
Mind how you go.	Act carefully; watch your step.
It has put my mind at rest.	I can stop worrying about this (another reference to feelings).
Never mind.	Do not worry; stop worrying; it is not important.

In each instance no meaning is lost, and in each, the translation is closer to behavior in that the statements relate to remembering, thinking, choosing, and feeling. Examining the language of mind in this way brings us closer to behavioral processes that we *can* submit to a scientific analysis. The conceptual system inherited in the language of mind diverts attention from these behavioral processes by implying a metaphysical or mental plane that is not susceptible to direct scientific treatment.

Learning in language. We inherit a conceptual system also in the language of learning, especially in the kinds of questions that are typically asked about learning. If the definition of learning is strictly maintained as "any relatively permanent change in behavior," we are likely to ask questions about changes in behavior. It is, however, more customary to ask, "What has this person learned?" than it is to ask, "What can or does this person now do?" The conceptual system suffusing the language of learning directs us away from changes in behavior toward the thing learned, and the thing learned becomes an entity possessed by the learner. This way of talking or asking questions about learning is grounded in the metaphor of storage and retrieval, a metaphor that informs the cognitive or information processing traditions in psychology: "Processing information is, of course, something people have done for thousands of years. They have made records of things that happen—on clay tiles, papyrus, vellum, paper, magnetic tapes, and now silicon chips—and they have stored them, retrieved them, and responded to them again more or less as they responded to the originals. Cognitive scientists have taken this practice as a model or metaphor" (Skinner, 1985, p. 292). In this tradition, the organism is conceptualized as a system that takes in information from the environment, processes it, stores it, and at some stage retrieves and acts upon that information.

If the metaphor is accepted uncritically (as it is by much of contemporary psychology), then the scientist is directed toward a stimulus-organism-response (S-O-R) account: environmental stimuli are taken in by the organism, processed and worked upon; these internal workings are then considered to guide responses. Skinner examined the metaphor and found it lacking: "When physical records are stored, the records continue to exist until they are retrieved, but is that true when people 'process information'?" (Skinner, 1985, p. 294). He argued that a storage battery might be a better metaphor to guide psychology. Electricity is put into a battery but is not stored there. Rather, the battery is changed, and it is a changed battery that puts out electricity. In a similar way, he argued, an organism is changed by its exposure to contingencies of reinforcement, and it is a changed organism that emits behavior: "Organisms do not acquire behavior as a kind of possession; they simply come to behave in various ways. The behavior is not in them at any time. We say that it is emitted, but only as light is emitted from a hot filament; there is no light in the filament" (Skinner, 1985, p. 295).

The language of learning and its metaphor of storage and retrieval directs scientific psychology in a particular way when adopted without critical examination. Once examined, however, and perhaps an alternative metaphor substituted, a new language can direct inquiry to behavioral processes that can be submitted to scientific analysis: "How organisms are changed by contingencies of reinforcement is the field of a behavioral analysis. What is happening inside is a question to be answered by neurology, with its appropriate instruments and methods" (Skinner, 1985, p. 295).

Language in language. We inherit a conceptual system also in the language of language, in the way we ordinarily talk about language. Like mind, the word, language, seems to elude both definition and reference when taken out of ordinary usage for the purpose of scientific analysis. Vicki Lee (1981), for example, noted that despite the familiarity of the word, language is notoriously difficult to define: "People know what 'language' means; that is, until they are asked to define the word, either nominally by stating its defiens, or ostensively by pointing to its referent. It then becomes apparent that the meaning of 'language,' despite the familiarity and usefulness of the word in everyday discourse, is uncertain and obscure" (Lee, 1981, p. 29).

On the way we ordinarily talk about language, Skinner noted, "Language has the character of a thing, something a person acquires and possesses. Psychologists speak of the 'acquisition of language' in the child. The words and sentences of which a language is composed are said to be tools used to express meanings, thoughts, ideas, propositions, emotions, needs, desires, and many other things in or on the speaker's mind" (Skinner, 1974, p. 88). The language of mind implies a thing or a place; the language of language implies a thing or a structure. As the language of learning implies the possession of knowledge, so the language of language implies a complex program of words and grammatical rules possessed by and stored inside the person, retrieved and used as a

31

tool when required. The metaphor of storage and retrieval has been discussed above, and a further question may be added here about its use in relation to language, that is to say, about the suggestion that language is stored, retrieved, and used as a tool.

Consider an analogy between the language of words and what is often called the language of dance. We are said to store words, retrieve them, and use them to convey meaning. In a dance context, we can comfortably talk about the language of dance conveying meaning to an audience. A skilled writer, public speaker, or lecturer shares several characteristics with a skilled dancer. Each is a performer, highly trained over several years to behave in a particular way. Barring physical disability, everyone is capable of dancing and speaking to some degree or other. In each instance, the level of skill and subtlety will depend largely on training and the language can either be performed or written. The analogy is useful because it highlights the way we are directed to study one kind of language, the language of words, by the way we generally talk about it. We would not comfortably talk about the acquisition of dance as though it were an entity taken in and possessed; we would more easily refer to the training of a dancer. Neither would we refer to storage and retrieval: where does the dancer store a pirouette, for example, or an arabesque? An arabesque is not *in* the dancer at any time. The pirouette, the arabesque, come into being in performance. These movements are not dormant, latent, stored inside the dancer awaiting recall. They are transient events existing in the moments of their performance.

We are also likely to say that a dancer *performs* a pirouette in preference to *uses* a pirouette, which helps to illustrate Skinner's argument that: "We have no more reason to say that a man 'uses the word water' in asking for a drink than to say that he 'uses a reach' in taking the offered glass" (Skinner, 1957, p. 7). The way we talk about the language of words needs careful consideration before we allow its conceptual scheme to direct our scientific inquiries.

The languages of mind, learning, and language illustrate some of the difficulties inherent in taking ordinary, everyday vocabulary as the starting point of a scientific analysis of behavior. Verbal behavior precedes scientific behavior and words therefore carry with them prescientific conceptual systems and metaphors that can block or hinder analysis by guiding scientists toward internal, inaccessible properties of organisms and away from more accessible properties—namely, relations between behavior and the context in which it occurs.

Grammar and the Syntax of Action

Conceptual systems are not the only controlling variables concealed in ordinary language. Other variables are embedded, in a sense, more deeply than the conceptual systems discussed above. Other aspects of ordinary language also encourage a particular way of looking at or thinking about behavior, and are even more obscure than the conceptual systems of mind, learning, or language because they comprise the syntax of our language.

Hineline (1980) argues that English grammar and syntax impose constraints on the way we view the subject matter of psychology, constraints that are "linguistic—as opposed to logical" (Hineline, 1980, p. 80). He identifies two linguistic constraints that guide scientists toward a particular way of dealing with behavior. The first lies in the failure of the English language to maintain a strict distinction between verbs (words that denote transient events) and nouns (words that denote things or objects that endure and have a kind of permanence). The second is the near impossibility of speaking of action in the English language without reference to an agent.

Grammatical categories. In his analysis of linguistic constraints, Hineline draws on the comparative linguistics of Benjamin Lee Whorf (see Whorf, 1956). Informed by his comparisons of grammar and syntax in English and several American-Indian languages, Whorf argued in *Language, Thought, and Reality* that Western science dissects the physical world along lines laid down by its language. Structures and processes are not given to Western science by the physical world but are to some extent already present in its language. He argued that speakers of languages with different kinds of grammars are led to dissect the world along different lines: "Formulation of ideas is not an independent process, strictly rational in the old sense, but is part of a particular grammar, and differs, from slightly to greatly, between different grammars. We dissect nature along lines laid down by our native language" (Whorf, 1956, p. 213).

Whorf examined the distinction between nouns and verbs in the English language and found that the traditional distinction between "doing" (or "happening") words and "thing" words is not well maintained in practice and that many words which should properly be in verb form because they describe transient events are in fact in noun form. Similarly, some words denoting stable and long lasting events, which because of those properties should be classed as nouns, are found to be verbs:

> If it be said that "strike, turn, run," are verbs because they denote temporary or short-lasting events, i.e., actions, why then is "fist" a noun? It is also a temporary event. Why are "lightning, spark, wave, eddy, pulsation, flame, storm, phase, cycle, spasm, noise, emotion" nouns? They are temporary events. If "man" and "house" are nouns because they are long-lasting and stable events, i.e., things, what then are "keep, adhere, extend, project, continue, persist, grow, dwell," and so on doing among the verbs?" (Whorf, 1956, p. 215).

Like scientific categories, grammatical categories are not handed to us by nature: "It will be found that it is not possible to define 'event, object, thing, relation' and so on from nature, but that to define them always involves a circuitous return to the grammatical categories of the definer's language" (Whorf, 1956, p. 215). Grammatical categories of other languages such as Hopi and Nootka express objects, transience, and duration in different ways from English. Hopi, for example, has a class of events roughly corresponding to our verbs that are grouped by duration type—lightning, wave, flame, meteor, puff of smoke, pulsation, which in English are more like nouns.

This grammatical tendency to express in noun form events that are properly verbs guides psychologists away from the study of what people do (processes, verbs) toward the study of structures denoted by the noun forms. People remember, think, talk, see, hear, and feel—all verbs. When these actions are transformed into nouns—memory, thought, language, sensation, emotion—as is common in the English language, then scientists are encouraged to look for the things denoted by the nouns. In this way, inspired by grammatical form, psychology becomes the study of structures (nouns) that are assumed to have some kind of permanence, rather than the study of ongoing processes or activities.

Agents for actions. Another linguistic constraint that Hineline draws from Whorf is the syntactic requirement of providing subjects for verbs, or as Hineline puts it: "the near impossibility, when speaking English, of expressing action without imputing an agent of the action" (Hineline, 1980, p. 80). To satisfy the requirements of English grammar our verbs must have substantives, they must have agents that perform the act described by the verb. For example, "there is rain" would be an unusual although more accurate way of describing what is going on when we say "it is raining"; for in logical terms, what is raining? The answer: rain is raining, or water is raining from the sky. The requirement of an agent is a linguistic rather than a logical requirement. In his study of the Hopi language, Whorf (1956) found that:

> Hopi can and does have verbs without subjects, a fact which may give that tongue potentialities, probably never to be developed, as a logical system for understanding some aspects of the universe. Undoubtedly modern science, strongly reflecting western Indo-European tongues, often does as we all do, sees actions and forces where it sometimes might be better to see states. On the other hand, "state" is a noun, and as such it enjoys the superior prestige traditionally attaching to the subject or

thing class; therefore science is exceedingly ready to speak of states if permitted to manipulate the concept like a noun. (pp. 243-244).

Whorf applied his notion of linguistic relativity to Western science, arguing that science divides the world along lines laid down within the structure of Indo-European languages. Hineline applies this argument to psychology to highlight some of the differences between the terminology of behavior analysis (the field of psychology informed by radical behaviorism) and the language of other types of psychology. "Given that patterns of English virtually disallow actions without agents," he writes, "when one describes an action that has no obvious external agent one gratuitously implies an agent. By convention the implied agent is usually internal or mentalistic" (Hineline, 1980, p. 81).

Because English language patterns require agents for actions, it is a matter of linguistic rather than logical necessity to supply an agent. In the case of behavior, agency is often ascribed to the organism itself. Behavior does not simply occur; the organism is taken to be the initiating agent. In the radical behaviorist formulation, if there is deemed to be an agent, that role is given over to the environment. To talk of the environment as an *initiating* agent, however, is still to thwart the real emphasis of the radical behaviorist formulation. To say "the environment selects behavior" is too strong a case, giving too much to the environment as though it were somehow an active entity. "Behavior is selected by the environment," the passive form, is a somewhat better expression since it de-emphasizes the notion of an initiating agent that is given prominence in the former expression. The passive form is not popular however. The *Publication Manual of the American Psychological Association,* for example, instructs writers thus: "Verbs are vigorous, direct communicators. Use the active rather than the passive voice" (American Psychological Association, 1983, p. 36). According to Whorf, the outcome of this grammatical necessity is that "We are constantly reading into nature fictional acting entities, simply because our verbs must have substantives in front of them" (Whorf, 1956, p. 243).

Ordinary Language and Science

Circumventing language traps. Hineline suggests three strategies for circumventing these "language traps," allowing us to talk about behavior in ways that deemphasize the notion of initiating agents and focus more on processes (verbs) than on structures (nouns).

(1) He argues that some nouns seem to have a more solid character than others and his first strategy is to try to choose nouns that are less solid for referring to events or changes. For example, he suggests that we might substitute *pattern* for *structure* and argues that this would have two advantages. First, pattern implies greater fluidity, change, and continuation than structure, carrying with it the notion that behavior is ongoing rather than fixed or static. Second, referring to patterns rather than structures helps avoid the practice of attributing causal status to descriptions. Consider the difference between *personality* and *patterns of behavior:* in referring to regularities in behavior as patterns we are likely to remember that we are describing something ongoing and fluid. Referring to regularities in behavior as personality (a word having a more solid character) encourages us to forget that we are describing behavior and to assume that we are giving a causal account, that in identifying some sort of structure for personality we can draw on it as a causal concept. The term, personality, has shifted in some areas of psychology from a description of regularities in behavior to the status of a causal entity or agent: "There is now much evidence that there are three major dimensions of personality *that determine* a good deal of our everyday behavior" (Eysenck, 1980, p. 52, emphasis added), a shift that is less likely to occur if regularities are referred to as patterns of behavior.

Hineline goes on to say, "Such differences of metaphor are not trivial. 'Cognitive structure,' to me, suggests a rigidity uncharacteristic of evolving human thinking; it is too easily reified in the absence of adequate facts. 'Cognitive patterning,' on the other hand, suggests fluidity and flexibility—the quicksilver phenomena of problem-solving, remembering, and recognizing or discriminating" (Hineline, 1980, p. 83). Indeed, the choice of metaphor is far from trivial since metaphors have the power to direct the way in which we study and talk about our subject matter, as the earlier discussion on the metaphor of storage and retrieval illustrates. Similarly, the pejorative expression, "this is just semantics," fails to recognize the profound consequences of opting for one kind of discourse rather than another.

(2) Hineline's second strategy addresses the problem of "what to do with the agent that our language patterns continually append to actions" (Hineline, 1980, p. 83). Instead of viewing the organism as agent, he suggests it might be viewed as the "host" of its behavior, a focal point of energy and activity and a "place" where variables come together. This unusual view differs from our traditional Western conception of the person as a contained self separate from its environment, operating *on* rather than *in* the environment, but it may provide a way of thinking about behavior that is less constrained by linguistic convention.

What is the self, asks Hineline, if it is not to be defined as the repertoire of the organism? "Even as behaving constitutes the uncanny difference between a live creature and a dead one, a person's repertoires define the person who is the locus of activity" (Hineline, 1980, p. 83). Skinner also used this metaphor of the person as a place where variables come together. In *A Lecture on "Having" a Poem* (Skinner, 1972*a*) he compared the process of creating a poem or a lecture to the process of creating a baby and asked of each case "who is to be given credit?" In the case of a woman having a baby there is a sense in which the woman should be given credit since it is she who undergoes this difficult and painful process. But having a baby can also be viewed as a biological process and the woman in this view is the place where biological variables come together. Similarly, the poet or lecturer may be given credit for going through the difficult process of creating text, but we may also see that person as the focus of genetic and environmental variables, as a combination of reinforcement history and present circumstances, as a place where all of these variables come together to produce poem or lecture. In this dynamic, interactive formulation there is no single initiating agent, but many variables acting together.

This distinction between the person as agent and the person as host is also not a trivial one, because if the person is the agent of creation, then it is the person who must be analyzed, dissected, and investigated in order to study the creative process. However, if the person is viewed as host, and the creation of a poem or lecture seen as the confluence of reinforcement history (experience) and present circumstances, then it is history and present circumstances that can more easily be analyzed, dissected, and investigated. Skinner concluded his lecture thus: "And now my labor is over. I have had my lecture. I have no sense of fatherhood. If my genetic and personal histories had been different, I should have come into possession of a different lecture. If I deserve any credit at all, it is simply for having served as a place in which certain processes could take place" (Skinner, 1972a, p. 355). The metaphor of the person as host rather than agent guides scientists to look at the *many* variables influencing creative processes (multiple causation) and to consider the person as a dynamic, interactive part of their environment.

(3) Hineline's third strategy involves careful rewording of nouns derived from adverbs, turning words that sound like things back into descriptions of behavior and using gerunds (in simple terms, usually words ending in "ing"). For example, intelligence has the character of a thing, whereas acting intelligently is a description of behavior. Similarly, knowledge and motivation sound like things and many attempts are made to study them as though they were. Hineline's strategy would convert knowledge to knowing, and motivation would become "motivated, or highly persistent, focused behaving" (Hineline, 1980, p. 84). Behavior itself becomes behaving: "We study remembering rather than memory, thinking rather than cognition—in short, behaving rather than behavior" (Hineline, 1980, p. 84).

Modifying language in this way brings us closer to a conception of behavior that guides behavioral science toward the study of processes (verbs) rather than structures (nouns), toward an interactive view of organisms and their environments, and toward a view of behavior as the confluence of many variables including past and present, organism and environment. To put the case in behavioral terms: without careful analysis of language patterns and the controlling variables in ordinary language, we continue to succumb to its influence. Understanding its influence provides a means to counter control by allowing us to see the constraints it places upon us and by presenting possibilities for change. Changing the words in which we talk about behavior will guide behavioral science in a different and perhaps more useful direction.

Directional Talk

In addition to the ways ordinary language influences our thinking about and investigating behavior, readers and listeners may be discomforted by what Hineline (1980) calls the "distinct dialect" of radical behaviorism. There are many examples in the dialect of radical behaviorism of what seem to be unnecessarily convoluted expressions for quite simple events. Hineline notes that the seemingly simple expression, "Knowing that we can predict future events, we act accordingly," becomes at first glance a more convoluted expression when translated into radical behaviorist terminology: "Predictability of events, apart from the events themselves, is a variable that affects our behavior" (Hineline, 1980, p. 71). And the simple phrase, "The child learns to catch someone's eye when needing assistance or attention," becomes in the radical behaviorist's dialect, "Eye-contact becomes both a reinforcer and a discriminative event setting the occasions on which the child's behavior is likely to be reinforced by another person" (Hineline, 1980, p. 71). In each example, note that the behavioral dialect avoids the difficulties involved in terms like knowing and learning and concentrates on simpler functional relations between discriminative stimuli, setting conditions, and reinforcement. Ironically, the seemingly more convoluted sentence actually expresses simpler relations than those involved in the conceptual systems inherent in the language of "knowing" and "learning." The phrases that *seem* so complicated in comparison to our everyday expressions, are in fact less problematic in terms of their conceptual systems.

Another difference between ordinary language and the language of behavior analysis has to do with the tendency to alter the directionality implied in accounts of behavior depending on whether the interpretation is of our own or of someone else's behavior. Again, Hineline (1990, 1992) was the first to point out this difference as well as its controlling variables.

First, he notes that interpretations and explanations of behavior have two characteristics; bipolarity and directionality, with forms like agent to action, cause to effect, independent to dependent variable. Second, he notes that psychological accounts occur in two basic modes: person based or environment based. In the former mode, the direction is from person (or some dispositional aspect of the person) to behavior:

Person ————————————> Behavior

In the latter mode, the direction is from some aspect of the environment to behavior:

Environment ————————————> Behavior

Hineline's analysis draws on the work of attribution theorists (for example, Jones and Nisbett, 1971; Storms, 1973) who found that the direction of action in interpretations or explanations of behavior differs according to the location of the person giving the account. Where an account is given of the behavior of another person, the typical direction of action is from person to behavior; an observer tends to explain the behavior of another person by alluding to internal characteristics of that other person as in some way causal. This tendency has become known as the "fundamental attribution error" (Ross, 1977). When describing their own behavior—when the observer and observed are one person—the directional mode is typically from environment to behavior. People ordinarily interpret their own behavior in terms of events or effects in the external context and interpret the behavior of others in terms of characteristics or events internal to the person:

Interpreting the Behavior of Others

Person ————————————> Behavior

Interpreting One's Own Behavior

Environment —————————————> Behavior

Radical behaviorists interpret the behavior of others using the directional mode normally reserved for accounting for one's own behavior and so reverse this tendency:

Interpreting the Behavior of Others
(behavior analytic account)

Environment —————————————> Behavior

As such, behavior analytic accounts violate a cultural norm. This, Hineline argues, may contribute substantially to clashes between behavior analysis and other viewpoints in psychology (Hineline, 1990).

Hineline makes a further point in his analysis of directional modes and the distinctiveness of behavior analytic accounts. Attribution theorists have also described circumstances that occasion a switch of directional mode from environment based to person based, even when the interpreter of action is both observer and observed (when a person interprets his or her own behavior). Hineline illustrates this by comparing two passages, one that maintains the culturally typical pattern and one that reverses it: "I have carried out an extensive set of observations, with myself as subject, and have discovered that wine is stronger than beer. Based on a comparable set of observations, I have discovered that I am more allergic to tulips than to roses." Here an observer interprets his or her own behavior, but the directional mode switches from environment based for the first observation to person based for the second observation. Each observation refers to the susceptibility of the person to some environmental event, and it turns out that the switch is occasioned by the extent to which an effect applies to many people or to isolated individuals (Hineline, 1990). Where situational events affect people similarly, directionality is environment based:

"Wine is stronger than beer"

Environment ————————————> Behavior

Where not everyone is similarly affected, where a response to situational events is more individual, directionality is person based:

"I am more allergic to tulips than to roses"

Person ————————————> Behavior

Reversing directionality illustrates the convention: "I have carried out an extensive set of observations, with myself as subject, and have discovered that I am more easily intoxicated by wine than by beer. Based on a similar set of observations, I have discovered that tulips are more allergenic than roses." Hineline directs us to consider how such statements might be received. "I am more easily intoxicated by wine than by beer" (a person based interpretation of a general effect) is likely to be dismissed as an uninteresting statement since the relative potency of wine and beer is well known and everyone is similarly affected. The observation, "tulips are more allergenic than roses," an environment based interpretation of an individual effect, is likely to be protested for precisely the reason that it is an individual effect and should not be generalized. It seems that where people are equally affected, the directional mode in ordinary parlance is environment based, but where people are not equally affected, the directional mode is person based.

Behavior analytic accounts also violate this cultural norm by referring to the behavior of individuals in the mode ordinarily reserved for instances in which everyone is treated as being alike. Behavior analytic experiments as well as educational and therapeutic interventions concentrate on individuals rather than on groups, but interpretive accounts in the Skinnerian tradition are couched in a language pattern that suggests that all individuals are alike or are equally affected. Hineline (1990, 1992) suggests that this violation of a cultural norm may also cause discomfort by threatening the individuality of the reader or listener.

Apart from grammatical and syntactic constraints, then, behavior analysts must also be concerned to note that the directional mode in their interpretations of behavior runs counter to cultural norms. Similarly, other traditions in psychology should also be concerned with deep rooted language patterns that inform and guide ways of thinking and talking about behavior, with the variables governing the directional mode of their own accounts, and with the possibility that vernacular language patterns may also influence their response to radical behaviorist accounts.

Ordinary language is not neutral with respect to the subject matter of behavioral science and the scientist is not exempt from the influence that ordinary language exerts on conceptualizations of behavior and on interpretive forms. Ordinary language terms and their conceptual systems function not simply as interpretations of the subject matter but also as guides to the way the subject matter will be treated. The conceptual systems inherent in the language of mind, learning, and language itself lead to a view that the important relations between organism and environment take place *inside* the organism. Apart from these conceptual systems, linguistic constraints also draw science toward the study of nouns (things, structures) and away from the study of verbs (activities, processes, patterns). Our way of talking about the direction of action appears to be influenced both by the location of the interpreter and by the locus of variability, a feature that sets behavior analytic interpretations apart from the cultural norm and that may cause discomfort to the reader or listener.

Much more can be said about the relation between ordinary language and science. Much more *should* be said, because if language continues to be the calculus of behavioral science, its practitioners need to understand its limits and constraints as well as the ways it guides their own behavior toward particular views of their subject matter and particular forms of interpretation.

Chapter 3

Science: Aims and Methods

Chapter 1 noted that although psychology is united by a commitment to scientific method, its subdisciplines are not all committed to the same kind of science. Methods and the general theoretical framework against which data are interpreted vary between sub-disciplines. Behavior analysis is distinct from much of contemporary experimental psychology in that its philosophical background, radical behaviorism, promotes a scientific method that is inductive rather than hypothetico-deductive.

The contemporary literature of mainstream experimental psychology gives little recognition to the fact that there is more than one way of legitimately doing science. Methodology is strictly prescribed within the hypothetico-deductive tradition (or the method of hypothesis, as it is also known), loosely adopting the logic of falsification, and emphasizing statistical analysis of data as a way of controlling for variability in behavior. These prescriptions and their rationale are presented to successive generations of students so as to seem the only legitimate methods of scientific inquiry.

Chapter 1 also noted that Skinner did not subscribe to the view that science is a straightforward and strictly logical pursuit, arguing instead that some very important aspects of the scientific process do not lend themselves to formal treatment. In his experience, science is rarely the formal process that historians and methodologists claim, and is only imperfectly described by the step-by-step logic of the hypothetico-deductive approach.

Radical behaviorist methodology belongs to a philosophy of science tradition that does not recognize the method of hypothesis as an essential requirement of scientific inquiry. Methodology is dictated by a number of concerns, and in the case of radical behaviorism is largely dictated by its views of the aims of science, its commitment to the individuality of organisms, and by the nature of its theoretical system. A later chapter will deal in detail with types of theoretical systems; this chapter concerns the distinction between hypothetico-deductive and inductive approaches to scientific inquiry and demonstrates that the dominance of the hypothetico-deductive method today is not related to logic or to the power of the method but to the types of explanatory accounts (theories) that dominate psychology. Hypothetico-deduction is required only to test particular types of theories and is not an essential requirement of scientific inquiry in general. The method continues to be undermined by an epistemological problem: it cannot logically or empirically confirm some of the kinds of theoretical claims it is invoked to test.

Methods in Contemporary Psychology

Students of psychology today are usually introduced early in their training to a set of procedures that provide a yardstick for their scientific community to evaluate research findings. The community demands adherence to a rigorous logic and trains successive generations of psychologists according to this logic.

For example, students need to be familiar with the rationale for using the same or different groups of subjects in experimental conditions (between subjects, within subjects, or matched pairs design). The logic of using a control group and an experimental group in some situations to test the effectiveness of a single variable also becomes a basic part of the student's understanding of research methods. Classification of data into parametric and nonparametric, related and unrelated, nominal, ordinal, interval, and ratio, provides the basis for choosing a suitable statistical test, as does the basic distinction of whether a research project looks for differences or correlations between scores.

Students also learn a rationale for the conduct of experiments that conforms to the hypothetico-deductive tradition and emphasizes the need for a formal hypothesis. A typical introductory text notes, "At some point a researcher will want to test out his theory. In order to do this, the researcher will make a *prediction* about the kind of behavior which would be expected to occur if the theory is true. A prediction of this kind is known as the *experimental hypothesis*" (Green and D'Oliveira, 1982, p. 7).

The rationale of hypothesis testing in psychology is loosely based on the logic of falsification. In its strongest form, this asserts that accumulated observations of the consequences of a theory cannot show it to be right or true but that the only route to confidence in a theory is through the failure of repeated attempts to falsify it. The more a theory withstands attempts to falsify it, the greater the confidence a scientific community may have in it. In other words, the experimenter must repeatedly set up situations capable of demonstrating that a theory is wrong in some respect: "In order to carry out a test of an experimental hypothesis, it must in principle be possible for the predicted effects either to occur or *not* to occur....this is a basic rule of experimental research. If there is no possibility that an experiment might go *against* the experimental hypothesis, then there is no point in doing the experiment at all. Consequently an experimental hypothesis is tested against a *null hypothesis*, that states that an experimenter will *not* find the experimental results he or she expects" (Green and D'Oliveira, 1982, pp. 7-8).

The null hypothesis in psychology is essentially a statement that the results of an experiment could have occurred *by chance*. Chance is an element added to the logic of falsification and is attributable to variations in behavior between individuals. Chance forms the basis of the rationale of statistical analysis. The underlying notion is that any group of people is made up of individuals who will show differences in behavior on a given measure. Since it is unlikely that individuals in a group will produce exactly the same test scores in an experimental manipulation, contemporary psychology bases its confidence in the significance of different outcomes between groups, or similarities between groups as in correlational designs, on the statistical laws of chance. It is against chance that the effectiveness of an experimental variable is measured: "According to the null hypothesis, any results found in an experiment are due to chance fluctuations in people's performance rather than to the predicted effects of the variable the experimenter is interested in" (Green and D'Oliveira, 1982, p. 8).

Psychologists turn to statistical analysis as a means of verifying whether a result could have been expected to occur by chance in the sample used and are usually required to state at the outset a probability level below which their results will be accepted as being due to the experimental manipulation and above which they will not. For example, in evaluating the effectiveness of a new teaching scheme a control group who had been taught in the normal way would perform the same test as an experimental group who had been taught in a different way. The experimenter sets the probability level at 0.05 (or five in every hundred) so that if after statistical analysis it transpired that the obtained results could have been expected at a probability of lower than 0.05, or less than five times in every hundred, the experimenter would conclude that the difference in scores between the control and experimental group was a function of the new teaching scheme rather than a chance result. It should be stressed that the 0.05 probability level is nothing more or less than a convention. There is no scientific or logical justification for choosing this probability level; it is merely "the done thing."

A large part of a psychology student's training consists of learning and practicing these methods. It is safe to say that both the hypothetico-deductive method and statistical analysis of data are the current ortho-doxy in experimental psychology. Contemporary psychology is charac-terized by a "methodological package" of formal procedures including hypothesis, null hypothesis, and statistical tests of significance. Results that are found to have a probability level greater than 0.05 (or some other arbitrary level) dictate rejection of the hypothesis and acceptance of the null hypothesis. This package of formal procedures helps psychology's scientific community to evaluate research findings, allowing the com-munity to establish some findings as part of psychology's body of knowledge and to reject others. This chapter extracts hypothesis testing from the package and considers it in contrast to a less formal and inductive approach. The following chapter will be concerned with the statistical aspect of the package and will consider some of the scientific and philosophical issues involved in statistical treatment of behavioral data.

Science: Aims and Methods

Hypotheses in Science

Given today's dominance and widespread promotion in student instruction packages of the method of hypothesis, it would be reasonable to assume that the method had always enjoyed a favored place in both the philosophy and practice of scientists. Its history, however, is not straightforward. Scientists and philosophers have vacillated and argued throughout other eras over the logic and utility of the method and continue to do so today. Some of the difficulties concern scientists and philosophers regardless of their special subject, while other problems are noted specifically by workers in the behavioral and social sciences.

An enduring problem with the method, regardless of subject matter, is that demonstrating the deduced observational consequences of a theory does not confirm the truth or accuracy of the theory itself. For example, from theory X an experimenter deduces and thus predicts that under certain circumstances C will be observed. This is the experimental hypothesis. If C is found to be the case, it cannot be argued that therefore X is the case because C could result from other processes or mechanisms included in a competing theory. To argue from the demonstration of the consequence C to the truth of the theory X is an error in reasoning—"the fallacy of affirming the consequent." The error lies in reversing the direction of validation, in appealing to a consequence to validate premises rather than using premises and the deductive process to validate a consequence.

In deductive logic, premises need not be true for a conclusion to be validly deduced. The following deduction, for example, is valid according to the rules of deductive logic.

Premise:
    Asthma is caused by factor x in the bloodstream.
Premise:
    Alice is asthmatic.
Conclusion:
    Alice has factor x in her bloodstream.

Regardless of the real-world accuracy of any statement in the argument, the conclusion is logically valid in relation to the premises. Verifying that Alice does have factor *x* in her bloodstream (observing the deduced consequence) does not, however, verify the initial premise that asthma is caused by factor *x* in the bloodstream.

Consider an example from psychology: a theoretical account of memory states that human memory is comprised of two stores, short term and long term. This is an initial premise. A second premise might be that the short term store has a maximum capacity of nine items. Together, these premises predict that under conditions of immediate recall of items on a list, most people will not be able to recall more than nine items.

Premise:
  Human memory is made up of a short term store and a long term store.
Premise:
  The short term store has a maximum capacity of nine items.
Conclusion:
  People will not be able to recall more than nine items from a longer list shortly after presentation of that list.

If the prediction is confirmed (which it is likely to be), the demonstration that most people cannot remember more than nine items from a longer list is not a demonstration that memory is made up of a short term and a long term store. All that can be known from confirming a prediction is that under a given set of conditions event C will occur. If a researcher concludes from the demonstration of C that therefore X is true, this reverses the direction of validation and is an example of the fallacy of affirming the consequent. In deductive logic, premises validate a conclusion, but a conclusion does not validate premises.

Nonoccurrence of the predicted event and consequences of the theory necessarily entails the falsity of the theory or of one or more of the statements that comprise the theory. If Alice does not have factor *x* in her bloodstream, the first premise is false; if people recall more than nine items from a longer list, then at least the premise relating to short term memory's capacity is false. In these circumstances, the experimenter must either reject the theory because it cannot account for the data or must modify the theory in some way that will lead to further experimental testing.

One of the consequences of this enduring problem, widely recognized in philosophy of science literature but rarely considered in psychology, is simply that no amount of confirming instances of a theory tested this way can confirm its accuracy, but one disconfirming instance guarantees the falsity of the whole or some of its parts. This method is asymmetrical in the sense that a theory can be shown to be false but not to be true. Thus, a theory is only as good as the number of times it has withstood falsification and can only be held tentatively. Explanations of events generated by hypothetico-deduction stand only as long as a particular theory withstands falsification.

Johnston and Pennypacker (1980) pointed out a practical difficulty specific to behavioral and social sciences, which is that the method of hypothesis requires for its success a clear correspondence between theoretical elements and empirical measures involved in testing and verifying the theory's consequences. Psychology's theoretical base, in contrast to that of the physical sciences, retains categories that are themselves the subject of continual debate and disagreement. Categories like emotion, arousal, personality, memory, schemata, motivation, intelligence, stress, and many others comprising the discipline of psychology are at best vague in their definitional and mensural outlines and therefore lack the predictive capability of theoretical categories in physical sciences. The theoretical base informing, for example, physics, chemistry, and the biological sciences consists of more clearly defined conceptual elements and relatively precise measurement techniques. These, to the extent of their coherence and precision, allow empirical outcomes to be compared to theoretical elements. Background knowledge in these sciences is extensive, so that outcomes are predicted from an already well-founded data base. Psychology's data base in comparison is inexact, lacking the conceptual clarity of these other sciences that have successfully employed hypothetico-deduction. At present, we cannot draw on well established behavioral principles with the same precision as other natural sciences to predict what should occur in an experiment.

At a practical level, radical behaviorists are concerned that this method entails wastage of both effort and data. Data tend to be considered valuable only if they conform to predictions, if results are positive—in favor of predictions. If they do not conform, and a theory is rejected or undergoes extensive modification, then those data so carefully collected in the research process have little or no meaning or value to the experimenter: "The working hypothesis of experiments designed to confirm predictions take the general form, 'When x occurs, y will occur.' Quite often y fails to occur, and little note is taken of what occurred instead" (Johnston & Pennypacker, 1980, p. 31). To the radical behaviorist it seems wasteful to expend time and energy on research in such a way that some data will turn out to be useless. Sidman (1960) argues that relatively little is known about behavior and therefore all data are in some sense significant, not in the statistical sense of that term but in the sense that they tell us something more about behavior: "All the significant data have not yet turned up in the laboratory. There is a wealth of behavioral phenomena still to be brought under experimental control for more precise study and analysis. That is, perhaps, why negative results seem wasteful" (Sidman, 1960, p. 9).

Radical behaviorists note that many facets of behavior are still not understood and the process of data collection and examination is necessarily slow. The theoretical base that now informs physical sciences did not develop overnight, nor in the hundred or so years of psychology's history. Unanswered questions in any science often await the development or improvement of methods and instruments. As Skinner put it, "To insist that a science of behavior give a rigorous account of such phenomena [for example, imagining, remembering, emotion, insight] in its present state of knowledge is like asking the Gilbert of 1600 to explain a magnetic amplifier or the Faraday of 1840 to explain superconductivity" (Skinner, 1969, p. 85). Radical behaviorists continue patiently with their scientific enterprise, avoiding wasted effort and negative data.

Induction

While psychology students continue to be trained mainly in the formal methods of hypothesis testing and falsification, radical behaviorism is characterized by a less formal inductive approach. This section seeks to clarify what is meant when radical behaviorists refer to their approach as inductive and considers some of the philosophical issues generated by induction.

The term, induction, as used by radical behaviorists refers primarily to a way of doing science that gives prominence to data rather than to theory. In contrast to the method of hypothesis, which takes theory as its starting point and seeks to test the truth or approximate truth of theory via its data, the inductive approach attempts to derive general theoretical principles *from* data. The simplest way to illustrate the difference between theory-driven and data-driven approaches is to distinguish the kinds of questions asked by each. Hypothesis testers tend to ask, "Is this theory true (or approximately true)?" and radical behaviorists tend to ask "I wonder what would happen if...." (Sidman, 1960, p. 8). Knowing that people ordinarily recall up to nine items from a list, a radical behaviorist might ask, "What would happen if all items in the list were repeated twice?" Or "What would happen if recall was delayed for one half hour?" Or "What would happen if we arranged words in the list by semantic categories?" In this way, the scientist is encouraged to look at what does happen, to collect information about behavior, rather than to consider what the data reveal about the shape or capacity of a hypothetical structure.

Second, induction refers to the process of reasoning from specific instances to general laws, a process that is based on two assumptions: a) that a number of specific instances counts as evidence of a general law, and b) that past regularities count as evidence of future regularities. Detailed and thorough accounts of methods for establishing generality are given in Sidman (1960), Hersen and Barlow (1976), and Johnston and Pennypacker (1980). Briefly, radical behaviorists seek to establish generality by the careful manipulation of experimental variables across a number of situations. If a single variable is shown to be similarly effective across several situations, this is taken to be a demonstration of the generality of that variable.

Philosophical problems inherent in the inductive method mainly concern the nature of evidence. Three problems of induction will be dealt with here—generalizing from specific instances, the assumption of continued uniformity, and induction to theories. The first two of these problems will be familiar as Hume's classic problems of induction.

Generalizing from specific instances. The first problem has been stated in the following way: "Given a universal empirical generalization and a certain number of positive instances of it, to what degree do the latter constitute evidence for the former?" (Laudan, 1981*a*, p. 73). In other words, how do we justify universal statements on the basis of a limited number of observations?

Quite simply, there are no logical grounds for believing that a finite number of observations demonstrate (are evidence of) a universal case. The observation of specific instances does not constitute a demonstration of universality. Generalizing from specific instances merely assumes that those instances are all examples of a single principle. Furthermore, there are no hard and fast rules to guide the scientist, no laws of scientific procedure that state the number of observations required to make a universal generalization. Establishing generality is a matter of judgment and the process of induction is "a behavioral process, not a logical one, which is the reason logical analysis has failed to account for it. Whether or not we make an inductive inference, and the degree of tenacity with which we cling to that inference, will depend upon our behavioral history [experience]" (Sidman, 1960, p. 59). The philosopher is correct in stating that there is no logical reason for assuming generality, but there is a behavioral reason, as the following section will clarify.

Assuming continued uniformity. The second problem of induction, also related to the nature of evidence, is a more general issue extending beyond science to everyday behavior. Hume posed the question, "How do we know that nature will continue to behave in the future as it has behaved in the past?" The fact that nature has behaved uniformly in the past does not logically guarantee that it will continue to do so in the future. Because the sun has always appeared in the morning does not assure that it will continue to appear in the morning; because metals always expand when heated does not assure that they will continue to do so. There is no solution to this problem of induction because uniformity into the future can never be demonstrated. Only the future can yield the evidence required to satisfy the issue and the future remains, forever, the future. Induction is again accounted for behaviorally: inductive generalizations are based on experiences in and observations of the world (behavioral history), and continued uniformity has been a part of those experiences and observations. There is no possibility of demonstrating that tomorrow will be as today or as yesterday, but our behavioral history is such that we have in the past experienced tomorrows being the same as yesterdays. That experience leads us to think about and act toward the world as if its uniformities will continue.

This way of behaving toward the world is sometimes said to rest on "the principle of the uniformity of nature" (for example, Hospers, 1956), which is given as the foundation of all science. The principle can never be demonstrated, but it makes sense in the light of our experience in the world, our behavioral history. As noted above, this second problem of induction is not confined to the scientific domain. In everyday matters it is common practice to assume generality, to behave as though aspects of the world that have hitherto been consistent will continue to be so. What could be the consequences of not assuming generality? Our worlds, our lives would have to be negotiated afresh in every moment, in every encounter. The assumption of continued uniformity is an everyday feature of human behavior and, as such, is accounted for by a behavioral analysis.

Induction to theories. Laudan urges that attention be given to yet another problem of induction, arguing that critical discussions of induction tend to overemphasize the two problems outlined above, thereby obscuring another equally important problem. He calls this the problem of "induction to theories" and states it in this way, "Given a theory, and a certain number of confirming instances of it, to what degree do the latter constitute evidence for the warranted assertion of the former?" (Laudan, 1981*a*, p. 74).

Laudan stipulates that the term, theory, in its usage here refers to statements postulating one or more unobservable entities and that this problem of induction relates to instances where such a theory or theoretical statement is tested. Statements that could arise as empirical generalizations are not affected by this problem, but theoretical statements as defined for this argument by Laudan are prone to the third as well as to the first and second problems of induction.

In principle, empirical generalizations could be confirmed by observing all instances of the phenomenon because the general statement amounts to no more than the sum of its single instances. Where a theory or theoretical statement includes reference to unobservable properties or entities, however, that statement goes beyond the sum of its single instances. Even if it were possible to observe all instances of the consequences of a theory, such evidence still could not reliably confirm the theory since one or more of its claims refer to unobservable phenomena. So, the testing of theories or theoretical statements is prone to the first problem of induction—how many single instances justify a generalization?—and to the second problem of induction—what evidence do we have that this generalization will continue to be the case in the future as it has in the past? It is also prone to the criticism that even if all observational consequences of the theory or theoretical statement could be collected, confirmation of the theory could never be claimed if it contained statements about unobservable properties.

For example, a well known and widely demonstrated phenomenon of human remembering goes by the name of the primacy/recency curve or the serial position curve (see Glanzer & Cunitz, 1966; Eysenck, 1984). Typically, subjects presented with a list of words and required to recall the list will reproduce more words from the beginning (primacy) and end (recency) of the list than from its middle. This is an example of an empirical generalization derived from repeated observations of the phenomenon, an assertion that contains no more than the sum of its single instances. Attempts to account for it have usually drawn on the type of theory alluded to earlier that postulates a two-store architecture of memory and additional processes like rehearsal and transfer. Words recalled from the beginning of the list are said to have been transferred into memory's long-term store through the process of rehearsal, while words recalled from the end of the list are said to be maintained in the system's short-term store and thus easily available for recall. Memory stores of this type are unobserved and, without physiological correlates, unobservable. They are additional to the observations and are thus prone to Laudan's problem of induction to theories. No matter how many times the phenomenon is demonstrated, the proposed two-store architecture of memory cannot be confirmed since the stores are unobservable entities.

The problem of induction to theories, as stated by Laudan, is of greatest concern for those areas of psychology whose aim is the verification of a theory that postulates unobservable entities. Indeed, Laudan makes this case when he argues that the first two problems are "a feature of only (but not all) those ampliative inferences which deal exclusively with observable events, objects, or processes" (Laudan, 1981a, p. 75), but with induction to theories, "we do not know—even in those cases where we have a confirming instance—that all the assertions made by the theoretical statement about a given state of affairs were true in the observed cases" (Laudan, 1981a, p. 74). Statements about unobservables cannot be confirmed by any number of demonstrations of the phenomenon. The problem of induction to theories is of no great concern to radical behaviorists since their accounts of behavior avoid explanatory statements that appeal to unseen or unseeable forces, mechanisms, or processes. Rather than testing a theory or hypothesis, radical behaviorists attempt to discover how behavior is related to aspects of the context in which it occurs. The task of analysis is to describe the particular effects (or functions) of discrete aspects of an experimental setting, and the inductive task is to formulate general principles applicable across a wide range of settings.

Radical behaviorists' accounts, like other inductive generalizations, are subject to the philosopher's criticism that they cannot logically be assured. The sun may not rise tomorrow, and perhaps not all metals will expand when heated a week from today. But like other inductive generalizations, they are supported by direct evidence, by positive instances of the general statement, and until new evidence is produced they continue to be reliable. Such generalizations are prone only to the first and second of the problems outlined above. Theories that postulate unobservable and/or hypothetical processes, mechanisms, or entities are also subject to the philosopher's criticism that they cannot be logically assured; any psychological theory of this type also has to deal with induction's first and second problems. Such theories, challenged further by the fact that supporting evidence is indirect rather than direct, are thus subject to the criticism that even if all possible consequences of the theory or theoretical statements could be observed, statements referring to unobservable or hypothetical properties cannot be confirmed. Hypothetico-deduction cannot confirm the accuracy of statements about unobservables.

Shifting Views of the Aims of Science

Science, whether nominally inductive or hypothetico-deductive, seems prone to the problem(s) of induction, with the third problem reserved for theories or theoretical statements that refer to unobservables. What would dictate the use of either method to a researcher and what criteria might scientists apply when deciding how to go about research in their field?

Laudan has been interested in the changing fortunes of hypothetico-deduction and argues that the current favoring of this method over induction is related not to logic or the power of the method but to views of the aims of science held by a scientific community during a particular era. If the aim of science is to reduce natural phenomena to fundamental mechanisms, to postulate structures or mediating entities as explanations, this will determine that their consequences must be deduced and tested for. If, however, the aim of science is to formulate general empirical laws based on observation, this will determine an inductive approach that attempts to generalize *from* data. Criteria for choosing a method will depend on what Laudan calls "our shared archetypes of significant science" that in our own era, he argues, "virtually all involve theoretical entities and processes which are inferentially far removed from the data which they explain" (Laudan, 1981*b*, p. 186). In other times, "speculative theories and unobservable entities were anathema" (Laudan, 1981*b*, p. 186) and at those times, an inductive methodology dominated the philosophy of science. Laudan, not only a philosopher of science dealing with contemporary issues (for example, Laudan 1977, 1984), is also a historian of the philosophy of science. He developed his concept of shared archetypes from a historical analysis of shifts in the nature of physical theory and epistemology in the late 18th and early 19th century. The concept is important for contemporary psychology, and recounting Laudan's historical analysis helps clarify the way changing views of the aims of science have influenced the development of speculative theories in experimental psychology.

The first phase: "aetherial theories." According to Laudan, a major shift in the philosophy of science occurred over the period 1740-1850. The philosophy of science of the early 18th century promoted a rigidly inductive methodology that was fiercely opposed to the method of hypothesis and especially opposed to any kind of theorizing that appealed to unobserved events, processes, or entities. Empiricism dominated and legitimate scientific knowledge was restricted to phenomena that could be directly observed. Newton's achievements gave the lead to succeeding scientists and epistemologists who barred hypotheses from the domain of science. "The [natural] philosophers of the present age hold hypotheses in vile esteem" (Benjamin Martin, 1748, quoted in Laudan, 1981*c*, p. 10) and "The world has been so long befooled by hypotheses in all parts of philosophy, that it is of the utmost consequence...[for] progress in real knowledge to treat them with just contempt" (Thomas Reid, 1785, quoted in Laudan, 1981*c*, p. 10) are only two examples of the general mood of the time. Of invisible entities or agents, Joseph Priestley wrote, "As the agent is invisible, every philosopher is at liberty to make it whatever he pleases, and to ascribe to it such properties and powers as are most convenient for his purposes"

(Joseph Priestley, 1775, quoted in Laudan, 1981*d*, p. 113). Epistemologists of the time were convinced that the fallacy of affirming the consequent rendered the products of hypothesis testing useless as scientific knowledge and were also aware of the dangers of appealing to unobservables as explanations.

The empiricist tone of the time became even more forceful in response to the development of a plethora of theories known as aether theories or aetherial theories, which argued the existence of a subtle fluid or aether through which action takes place. Although aethers were unobservable, they could be invoked to explain a large number of mysterious phenomena, and by the 1760s scientific literature was replete with explanations claiming that light, heat, magnetism, gravity, and most other physical processes resulted from movements or vibrations in an imperceptible aether.

David Hartley and George LeSage gave the initial impetus toward acceptance of the method of hypothesis (Laudan, 1981*d*). Hartley articulated a theory of mind and perception that postulated a subtle fluid or aether in the central nervous system through which vibrations took place. LeSage's theory concerned an invisible aether of particles that bombarded bodies and caused them to move. He argued that bodies were attracted to one another because their facing surfaces partially shielded those surfaces from particle bombardment and, consequently, the greater pressure exerted on their outer surfaces forced them to move closer together. In this way, LeSage's aether theory attempted to explain, among other things, gravitation.

Not surprisingly, the theories of Hartley and LeSage were condemned by empiricist philosophers and scientists of the time for all of the reasons given above. Hartley and LeSage knew that if their theories were to be accepted, the dominant empiricist philosophy had to be weakened and support for the method of hypothesis strengthened. Consequently, they turned their efforts toward epistemological issues.

Hartley began by acknowledging induction as the soundest method for establishing reliable scientific knowledge (Laudan, 1981*d*). Having stated his recognition of the power of the inductive method, he proceeded to argue that it should not be considered to be the only method available to science and that the method of hypothesis also had much to offer. Hartley's main defense was that, although confirmation could not *guarantee* a theory, nevertheless a wide range of confirming instances rendered a theory probable and—in the case of his own theory—its wide explanatory scope rendered it useful to natural knowledge. Hartley also appealed to the heuristic value of hypotheses, arguing that they could lead quickly to confirmation and refutation and therefore to the production of new and useful facts about the world.

But he failed to convince his critics chiefly because he could not give a rational account of why hypotheses concerning unobservables should be believed. For Hartley's contemporaries it was a necessary condition of a legitimate theory that it should fit all of the available data. Hartley, however, went a step further and made it a sufficient condition of legitimate theorizing, a position his contemporaries could not accept. For them, there remained the central problem that theoretical statements concerning unobservable phenomena could not be admitted into the realms of natural knowledge since those statements could not be confirmed by observation.

George LeSage mounted a more robust attack than Hartley, who may have conceded too much to the inductivists by allowing initially that induction is the best route to sure knowledge. Convinced that his theory was dismissed on methodological rather than substantive grounds, LeSage knew that the method of hypothesis had to gain epistemic credibility before his aether theory would get what he considered to be a fair hearing. LeSage conceded far less to the inductivists than Hartley, arguing that inductive methods were not as foolproof as their proponents claimed. His argument revolved around the notion of what is and is not observable, since the inductivists claimed that theories that stayed close to data and dealt only with observables had a greater degree of certainty than theories that were inferentially far removed from their data. LeSage argued that *all* scientific theorizing went beyond observation and that there was no clear point at which, once crossed, one theory could be said to be further removed from direct observation than another. In other words, there is no viable distinction between theories which go beyond the evidence and those which do not.

Having dispensed with the core presumption of inductivist argument, LeSage proceeded with his thesis that both methods, induction and hypothesis, had merits and demerits and therefore neither method should be outlawed from the scientific domain. Hypotheses with a large number of supporting instances and few or no contrary instances have a high degree of confirmation. Thus, he argued, confirming instances *count as evidence* in favor of a hypothesis. LeSage was as concerned as his inductivist contemporaries about the admission of untestable hypotheses. Hypotheses should be subjected to a rigorous process of verification, and those that could not be submitted to this process were unacceptable. But, he added, because *some* hypotheses could not be verified and should be dismissed, it would be a mistake to condemn the method in its entirety. Given suitable empirical constraints, the method of hypothesis had much to contribute to science. Neither its fallibility nor the fact that it sometimes produced false theories should force a decision to abandon the method, LeSage argued, since its achievements could be of great value to the growth of knowledge.

The inductivists continued to rest their case on the observational requirement, rejecting theories that sought to explain phenomena by an appeal to unobservable mediating fluids or aethers. Laudan notes that the Scottish philosopher Thomas Reid maintained a rigid inductivist stance by rejecting Hartley and LeSage's contention that a large number of confirming instances count as positive evidence in favor of a theory. By demanding too much, however, Reid's epistemology "was altogether unable to come to grips with the contemporary theoretical sciences" (Laudan, 1981*d*, p. 127) and by the late 18th century the debate was at a standstill, with neither side having convinced the other of the case for or against the method of hypothesis.

The second phase: a new epistemic criterion. The debate was given renewed impetus in the period 1820-1850 by the simultaneous emergence of a new epistemological criterion for evaluating hypotheses and the success of the developing wave theory of light (Laudan, 1981*d*). The new criterion is familiar in modern philosophy of science but did not form part of the earlier debate between Hartley, LeSage, and the inductivists. The criterion is that of the independent test: an acceptable hypothesis became one that not only had wide explanatory scope and a large number of confirming instances but was required also to be able to predict novel or unlikely phenomena and to demonstrate its predictions. Note that this criterion is essentially a reconstrual of the nature of evidence. For Hartley and LeSage, a large number of confirming instances counted as evidence. For the inductivists, observables alone counted as evidence and they rejected Hartley and LeSage's definition of evidence on the grounds that there were many patently false theories that, with suitable modification, could garner to themselves a large number of confirming instances. The independent test criterion shifted the responsibility of evidence from that of accounting for the already known, to that of predicting the unknown. Hypotheses were required, in the emerging philosophy of science of the early to mid-19th century, to predict and explain aspects of the physical world that were significantly different from those aspects they had originally been invented to explain.

As with the earlier debate, this debate, too, was informed by both epistemological concerns and developments in physical theory. Two competing theories of light, corpuscular theory and wave theory, required the method of hypothesis and it was the ability of the wave theory to predict and explain surprising or unexpected phenomena that encouraged the two major proponents of the hypothesis, John Herschel and William Whewell, to establish the modern criterion of independent testing as the crucial justification for this method. For Hartley and LeSage, it was sufficient that a hypothesis should be able to explain all of the relevant phenomena and be consistent with all of the observed facts. For Herschel and Whewell, this was only one necessary condition. Sufficient conditions for them included the criteria of Hartley and LeSage, with the addition of the criterion of the independent test. By the middle of the 19th century, an acceptable hypothesis was one that a) accounted for all of the observed facts and b) predicted and explained phenomena not yet known, or phenomena that were unexpected.

This new criterion had its critics, notably John Stuart Mill, who argued that being impressed by successful and surprising predictions had more

to do with human psychology than with epistemology. Epistemologi-
cally, hypotheses continued to suffer from the possibility that although
they may account for a large number of observed phenomena, they may
still be false. To argue for the superiority of hypotheses that successfully
predict novel and sometimes surprising phenomena was, in Mill's
opinion, to confuse the psychology of surprise with epistemological
questions on the nature of evidence. Mill accepted that many people are
impressed by a theory that makes successful predictions, and are especially impressed if those predictions are novel or surprising in some way,
but he called for epistemological support for the criterion of independent
testing rather than a justification based on psychology.

By the end of the 1850s, however, the method of hypothesis had gained
the unprecedented credibility it retains today. Acceptance of the method
of hypothesis was essential to allow physical theories concerned with
fundamental and usually unobservable structures to be admitted into the
realms of legitimate scientific knowledge. Today's shared archetypes of
significant science mainly involve the search for theoretical entities,
processes, or structures, whose observational consequences must be
deduced and tested for. The method of hypothesis goes unquestioned
today, and it would be interesting to consider what the shape of our
present scientific knowledge might be if the proponents of the method
of hypothesis had been less successful in their drive to establish its
epistemic credibility.

Shared Archetypes in Contemporary Psychology

Applying Laudan's notion of "shared archetypes of significant science"
to contemporary experimental psychology can help to resolve some of
the confusions between the radical behaviorist approach and others
because it directs us to look for some of those shared archetypes that
govern the choice of method. For example, the cognitive or information
processing approach concerns itself with hypothetical inner structures or
processes that mediate between input and output. This approach shares
the broad features of other speculative sciences in that it appeals to

fundamental structures as explanations of action. Like them, it must use the method of hypothesis because the only way to proceed with these kinds of structural theories is through deducing their observational consequences and testing for them. Evidence is indirect, and the approach suffers from the classic (Humean) problems of induction as well as from Laudan's problem of induction to theories. Again, as with other speculative sciences, each theory awaits its downfall as the process of matching theory to real-world phenomena proceeds. Such theories in all sciences can only be tentatively held.

Radical behaviorism's shared archetypes differ from those of contemporary psychology. Radical behaviorists do not concern themselves with mediating processes and structures but with behavior-environment relations. They seek general behavioral principles, derived *from* data and based on direct observation. Theirs is a philosophy of science closer to the period when "speculative theories and unobservable entities were anathema" (Laudan, 1981*b*, p. 186) than to the shared archetypes of our own era that "virtually all involve theoretical entities and processes which are inferentially far removed from the data which they explain" (Laudan, 1981*b*, p. 186). As an approach based on direct evidence, giving prominence to data rather than to theory, radical behaviorist methodology does not require the method of hypothesis. Speculative theories cannot function without the method; radical behaviorism does not rely on it and rarely, if ever, calls on it.

The Context of Scientific Behavior

Skinner freely admitted that in some circumstances the method of hypothesis is useful, but rejected it as an essential component of science and noted that in his own research experience he had "never faced a problem that was more than the eternal problem of finding order" (Skinner, 1959, p. 369). It is true that a researcher may approach an experiment already guessing its outcome or with a hunch (perhaps based on background knowledge) about how the variable of interest will be effective, but as Skinner also noted, "The guesses and hunches with which the experimenter proceeds...are not the formal hypotheses of scientific method; they are simply tentative statements for which further support is sought" (Skinner, 1969, pp. 82-83).

A good example of the way radical behaviorists proceed without the formal methodology of prediction and hypothesis testing can be seen in a report by Matthijs, whose research is in a field known as stimulus equivalence or equivalence relations and involves questions about the way words and symbols become semantically related. Matthijs (1988) states that his research "is in the first place an attempt to expand and to systematically replicate the findings on stimulus equivalence in a schizophrenic population." He reports that his research both *replicates* and *expands* on background knowledge. After describing his procedures, he continues: "After a subject has been taught all these conditional relations, the question arises whether he has learned anything more than simple conditional if-then performances, or whether the contingencies have been successful in establishing in the subject's behavior a class of verbal, symbolic, or equivalent stimuli" (Matthijs, 1988). Note that Matthijs makes no predictions about the sort of behavior that will be generated by the contingencies, but asks Sidman's "I wonder what would happen if" question (Sidman, 1960, p. 8). Some facts are already known about the development of equivalence classes, and Matthijs tries to see whether they continue to hold true (by replication) and whether the knowledge base can be expanded by examining the generation of equivalence classes under more complex contingencies. The knowledge base grows through replication and expansion, and when more of the significant data (in Sidman's use of that term) are compiled, radical behaviorists will be in a position to derive general principles from those data. Note also that in Matthijs' experiment nothing is wasted. Such an experiment cannot produce negative data because, as Sidman put it, "Data can be negative only in terms of a prediction. When one simply asks a question of nature, the answer is always positive. Even an experimental manipulation that produces no change in the dependent variable can provide useful and often important information" (Sidman, 1960, p. 9). It is true that Matthijs could state *post hoc* several hypotheses and report whether these were confirmed or not, but it is also true that this is not the way his research was conducted.

Green and D'Oliveira (1982) and others continue to present students with a straightforward, logical, and rational vision of the research process. Skinner, however, argued that this ideal vision does not correspond to the everyday reality of laboratory research. It is more appropriate to recognize the somewhat disordered nature of the process than to describe (or prescribe) science as a series of logical steps: "The behavior of the scientist is often reconstructed by scientific methodologists within a logical framework of hypothesis, deduction, and the testing of theorems, but the reconstruction seldom represents the behavior of the scientist at work" (Skinner, 1974, p. 236). In the early 1950s a project was initiated that attempted to identify the progress psychology had made in understanding and accounting for human behavior by looking at some of the major theoretical approaches then current. Skinner, along with other major theorists of the time, was invited to give an account of his position in systematic and formal terms. Themes to be discussed in "Project A" included: Background and orienting factors; Structure of the system as thus far developed; Initial evidential grounds for assumptions of the system; Construction of function forms; Mensurational and quantificational procedures; Formal organization of the system; Scope and range of application of the system; History to date in mediating research; Evidence for the system; Specific methods, concepts, or principles of the system believed valuable outside the context of the system; Degree of programmaticity; Intermediate and long-range strategy for the development of the system (Koch, 1959, pp. 666-673). The organizers of Project A felt the time had come to consider how psychology had developed as a system of knowledge, what advances had been made, and how each part of psychology contributed to the overall discipline: "Knowledge has grown rapidly in the short history of man's efforts to develop a science of behavior, and the time seems appropriate for a major effort to examine the progress that has been made in attempting to find a way, or ways, to the attainment of the explanatory power that we like to think of as characteristic of science" (Wolfle, 1959, p. v).

Other contributors attempted to describe their systems in the formal terms given above, but Skinner argued that scientific behavior could not easily be described in formal/logical terms and gave instead an account of the development of his system by looking back at his own scientific behavior and at other features of his research experience that contributed to new findings (Skinner, 1959). In doing this, he summarized five "unformalized principles of scientific practice": "when you run into something interesting, drop everything else and study it"; "some ways of doing research are easier than others"; "some people are lucky"; "apparatus sometimes breaks down"; and "serendipity," or "the art of finding one thing while looking for something else" (Skinner, 1959). These unformalized principles would not sit comfortably within an account that presents the scientific process as the deduction of predictions and the testing of hypotheses, but they nevertheless describe aspects of Skinner's own research experience and possibly the experience of other scientists more accurately than formal accounts.

Skinner's reaction against formalism should not be interpreted as a call to abandon scientific method; being opposed to excessive formalism is not equivalent to an absence of definable methods. The two broad conclusions of Skinner's analysis are that: a) certain features of his behavior contributed to the production of new findings, and b) that some inevitable occurrences (for example, accidents) in the course of research can also bring to light an effect or result not planned for. It is well known that the process of classical conditioning did not come to light through the formal procedures described so clearly in methodology textbooks. Pavlov and his students were measuring digestive secretions in dogs, and the fact that the dogs began to salivate when Pavlov entered the room was initially an irritation because it corrupted his careful measures of the relation between food and salivation (Rachlin, 1970). By dropping everything else and studying it, Pavlov revealed important processes and relations that generated new fields of research and allowed for the development of new therapeutic techniques in applied settings.

In his own scientific practice, Skinner dispensed with the method of hypothesis. He also rejected descriptions of the scientific process that present it as a straightforward and strictly logical pursuit. The scientist, for Skinner, is part of a complex set of contingencies including subject matter, language (the concepts of ordinary language as well as scientific laws and theorems), laboratory spaces, instruments, other people, and so on that interact in the production of new findings. The traditional view of the white-coated scientist operating *on* an environment rather than *in* an environment is an imperfect view for Skinner, who did not separate the scientist, the person, from the context in which scientific behavior occurs. For Skinner, as for other radical behaviorists, science is imperfectly presented when it is described as a series of rigorous, logical steps.

When we speak of science or attempt to describe (or prescribe) its methods, we must be careful not to imply that the dominant methodology (in our own era, the method of hypothesis) *is* science or is the only way of doing science. Hypothetico-deduction has not always enjoyed a favored place in the philosophy of science; its dominance in our own era is related to developments in physical theory and the establishment of new epistemic justifications that took place between 1740 and 1850. Methodology is dictated by a number of concerns, and the choice of hypothetico-deduction is not dictated by logic or by the power of the method; contemporary views of the aims of science render it indispensable despite its enduring flaws, because it is the only method available for testing speculative theoretical statements involving unobservables. The method continues to suffer the charges that it can only provide indirect evidence for such statements and, in the final analysis, that observing predicted events does not confirm these speculative statements. Induction is not without its logical problems, but principles derived inductively have the advantage of being based on direct evidence and thus providing reliable knowledge until contradictory evidence is produced. A large part of contemporary psychology shares the view that mechanisms and structures are science's important explanatory concepts. Approaches that concern themselves with hypothetical structures or mechanisms must necessarily adopt the method of hypothesis, with all its flaws, as LeSage and Hartley were forced to do. Such speculative theories cannot function without it. Radical behaviorism does not appeal to mechanisms or structures as explanatory concepts and its science does not, therefore, rely on hypothetico-deduction.

Speculative theories, in conjunction with the method of hypothesis, have two major effects on scientific psychology that again do not concern radical behaviorists but that should be noted. First, they encourage a style of inquiry whereby theories and theorists compete for verification and falsification: "The deductive mode tends to encourage an advocacy style of inquiry wherein experimental results are marshalled in support of propositional statements, whereas the inductive strategy promotes attention to any properly obtained data" (Johnston & Pennypacker, 1980, p. 31). Scientists are encouraged to ask questions about the accuracy or otherwise of theories or theoretical statements rather than questions about behavior itself. Second, it encourages in contemporary psychology the same practice that pervaded physics during the decades of aetherial theories; that is to say, a "proliferation of personal theorizing" (Watkins, 1990), in the sense that if hypothetical systems and mechanisms are the important explanatory concepts, then any number of modifications to those concepts can (and frequently do) produce whole new theories with new experimental tests and yet more attempts to verify or falsify competing theories. In this way, much of scientific psychology expends enormous energy attempting to establish theoretical supremacy.

Chapter 4

Aims, Methods, and the Individual

By extracting the method of hypothesis from psychology's methodological package and comparing it with induction, the previous chapter highlighted an overall view of the aims of science that informs and guides the methods used by radical behaviorists. It noted that psychology students are trained in the method of hypothesis and the mastery of experimental design and statistical analysis of data. This chapter considers in more detail some of the philosophical and scientific issues related to the statistical treatment of behavioral data, and contrasts radical behaviorism's views on methods for analyzing behavior.

Psychology relies extensively on inferential statistics for drawing conclusions about the effects of independent variables. This type of analysis is rooted in the concepts of variation, the average, and the normal distribution. The statistical view considers variation to be an undesirable feature of psychological data, and requires individuality to be suppressed in favor of the average. Furthermore, it is based on an assumption that variation conforms to the normal distribution, that measures of psychological attributes in a population cluster around a mean and trail off in the direction of excess or deficiency. The statistical view of variation encourages the use of large numbers of subjects and the group comparison approach to experimental questions. This view of variation and of how to cope with it is the starting point for experimental design and data analysis in many areas of experimental psychology, providing justification for that ubiquitous feature of contemporary psychology—the test of significance. If the subject matter is variable, it is argued, then the probability of an outcome being due to variation needs to be assessed, and this can be done using statistical tests of significance.

This view differs from the biological concept of variation. There, variation is far from being an undesirable deviation. It is the raw material for selection and evolution. Variation as a fundamental biological phenomenon is central to radical behaviorism's view of organisms and their behavior. Organisms—rats, pigeons, or people—comprise a unique genetic endowment and a unique reinforcement history (life experience). Starting from the biological rather than statistical viewpoint, radical behaviorists do not rely on the concepts of average and normal distribution and do not derive statements about effects of independent variables from statistical tests of significance. Psychology adopted and adapted methods that were developed for making statements about populations, statements that cannot be applied to individuals and that are useful where the behavior of individuals is of no interest. Maintaining the biological tradition, radical behaviorists developed methods that accept and incorporate notions of individuality. In this way, they derive statements that can be applied to the behavior of individuals.

The move toward what is now psychology's orthodoxy—large numbers, statistical treatment, and tests of significance—began roughly at the turn of the century, partly as a result of newly emerged statistical concepts and methods. The importance of the average and the normal distribution as concepts that are assumed to describe the shape of variation in large groups, so much a part of contemporary thinking in psychology and other disciplines, was introduced by Adolph Quetelet in 1844 (Hacking, 1990). These ideas underpin the sophisticated statistical techniques developed in the 1930s by R. A. Fisher, whose statistical innovations "were one of the more important developments of the century for psychology" (Hersen & Barlow, 1976, p. 7)

From Individual To Average

Most psychological texts carefully elucidate the mathematical concept of normal distribution or the bell shaped curve, and imply (if not explicitly state) that psychological attributes tend toward a mean with smaller and smaller numbers tailing off in the direction of excess or deficiency. The assumption that variations in behavior conform roughly to the bell shaped curve provides the basis of statistical tests leading to inferences about the effect of an independent variable as opposed to chance fluctuation.

In *The Taming of Chance*, Hacking (1990) documents the development of statistical reasoning as a means of imposing order and predictability on social phenomena, and traces how Quetelet developed the assumption that aspects of human behavior are normally distributed. Hacking's research deals with Quetelet's reasoning in fine detail and thus throws new light on the assumption by showing how Quetelet transformed abstract mathematical properties into true values, into properties of a collective. Quetelet simply leaped from the distribution of measurement errors to the assertion that this distribution was characteristic of biological and social phenomena.

According to Hacking, Quetelet's reasoning derived from two sources: First, from repeated observations of a single astronomical quantity measured over a four year period. These measures of a physical (but unknown) quantity clustered around a mean, so the real measure could be assumed to be somewhere around that mean. Second, from the published measurements of 5,738 soldiers from eleven Scottish regiments. Quetelet combined the chest measurements from all eleven regiments and found the largest number of measurements at thirty nine inches (1073) and forty inches (1079) (Hacking, 1990). He then introduced a strange step into the reasoning; he made a surprising link between errors in measurements of physical quantities and measurements of abstract properties by arguing that if an individual chest of approximately forty inches was measured 5,738 times, these measures would show the same regularity, clustering around the real value in the same way.

Quetelet argued that measures from many individuals were indistinguishable in distribution from many measures of the same individual, and thus claimed the same status for abstract statistical properties as for real values. He equated statistical abstractions with real physical quantities by subjecting them to the same formal techniques (Hacking, 1990). In measuring the chest of one individual many times, or taking many measures of an astronomical event, there is an objectively real quantity being measured: however, "[Quetelet] transformed the theory of measuring unknown physical quantities, with a definite probable error, into the theory of measuring ideal or abstract properties of a population. Because these could be subjected to the same formal techniques they became real quantities. This is a crucial step in the taming of chance. It began to turn statistical laws that were merely descriptive of large-scale regularities into laws of nature and society that dealt in underlying truths and causes" (Hacking, 1990, p. 108). Quetelet took the shape of errors in measurements of physical properties and simply claimed that this shape could also be applied to the distribution of social phenomena: "The celestial position being measured is a real point in space, and the distribution of errors, we suppose, is an objective feature of the measuring device and the measurer. Quetelet changed the game. He applied the same curve to biological and social phenomena where the mean is not a real quantity at all, or rather *he transformed the mean into a real quantity*" (Hacking, 1990, p. 107).

The concept of the average as a real (and ideal) property was important to Quetelet as part of his doctrine of the Average Man (Quetelet, 1969), wherein he assumed that nature aimed at a fixed point in creating human beings but that, just as an individual makes errors in measurement, so nature also makes errors and produces clusters around the fixed point. Fashing and Goertzel (1981) point out that to Quetelet "the mean in any distribution of human phenomena was...not merely a descriptive tool but a statement of the ideal" and "extremes in all things were undesirable deviations" (p. 16). This view differs from the biological concept of variation in that variation to a biologist is far from being an error of nature, an undesirable deviation from an ideal, fixed point. It is the raw material for selection and evolution. Concepts like average and ideal do not enter into a Darwinian, biological formulation, but they continue, in the tradition of Quetelet, to form part of the background to psychology's treatment of its data. The assumption that measures from many individuals will cluster around a mean, and that there is somewhere in the data an average or ideal subject, is the basis of psychology's treatment of variation.

Aims, Methods, and the Individual

The myth of the normal curve (Fashing & Goertzel, 1981), with its attendant concepts of deviation, the average, and the ideal, entered the philosophy of social phenomena, allowing the development of new statistical techniques that were eagerly drawn upon by sociologists and psychologists in their attempts to quantify behavior and develop causal analyses. Paradoxically, while psychology recognizes variation and thus individuality, it considers variation (and thus individuality) to be an undesirable feature of its data. The average is a center from which deviation departs, and deviations from the normal state are unwelcome and considered to be unrepresentative of the average person. But, as other authors have also noted (Sidman, 1960; Hersen & Barlow, 1976; Fashing & Goertzel, 1981; Hacking, 1990), there is no such real quantity as the average person. The normal distribution is a mathematical conceptualization of an idealized distribution. Large numbers of scores, like large numbers of measuring errors, produce statistical averages with clusters around a mean. These statistics do not describe an average individual or any objectively real property. The numerical average is only that. All individuals in a psychology experiment or any other collection of statistical information, whether their behavior measures close to a mean or far from it, are just that—individuals. Psychologists using large groups and the statistical approach can only draw conclusions about independent variables and their relation to behavior by silencing differences between individuals. Such an approach begs the question, "Whose behavior does this independent variable influence"? Quetelet derived the notion of the average or ideal from massed observations of many individuals and claimed that such observations took the same form as if they had been measures of one individual. In this startling step, he turned abstract mathematical properties into real quantities. Using statistical techniques based on Quetelet's mean and curve, psychologists are forced to see their massed data as though they were drawn from one individual—the average, ideal subject. Although there is no such phenomenon in reality, the notion of the ideal or average person lurks behind all such experimentation.

Psychology's "Methodological Keystone"

Until the 1930s, statistical analysis of data from large numbers of individuals remained primarily in the domain of the study of individual differences. The development of a more sophisticated range of statistical tests had a profound influence on the direction of experimental psychology. R. A. Fisher, geneticist and statistician, is one of the key figures who have influenced psychology's present-day reliance on statistical procedures (Guilford, 1950; Hersen & Barlow, 1976) and its appeal to the test of significance as a form of evidence. In *The Design of Experiments*, Fisher (1947) advocated rigor in experimental design, instructing that all possible outcomes must be predicted prior to conducting an experiment and an unambiguous decision made about how those outcomes are to be interpreted: "In considering the appropriateness of any proposed experimental design, it is always needful to forecast all possible results of the experiment, and to have decided without ambiguity what interpretation shall be placed upon each one of them" (Fisher, 1947, p. 12). Fisher claimed that the null hypothesis is "characteristic of all experimentation" and stressed that "much confusion would often be avoided if it were explicitly formulated when the experiment is designed" (Fisher, 1947, p. 16). Note that Fisher's conception of the research process differed considerably from the radical behaviorist approach in that he advocated hypothetico-deduction and the testing of predictions against a null hypothesis.

On acceptable levels of probability Fisher wrote, "It is usual and convenient for experimenters to take 5 per cent as a standard level of significance, in the sense that they are prepared to ignore all results which fail to reach this standard, and, by this means, to eliminate from further discussion the greater part of the fluctuations which chance causes have introduced into their experimental results" (Fisher, 1947, p. 13). Most of the contents of the methodological package of contemporary experimental psychology are to be found in Fisher's *The Design of Experiments*, along with their rationale, to which the majority of texts dealing with statistical treatment of psychology's data remain faithful. The ubiquity of the test of significance in contemporary experimental psychology is noted by David Bakan (1967) who refers to it ironically as psychology's methodological keystone: "The vast majority of investigations which pass for research in the field of psychology today entail the use of statistical tests of significance" (Bakan, 1967, p. 1). He also notes that the test of significance "bears the essential responsibility" for conclusions drawn from psychological experiments and observes that significance testing "constitutes a critical part of the total cultural-scientific tapestry. To pull out the strand of the test of significance would seem to make the whole tapestry fall apart" (Bakan, 1967, p. 12). In other words, given the extent of reliance on significance testing today, it is difficult to imagine a scientific psychology proceeding without it.

Rigor and convention. Fisher made an important claim about the scientific value of statistical treatment of data that deserves careful consideration because it appears to resolve one of science's central philosophical problems—the problem of induction. He stated that statistical procedures not only assist the researcher in making sense of data, but also serve the more important function of supplying "the machinery for unambiguous interpretation" (Fisher, 1947, p. v). He further argued that mathematical treatment of data resolves the uncertainty of induction by making that process "perfectly rigorous": "We may at once admit that any inference from the particular to the general must be attended with some degree of uncertainty, but this is not the same as to admit that such inference cannot be absolutely rigorous, for the nature and degree of the uncertainty may itself be capable of rigorous expression" (Fisher, 1947, p. 4). Put simply, Fisher's argument proceeds as follows: there is always a degree of uncertainty in moving from the particular to the general; this uncertainty can be mathematically stated as a probability; therefore, applying probability testing (the laws of chance) to experimental data provides for a mathematical (rigorous) inductive inference. Fisher concluded: "The mere fact that inductive inferences are uncertain cannot, therefore, be accepted as precluding perfectly rigorous and unequivocal inference" (Fisher, 1947, p. 4).

The previous chapter noted three uncertainties normally attributed to induction: a) there is no logical basis for assuming that a number of specific instances demonstrate a general law; b) there is no logical assurance that a general law will continue to hold true in the future; and c) no matter how many times the deduced consequences of a theory are observed, the theory cannot be confirmed if it contains statements about unobservables.

Fisher's solution to the uncertainty of induction was to make uncertainty synonymous with probability and to apply mathematical laws of probability to the single instances from which general assertions are to be made. Such assertions, however, are still not exempt from the foregoing uncertainties of induction. Assertions derived from Fisher's statistical inference model are no more assured in terms of the three points above than are those derived from other scientific procedures because, strictly speaking, inferences using this model are not inductive inferences. Inductive inferences are drawn from many observations of a single phenomenon and are statements of the form "these observations exemplify a scientific law." Statistical inferences can be made on the basis of only one observation of a sample and the process of generalization is to the population from which the sample was drawn: a statement of the form "what has occurred in this sample is asserted to occur in the larger population from which it was drawn." Although Fisher's reasoning concerning the problem of inductive inference and its solution is persuasive, his technique is not closely related to inductive inference.

Fisher's wording when advocating statistical treatment of data is generally impressive and persuasive and may in itself contribute to widespread confidence in the method. By equating uncertainty with probability and using terms like perfectly rigorous and unequivocal, Fisher conveyed a sense of confidence that any uncertainty can be accounted for by calculating the probability at which a given result might be expected to occur naturally—without the intervention of an experimental variable. For him, the mathematical precision of laws of chance guaranteed that inductive inferences could be made unequivocally. But this language of certainty and assurance may serve mainly to overcome or conceal a serious contradiction in Fisher's rationale, which at a later stage admits that "It is *usual* and *convenient* for experimenters to take 5 per cent as a standard level of significance" (Fisher, 1947, p. 13, emphasis added). The terms, usual and convenient, are quite at odds with terms like perfectly rigorous and unequivocal, and reveal that the body of knowledge constituting much of contemporary psychology could be overturned not by the introduction of *new* evidence, but by a simple change in procedure. By shifting the usual and convenient level of significance from 5 per cent to 3 per cent or 1 per cent, much of what currently constitutes the body of knowledge of experimental psychology—"rigorously derived" and "unequivocally" inferred—would change according to the new level of significance.

While offering a guarantee against the uncertainty of induction, Fisher's statistical rationale is contradicted by the admittedly arbitrary adoption of a 5 per cent level of significance; how certain are conclusions that could be reversed as a direct consequence of changing the level of significance? The language of certainty may be appealing, but here, certainty is nonetheless directly related to an arbitrarily chosen level of significance. Furthermore, reliance on the results of significance tests as a form of evidence for or against scientific assertions brings into question the meaning of the term, evidence, when that evidence may be reversed from one level of confidence to another. At one level of confidence, a result may favor a scientific assertion, while at another level the same result may go against the same assertion. Evidence in favor of assertions that constitute much of the present body of knowledge of experimental psychology rests on a convention. Should the convention change, the same data could become evidence against those assertions.

Flaws in the body of knowledge: Type I error. David Bakan points out another problem for psychology's body of knowledge, a problem that arises from its reliance on significance testing as a form of evidence; the admission of Type I errors (rejecting the null hypothesis when it is true) into scientific literature. The logic of significance testing itself allows for the occurrence of the Type I error. Fisher was aware of this and cautioned that no matter how surprised we may be that the rare event happens to *us*, we must nevertheless be aware that it will occur "with no less and no more than its appropriate frequency" (Fisher, 1947, p. 14). Fisher could not predict that it would become the practice of journal editors in psychology to publish only those papers which report statistically significant results, but this is now done (Bakan, 1967). As a consequence, the psychological literature itself contains examples of the Type I error at "no less and no more than its appropriate frequency." Bakan suggests the following scenario for an instance in which the null hypothesis is actually true: one hundred researchers examine a psychological phenomenon; ninety five of these investigators accept the null hypothesis and five reject it; of the hundred investigators, the five who demonstrated statistical significance will write up their results and publish. Bakan notes, "One might imagine interesting quarrels arising among [the investigators] concerning priority of discovery, if the differences came out in the same direction, and controversy, if the differences came out in different directions. In the former instance, the psychological community might even take it as evidence of 'replicability' of the phenomenon, in the latter instance as evidence that the scientific method is 'self-corrective.' The other ninety-five experimenters would wonder what they did wrong" (Bakan, 1967, p. 12).

The assurance of rigor and unequivocation conveyed by Fisher in making his case for statistical treatment is undermined by the procedure itself, which rests on no more than a useful and convenient level of significance. Significance testing is a peculiar form of evidence for scientific assertions since the same measures could count both for or against such assertions in direct relation to the level of significance adopted. Furthermore, as Bakan points out, even if experimental psychologists are able to live with a contradiction between rigor and convention, the body of knowledge is likely to be flawed by the admission of Type I errors into the scientific literature—a consequence of the logic of significance testing itself and of the practice of publishing only those research findings that report statistically significant results. Results that do not demonstrate significance at the convenient level are assigned to chance.

The status of chance. Chance has attained the status of an explanatory concept in contemporary psychology. If results do not demonstrate a statistically significant relation between two or more variables, chance is invoked as an explanation of the outcome. Sidman notes, "The chief antagonist of statistical reliability is 'Chance.' Modern psychology has set Chance up as its devil. All data are, at birth, considered to bear its taint, and any data that cannot be proved to be independent of Chance are forthwith and irrevocably assigned to its hell" (Sidman, 1960, p. 43). He adds that only data with a low probability of belonging to chance are admitted into science: "If they do not belong to Chance, they belong to Science. Thus data are accepted into science by exclusion. They possess no positive virtues, only the negative one of being due to chance with a low level of confidence" (Sidman, 1960, p. 43).

Sidman examines the meaning of chance and finds that it may be used in at least three ways. First, it may be used to describe the combined effect of uncontrolled variables and, in this usage, it is "simply an excuse for sloppy experimentation" (Sidman, 1960, p. 45). Second, it may be used to describe a situation in which unknown variables have played a part and, in this usage, it is synonymous with ignorance. Sidman takes the view that scientists dedicate themselves to overturning ignorance, and that to accept chance in this second meaning of the term "is a curious negation of the professed aims of science" (Sidman, 1960, p. 45). The third meaning Sidman finds for chance equates it with unpredictability, but to accept unpredictability as an *a priori* assumption "would put a natural scientist out of business" (Sidman, 1960, p. 46). If there are elements of behavior or other natural phenomena that are unpredictable, the extent of unpredictability cannot be discovered without first uncovering the extent to which they are predictable, and "We have a long way to travel before we can argue convincingly that the variability observed in any given experiment is irreducible" (Sidman, 1960, p. 143).

The contemporary practice of admitting chance as an explanatory concept is similar to an earlier practice in reflex physiology of admitting spontaneity as a form of explanation for the behavior of intact organisms, and to the later practice of describing the remission of a clinical disorder as spontaneous remission. Skinner took issue with the explanatory status of spontaneity when he wrote, "Spontaneity is negative evidence; it points to the weakness of a current scientific explanation....By its very nature, spontaneity must yield ground as a scientific analysis is able to advance" (Skinner, 1953, p. 48). The same is true of the explanatory status of chance, as a paraphrase of Skinner will show: "Chance is negative evidence; it points to the weakness of a current scientific explanation. By its very nature, chance must yield ground as a scientific analysis is able to advance." As behavior is brought under refined experimental control more and more of the phenomena currently assigned to chance will be explicable in terms of controlling variables and chance, like spontaneity, will recede.

Orderly Relations and Experimental Control

Concepts like chance and the average or ideal subject do not enter into radical behaviorism's formulation of science in general or psychology in particular. Like other psychologists, behavior analysts recognize variation in human behavior, they recognize the individuality of people and other organisms. But they approach variation from the biological perspective, not from the statistical, Quetelian perspective. Rather than considering variation (and thus individuality) to be an unwelcome aspect of behavioral data, as in the Quetelian approach, they argue that it is fundamental to all scientific phenomena and that the task of science is to account for variation, to seek out the order in variability rather than to silence it: "Variation is the rule, not the exception, of all that exists. In the most general sense, the subject matter of all science is variability....Like all other natural phenomena, behavior displays variability, and like the other sciences, the science of behavior has as its task the explanation of that variability" (Johnston & Pennypacker, 1980, pp. 201/202).

In considering the subject matter of natural sciences in the late twentieth century, it may be difficult to appreciate that before the development of experimental control, aspects of the physical universe that are now the subject matter of physics, biology, and chemistry also seemed infinitely variable. Scientific chemistry ordered our human understanding of a seemingly infinite array of substances into a finite number of elements, and prior to Galileo it was perhaps inconceivable that only a few laws of motion could equally describe the movement of celestial and terrestrial bodies. But, as Sidman (1960) notes, the natural sciences assumed that underlying the variability was some kind of constancy, some order, and methods of *experimental* control were developed for coping with the subject matter and uncovering orderly relations. Psychology, on the other hand, begins with the assumption that its subject matter is intrinsically variable and has developed methods that apply *statistical* control and rely on tests of significance as a form of evidence for its scientific assertions.

The assumption of underlying order and the techniques growing out of that assumption have demonstrated in the natural sciences that nature can be described and interpreted in terms of orderly relations. In contrasting the basic assumptions of order and intrinsic variability, Sidman (1960) argues that if we take intrinsic variability as a starting point, we are led to develop methods that mathematically control variability and in doing so, close off the possibility of finding further order. He notes that although modern physics has reached a stage of development that suggests an element of chaos or randomness in nature, it has reached this stage only after the most careful exploration of sources of variability and control of experimental error. If there is randomness in nature, physics has attained a degree of control over its subject matter that may allow its confident admission. But starting from the assumption of variability, psychology closes off the possibility of attaining the same degree of experimental control. As Sidman has put it, "Modern physics is deeply involved in a realm of phenomena in which variability is the rule. But this shift was not a matter of philosophy; it was forced by the data. And the data which necessitated the change could never have been obtained if natural variability had been accepted from the start. The hard core of intrinsic variability was accepted only after errors of measurement had been reduced to quantitative insignificance and after exploration of possible contributory factors failed to eliminate the variability" (Sidman, 1960, p. 143). Psychology reverses the core philosophical presumption of physics and other natural sciences in accepting variability prior to experimental control of its subject matter.

Radical behaviorists take order as their starting point. Skinner wrote of science that it is "a search for order, for uniformities, for lawful relations among the events in nature" (Skinner, 1953, p. 13), and that in his own research experience he never faced a problem "that was more than the eternal problem of finding order" (Skinner, 1959, p. 369). These statements are at the heart of radical behaviorism's treatment of variability in psychological data. Science is a form of human behavior that seeks to demonstrate uniformities in nature by isolating aspects of it, controlling those aspects and their relations with other parts of nature, and formulating universal laws that summarize and describe classes of events. The enterprise of science is a search for order, and variation or variability has an important part to play in that search by directing the scientist to look for its source. Variability, to the radical behaviorist, raises the important scientific question, "Of what is this variability a function?" Variability is not viewed as an interference, a nuisance to be dispensed with by the use of statistical techniques, or silenced by averaging measures from large numbers of subjects and assuming an ideal average subject whose behavior is affected by an independent variable. Rather, variability itself poses research questions and guides the scientist toward greater refinement of techniques for gaining control over the multitude of factors influencing a given situation: "The process of systematically tracking down sources of variability, and thus explaining variable data, is characteristic of the scientific enterprise" (Sidman, 1960, p. 192).

Working with individuality. Radical behaviorists accept the unique individuality of people and other organisms and incorporate it into their experimental techniques. Discovering or establishing baselines in the behavior of individual subjects, either by recording data across time as it occurs prior to any intervention, or by manipulating contingencies so that behavior develops a steady state, behavior analysts begin with a measure of behavior for each of the subjects involved. The effect of an independent variable is assessed against each subject's individual baseline. If rates of behavior vary in an upward direction for three subjects and in a downward direction or not at all for one subject, the experimenter attempts to trace and control the source of this variation by experimental means rather than silencing it in a statistical average. Having identified and controlled it, the experimenter can proceed to test the independent variable again, and if on this occasion it is equally effective across four subjects, a degree of generality has been established. Behavior analysts are aware that a single demonstration of the effect of an independent variable on three or four subjects is not sufficient to justify an inductive inference, which is why the literature dealing with scientific method consistently emphasizes the importance of replication (Sidman, 1960; Hersen & Barlow, 1976; Johnston & Pennypacker, 1980).

A psychologist trained in another tradition might be surprised, on reading *Journal of The Experimental Analysis of Behavior* or *Journal of Applied Behavior Analysis*, to discover graphs and data points referring to the behavior of perhaps two, three, or four subjects, with each subject's behavior shown individually. Such a psychologist may be even more surprised to discover that this strategy is equally applied to pigeons and rats, as well as to human subjects. But this application is consistent with the principle of individuality: "The complex system we call an organism has an elaborate and largely unknown history which endows it with a certain individuality. No two organisms embark upon an experiment in precisely the same condition nor are they affected in the same way by the contingencies in an experimental space" (Skinner, 1966, p. 20).

Generalization and the individual. Radical behaviorism was described in the previous chapter as an inductive science giving prominence to data rather than to theory and attempting to derive principles of behavior from accumulated observations. Its principles conveniently summarize classes of events and take the form of universal laws in the sense that they apply to all members involved in a class of events. The kinds of laws that are a goal of science, as the radical behaviorist views it, are unlike the general statements derived from statistical treatment of data that summarize an average effect of experimental variables. The distinction between these two kinds of generalizations can be illustrated by applying each to a phenomenon from physics. The universal law, "all metals expand when heated," is the kind of law that is the goal of science as the radical behaviorist views it. It is a universal empirical generalization, a formula that describes the behavior of all (universal) members of the class to which it is applied (metals). A statement derived from statistical treatment of the phenomenon would state that "in general, metals expand when heated" and would not necessarily apply to all members of the class; it would not be a universal empirical generalization. In the same way that statistically derived general statements referring to behavior are not predictive of the behavior of individuals, it would not predict the behavior of an individual member of the class. Universal laws are derived inductively from accumulated observations, from *many* instances of a single phenomenon. Statistical statements, on the other hand, can be derived from a single experiment, a *single* instance of the phenomenon to which the statement applies.

Statistical generalizations offer no comment on the behavior of the individual in a given situation: "The physician who is trying to determine whether his patient will die before morning can make little use of actuarial tables, nor can the student of behavior predict what a single organism will do if his laws apply only to groups. Individual prediction is of tremendous importance, so long as the organism is to be treated scientifically as a lawful system" (Skinner, 1938, pp. 443-444). Such generalizations were developed for a different scientific purpose, for population genetics, agricultural research, and industrial quality control, where the behavior of individual members of the class is of little concern (Johnston & Pennypacker, 1980).

Scientific Plans

There are contexts to which the statistical inference model can be applied, and problems that it can expedite effectively. Consider a problem in the field of educational psychology where the statistical model can be effectively applied: a local education authority seeks to improve the reading skills of its primary school population and commissions an educational psychologist to develop a new teaching method that can improve on the method already in use. The amount of time and money available to the psychologist are limited because the education authority needs to implement the new reading scheme by a fixed date. The most effective research strategy available, taking into account limitations in resources, accepts uncontrollable variability and takes account of the poor prospects for experimental control by adopting statistical methods. A typical experimental design for testing the effectiveness of a new reading scheme would be to select two groups of children: control and experimental groups. One group would be taught to read using the newly designed method and the other by the old method. A comparison of reading scores between the two groups would give an average measure of the effectiveness of the new reading scheme and a test of significance would demonstrate at what level any difference might have occurred naturally (by chance). If the new reading scheme provides measures that are statistically significant in comparison to the traditional teaching method, then the educational psychologist has satisfied the needs of the local education authority by providing a teaching method that will *on average* be an improvement over other methods.

Tracking down variability. A psychologist engaged in the scientific enterprise as Sidman has characterized it would be interested not in accounting for variability statistically but in tracking down sources of variability, first examining any variability in the data and then asking, "Of what is this variability a function?" It may be that the new method of teaching children to read had more subtle effects on individual children than the blanket effect that the differences between averaged scores suggested. For example, children who were already good readers may have improved rapidly with the new scheme while children who were already poor readers improved at their same slow rate, and the final, statistically demonstrated difference was the result of this rapid advance by one set within the experimental group.

This psychologist would want to look more closely at individual scores both before and after the new reading scheme and would be especially interested in whether or not there was some order or trend in those scores. Other factors may be involved in the success or failure of the new reading scheme for individual children: for example, the interference of another language in children growing up in a bilingual household. A different kind of reading scheme may be more appropriate for such children. The effect of another language on a subgroup may not be visible in the classic experimental/control group design but may only show up by more careful examination of data from individuals. Variations are interesting to this scientist because they set the challenge of discovering the source of variability by further refining experimental control. It is true that the statistical model may further break down the global group in this way. But a statistical generalization only allows for prediction of the percentage of occurrence of an item in a group in the future. It cannot specify which individuals will be included in that percentage and cannot, however well refined, be applied to the behavior of individuals.

Basic science problems, engineering problems. Both Skinner and Sidman argue that the practices of tracking down sources of variability and of controlling it statistically represent different scientific plans and lead to different results. They equate these plans in psychology to the difference between dealing with basic science problems and dealing with engineering problems. Sidman adds to his statement that "The process of systematically tracking down sources of variability, and thus explaining variable data, is characteristic of the scientific enterprise" (Sidman, 1960, p. 192) a warning that this enterprise should not be confused with the engineering approach that involves the search for solutions to immediate, pressing, and everyday problems.

Sidman argues that the basic scientist has available a luxury that should be taken advantage of, "the luxury of being able to refine experimental conditions until they bear only the most abstract relation to the world as we normally see it. It is a luxury because it requires an amount of time not usually permitted by the pressing demands of immediate practical problems; because it requires a long-term financial investment that could not ordinarily be tolerated if that expense had to be included in the cost and sometimes in the market price of an engineered product" (Sidman, 1960, p. 193). In Sidman's opinion, the basic scientist has an *obligation* to take advantage of this luxury, for at least two reasons.

First, the careful elimination of variability through refined experimental control "has been found to pay off both in contributions to our understanding of natural phenomena and in practical applications to engineering problems" (Sidman, 1960, p. 193). In other words, principles derived from the basic science plan (its universal laws) not only add to the body of knowledge but also feed into the technology that helps resolve engineering problems, making it more effective. In the hypothetical case above, a refinement of experimental control capable of uncovering order in variability adds an important new piece to the complex puzzle of how children learn to read and of how best (most effectively) to teach them.

With its initial assumption of order and its attempt to seek out and experimentally control sources of variability, radical behaviorism concerns itself with the basic science plan of discovering general principles (or laws) applicable to the behavior of individuals. One example of such a general principle may be stated as: "behavior that is reinforced intermittently takes longer to extinguish than behavior that is reinforced continuously." So far, this principle continues to hold and is applicable to individuals' behavior. It has been inductively derived from accumulated observations of the phenomenon across differing situations and may be called upon by the behavioral engineer in cases where long term maintenance of behavior is required.

Another example of a general principle relates to temporal patterning of reinforcement and the effect such patterning exerts on behavior. The principle may be stated as: "behavior over time develops a pattern determined by the temporal pattern of reinforcement." Again, the principle has been derived inductively, is applicable to individuals, and forms part of the technology available to behavioral engineers attempting to shape or maintain specific kinds of behavior. For example, one of the cases reported by Martin and Pear (1983) concerns an eleven year old severely retarded boy in an institution, whose behavior after the announcement of some ward activity posed a problem to nursing staff. As soon as an activity was announced, the boy would run to nurses and continually beg them to begin the activity. The nurses designed a program to shape the boy's behavior so that he would sit quietly between the announcement and start of an activity, allowing them to arrange the start uninterrupted. They did this by using a variable interval/limited hold (VI/LH) schedule of reinforcement: if he was seated in his chair outside the nurses' office at the moment a timer sounded, a reinforcer (candy) would be available. Since the intervals varied and thus the sounding of the timer was unpredictable, the boy remained in his chair for the entire interval. Martin and Pear (1983) note that had other schedules been used, other patterns of behavior would have been produced: "Suppose that the nurses had used a FI 5-minute/LH 2-second (fixed interval 5-minute, limited hold 2-second) schedule with Benny. The boy would have been on the chair a good portion of the five minutes, and the nurses would not have had to monitor his behavior continuously. However, he might still have bothered them for the first several minutes or so of the interval. Furthermore, this schedule would not have taught Benny to sit on the chair for much longer than five-minute periods on each occasion" (p. 87).

Inductively derived principles applicable to the behavior of individuals are useful not only to the behavioral engineer in applied contexts; they also provide a base of background knowledge for further scientific investigation. For example, details of the extinction of a specific behavior may be studied against a background of either continuous or intermittent reinforcement with confidence in the principle that continuously reinforced behavior will extinguish more rapidly than intermittently reinforced behavior. Details of the effect of a single variable may be studied by establishing a reliable (schedule controlled) pattern of behavior and measuring changes in that pattern with the introduction or withdrawal of a variable. General principles become part of the background knowledge for both the investigations of the basic scientist and the technology of the engineer.

Second, basic science is less restricted by the limitations of time and financial resources governing the engineer. In adopting the assumptions and techniques of the engineering plan, the basic scientist fails to carry out the plan for which extended resources are made available and takes up "a peculiar, in-between position" (Sidman, 1960, p. 194) in the sense that although the nominal goals are those of fundamental research, the techniques "are those appropriate to the solution of immediately practical problems" (Sidman, 1960, p. 194).

Aims, Methods, and the Individual

It is important to clarify that the terminology "basic science plan" and "engineering plan" is not meant to imply that the former amounts to science and the latter amounts to something other than science. The terms are useful only to draw attention to different sets of assumptions, conclusions, and contexts in which the two plans are carried out. It may be possible to substitute the terms basic science and applied science respectively, but these terms are not sufficiently descriptive of the distinction between initial assumptions or of the different kinds of generalizations to which each of the programs gives rise. Applied science may give an impression that it is the principles (the universal laws) of basic science that are used to solve practical problems and would not highlight Sidman's point that the engineering plan, as it is carried out in experimental psychology, gives rise to generalizations of a different sort than the basic science plan. The engineering plan is useful in certain contexts and for the resolution of certain kinds of problems; but its general conclusions, since they are not predictive of the behavior of individuals, must not be mistaken for the general (universal) laws characteristic of the basic science plan.

In the process of locating sources of variability, the basic scientist moves toward the kinds of general laws predictive of the behavior of individuals of the class to which the law applies. Such laws will be of further use to the engineer in designing subsequent programs of behavior change; they become part of the technology available to the engineer. Each scientific plan serves a different function. Sidman cautions that they should not be confused, and that the general statements arising from designs engendered by the engineering plan should not be mistaken for the lawful statements generated by the basic science program. Similarly, the basic scientist should avoid adopting engineering designs that inevitably lead to general statements; these designs close off the possibility of locating sources of variability and establishing general behavioral principles. Most of contemporary experimental psychology, with its acceptance of intrinsic variability, its emphasis on large samples and on statistical analysis of data, imitates the engineer and often confuses the two plans by treating basic science questions with methods appropriate to engineering problems.

The statistical inference model promoted by Fisher and wholeheartedly adopted by mainstream experimental psychology serves a useful function in answering particular kinds of questions and in dealing with particular kinds of data. Statistical methods are appropriate in situations where variability is accepted as an uncontrollable feature of data and, consequently, where "chance" factors are allowed to enter into experimental situations. They are useful for identifying average effects and thus for solving immediate problems for which extended resources are not available.

In adopting methods appropriate to the solution of practical problems, contemporary experimental psychology carries out the engineering plan. The basic science plan requires an assumption of underlying order and the development of methods capable of tracking and eliminating sources of variability rather than the "fatalistically accepted conception of intrinsic variability" (Sidman, 1960, p. 194) that the engineering plan proceeds with.

Principles derived inductively constitute reliable background knowledge insofar as they continue to hold true until contradictory evidence comes to light. Unlike the body of knowledge—derived from the statistical inference model—that may be altered or modified by a simple change in procedure, a change in the usual and convenient level of confidence, principles derived from accumulated observations are held to be reliable until *new* evidence contradicts them. It has been noted above that the result of a test of significance counts as evidence for or against scientific assertions, and that the same data (evidence) may either be in favor of or against a scientific assertion in relation to a level of confidence—a matter of procedure. Inductively derived general principles are so derived by virtue of evidence from many sources and many instances of observation and are only contradicted by *independent* evidence. They hold true by observation rather than by procedure.

Again, radical behaviorism is distinct from the mainstream of contemporary experimental psychology in its preference for experimental rather than statistical control, and for inductively derived principles that are predictive of the behavior of individuals. Establishing baselines in the behavior of individuals, measuring the effectiveness of experimental variables against them, reversing experimental treatments and observing whether or not aspects of behavior reverse, tracking the behavior of individual organisms across time, examining data from individual subjects in detail and presenting individual data in published form all demonstrate behavior analysts' commitment to respect and work with the fact that people and other organisms are unique.

Chapter 5

Concepts of Causation

The concept of causation is explicitly or implicitly woven into many of our ways of talking about the world and into the practices of many of our legal, political, economic, educational, and scientific institutions. Despite its widespread use, the concept of causation is surprisingly difficult to pin down, even in science, which rigorously demands carefully derived evidence for its assertion of causal relations.

There are various ways of considering causation:

By what means can we safely say that one event causes another?
Are causal relations sequential?
Can events be causally related over time and space or are causes contiguous with their effects?
Is it more useful to think of causal relations as chains or as more complex webs or networks?
By what means do we identify conceptual units to test for causal influences?

Questions of this kind are equally as applicable in physics, chemistry, biology, medical science, and so on as in the behavioral sciences. But behavioral sciences are uniquely asked whether their subject matter can be described within the realms of causation as understood in the natural sciences. This chapter considers some aspects of causation both in science as a whole and in the science of behavior informed by radical behaviorism, including the question of whether human behavior is amenable to causal description. In examining various features of causation and causal thinking, it will become clear that this aspect of science is fundamental to one of the main issues of this book—mechanistic views of the subject matter of psychology. Radical behaviorism's causal mode separates it from most of contemporary experimental psychology in that it does not require links-in-a-causal-chain to explain the relations of its subject matter. Its concept of causation belongs to a philosophy of science tradition explicitly opposed to mechanistic thinking and to mechanistic interpretations of causal events in nature. Furthermore, this chapter asserts that more conventional forms of contemporary experimental psychology rely on a traditional view of the person as a duality, a view dispensed with in the radical behaviorist formulation of behaving persons.

The discussion begins by examining a way of thinking about persons and their behavior that is common in Western cultures. Initially, this may seem to have little bearing on causation, but our Western cultural view of the person exerts a profound influence on the way we search for causes of human behavior, the direction in which we look for those causes, and the causal mode by which we interpret evidence and thus provide scientific explanations.

The Behaving Person

The view that behavior is an indication, manifestation, or expression, *of something else* is predominant in western thinking about behavior. In psychology, as in the culture at large, behavior is most commonly given the status of an appendage to thoughts, feelings, underlying physiological and/or neurological mechanisms, instincts, personality, intelligence, motivation, mental states and so on. It is considered to be:

1) an *indication of* processes taking place inside the behaving person— for example, physiological and/or neurological processes, mental processes such as encoding, storage, retrieval, internal computing, decision making, choice, discrimination, attribution, attitude, and so on; or

Concepts of Causation

2) a *manifestation of* other kinds of events taking place within—for example, expectations, desires, intentions, feelings, and so on; or

3) an *expression of* an essential self or core being, a bounded individual separate from and standing behind behavior. In this view, what the person does is of secondary importance to what the person *is.* The person, the essential self, is both the organizer and initiator of behavior, with behavior standing in a dependent variable position to the self as independent variable.

As well as subtly pervading much of everyday discourse, literature, drama, and art, the view continues to be overtly expressed in several areas of psychological theory and remains a background assumption in others. Deese, for example, captures this view in his succinct statement, "Behavior is only the outward manifestation of what really counts" (Deese, 1972, p. 99), and even the social learning theorist, Bandura, has written that behavior is generated by a core self, explicitly ascribing to it causal status: "Self-generated activities lie at the very heart of causal processes" (Bandura, 1989, p. 1175). Perhaps Carl Rogers best exemplified this view when he wrote, "Below the level of the problem situation about which [an] individual is complaining—behind the trouble with studies, or wife, or employer, or with his own uncontrollable or bizarre behavior, or with his frightening feelings, lies one central search. It seems to me that at bottom each person is asking, 'Who am I, *really?* How can I get in touch with this real self, underlying all my surface behavior?'" (Rogers, 1967, p. 108).

Rogers unequivocally expressed the dualism in western cultural thinking on the nature of persons and their behavior. Capra compared this with views held by other cultures, notably Buddhist. In the western view, he writes, "Most individuals are aware of themselves as isolated egos existing 'inside' their bodies. The mind has been separated from the body and given the futile task of controlling it, thus causing an apparent conflict between the conscious will and the involuntary instincts. Each individual has been split up further into a large number of separate compartments, according to his or her activities, talents, feelings, beliefs, and so on, which are engaged in endless conflicts generating continuous metaphysical confusion and frustration" (Capra, 1975, p. 28). Capra contrasts this with the Buddhist doctrine of impermanence, which includes the notion "that there is no ego, no self which is the persistent subject of our varying experiences. Buddhism holds that the idea of a separate individual self is an illusion…an intellectual concept which has no reality" (Capra, 1975, p. 107). He draws attention to the Buddhist view of material substance and goes on to emphasize that this aspect of Buddhist philosophy also holds that "the idea of a constant 'self' undergoing successive experiences is an illusion" (Capra, 1975, p. 235). This contrast, as Capra has described it, illustrates that the bounded and essential self is a property of cultural thinking rather than an ontological reality and that there are ways outside western culture of talking about the behaving person.

A consequence of the predominant self conception in western culture is that a concern with behavior is not a concern with what is important about persons, with what counts, but with the trivial and superficial, the surface of the person. The person or the self in western thinking is made up of something other than behavior, which is merely an appendage to another system; that other system is considered to be of primary importance.

This separation of person from behavior predates and extends beyond western psychology. It informs and guides so much thinking about behavior in various areas of psychology that many psychologists do not study behavior but are drawn instead to inferences about systems and processes that are said to *underlie* it. *Remembering* (the behavior) is of secondary importance to *models of memory*. *Perceiving* (the behavior) is of secondary importance to *information processing* systems. *Thinking* is of secondary importance to *intentions, will* or *attributions*, and *behaving* toward something is of secondary importance to *attitudes* toward that same thing. *Aggression* or a*ggressive personality* steals the stage from *behaving aggressively*. And feeling and acting in a hostile way toward one's siblings is not as important as, for example, intra-psychic conflicts between id and ego that are said to generate such hostility. In each instance, behavior—what the person does—is at one and the same time an appendage to another system and "merely" evidence of that other system.

Radical behaviorism's strikingly different view of persons and their behavior was referred to in Chapter 2. Skinner's philosophical position does not separate person (an essential self) from behavior. Rather, persons are defined *in terms of* their behavior with no other entity, no bounded individual, standing behind. The person in radical behaviorism is a unity rather than a duality, an interactive part of the environment rather than a thing separate from the environment. The person in radical behaviorism operates *in* rather than *on* an environment. With this view, behavior takes primary rather than secondary place, since the person *is* behavior.

Instead of looking for mechanisms or entities that underlie behavior, the interesting question becomes, "How is this person, this unity, related to her or his environment?" Causal explanations are given in terms of interactive relations between person and environment, and both behavior and environment are broadly defined. Behavior, as Chapter 2 noted, is everything the person does, focusing on verb forms rather than noun forms, and including thinking, feeling, remembering, talking, acting intelligently, acting aggressively, and so forth. Environment consists not only of the inanimate world of desks, chairs, houses, motor cars, roads, trees, fields, sky, sun, rain, and so forth, but includes the other people that make up the world of the behaving person, what is often called the social environment. Dependent relations are bidirectional, between behavior (the person) and events in the environment, with the emphasis on future probabilities of behavior resulting from (caused by) the setting conditions and consequences of behavior. Present behavior (the person) in this view consists of a unique genetic endowment, a unique reinforcement history (life experience), and relations to a present environment. From a wide range of possibilities, patterns of behavior are selected, maintained, and strengthened by antecedent and consequent events— they create the person. The person stands in a dependent variable relation to environmental contingencies as independent variables, with special emphasis on the consequences of behavior.

Determinism and Human Behavior

Causal explanations are as fundamental to psychology as to other sciences, and the concept of causation implies an initial deterministic view of the subject matter of science, a background assumption that nothing in the universe occurs spontaneously or by accident. All events are assumed to be interrelated, with discrete events reliably linked to other, prior events. In sum, science assumes that all phenomena are dependent and this deterministic assumption in most sciences is unproblematic.

In relation to human behavior, however, there exists a continuing tension between the assertion that human behavior is subject to causal laws and the assertion that it is so radically different from the subject matter of other sciences that it is not amenable to deterministic causal explanation. Grünbaum (1953), for example, notes, "It is not uncommon to find that even those who have complete confidence in the continued success of the scientific method when applied to inanimate nature are highly skeptical of its applicability to the study of human behavior. Some go so far as to assert quite categorically that the methods of the natural sciences are in principle incompetent to yield predictions of man's individual or social behavior" (Grünbaum, 1953, p. 766). One of the immediate consequences of such a view, according to Grünbaum, is to permanently bar all social studies, including psychology, from achieving the status of science because the essence of science is to explain phenomena both in relation to prior events and as instances of a causal law. Further, it presents a futile scenario for the future: if human behavior does not exhibit causal relations then we are denied the possibility of learning anything from the past that may be of use in managing the future. As Grünbaum puts it, "To deny the existence of uniformities in human behavior, individual and social, is to assert that significant lessons cannot be drawn from the past and that man's future is capricious and elusive" (Grünbaum, 1953, p. 767). Alternatively, the assumption that human behavior is causally determined and thereby susceptible to causal description suggests a route toward alleviating problems directly created by human behavior. The gap between mastery of our physical environment and mastery of social, economic, and political systems, may be considerably narrowed by the application of the deterministic assumption common in other sciences to human behavior.

Skinner (1971) expressed this when he argued that our understanding of human behavior has not appreciably advanced since the time of the Greeks and that we could go a long way toward solving "the terrifying problems that face us in the world today" (Skinner, 1971, p. 1) through the application of science in the field of human behavior. Such an endeavor, however, calls for a major shift in some of the ways we commonly view human behavior. The popular view of human behavior in western cultures will be discussed below. This section concerns the scientific merit of arguments against causal determinism in human behavior. It is one thing to assert that we *might* move forward to a brighter future *if* human behavior could be shown to be causally determined, and quite another to demonstrate that the arguments against determinism have no merit. The former is simply optimism, requiring the latter for practical support.

Grünbaum describes four arguments for indeterminacy, three of which will be treated here:

1) the argument from individuality (since each individual is unique, unlike any other individual, this precludes the possibility of prediction and generalization);
2) the argument from complexity (human behavior is so intricate and complex that causal relations are not discoverable); and
3) the argument from purposiveness (human behavior, being directed toward the future, is not controlled by antecedent events and is thus not subject to the causal laws of science).

Grünbaum notes additional objections to a deterministic view of human behavior that in a sense move away from scientific arguments toward larger social/cultural issues: objections, for example, that relate to moral/legal questions such as personal responsibility and justifications for punishment. Although such questions are of the utmost importance to the culture as a whole, they will not be dealt with here because they do move so far away from scientific arguments. The three objections briefly outlined above relate directly to philosophy of science and will be assessed here on their scientific merit.

The argument from individuality. To appeal to the unique individuality of humans as an argument against determinism, as if it applied only to this special case, is a mistaken view of the subject matter of other sciences and of the nature of causal laws. It implies that the subject matter of other sciences does not also have unique properties, but in reality every event or phenomenon dealt with by other sciences is also unique. Every tree, flower, particle, element, member of a species, swing of a pendulum, tick of a clock, is a unique event or object. But its uniqueness does not preclude classification, generalization, or prediction. There may of course be some limitations to any of these processes, but uniqueness does not in itself place events outside the realms of causal determinism. Human biological characteristics, for example, are unique in the sense that no two stomachs are exactly alike, no two hearts precisely the same shape or size, no fixed ratio between height and length of spine or size of feet has been demonstrated. But this does not prevent biological science from classifying the basic similarities between people, generalizing biological properties, or establishing causal laws and predicting outcomes where initial conditions are known. The same is true of the entire subject matter of biology and botany. Uniqueness does not hamper the search for causal relations in these or in any other sciences; causal laws do not negate uniqueness.

The function of causal laws is to relate sets of properties of events, systems, or objects with other sets of properties, demonstrating in what ways they affect each other. Causal laws do not imply that all properties of a system need to be reproduced for the effect to take place, only the particular set of properties used to define a particular law. Photosynthesis is a process common to all green plants, regardless of their shape or size or what kind of soil they grow best in. In species of animals sharing a particularly defined set of structures, respiration takes place by the same process, regardless of whether the species can fly or lives in water or on land. To demonstrate photosynthesis or respiration does not require that other features of plants or animals be referred to, and the fact that such processes can be causally construed does not imply that each plant or animal is not unique. Humans are no more or less unique than the subject matter of any other science, and causal laws do not negate the uniqueness of humans any more than they do the subject matter of other sciences. Appealing to the uniqueness of humans as if they were a special case does not therefore justify claims of indeterminacy.

The argument from complexity. The argument from complexity to indeterminacy could equally have been applied to any science in the early days of its development. It requires us to accept the assumption that what is unknown cannot be known, but the development and success of science itself provides contrary evidence. As the previous chapter noted, there must have been a time before the development of scientific chemistry when the reduction of thousands of chemical compounds to a small and finite number of elements seemed merely fanciful. Early astronomers could not have known that it would one day be possible to express the complex movements of celestial bodies in a few simple equations. The argument from complexity to indeterminacy flies in the face of scientific evidence, since science proceeds in the opposite direction, from complexity to order. That we understand relatively little today about the causal relations among properties of human behavior does not count as evidence that such causal relations either do not exist or can never be known.

The argument from purpose. In explaining human behavior we often ascribe causal status to future events, a kind of causation not encountered in other sciences. This special relation between future events and present behavior suggests that the antecedent causal determinism assumed by other sciences is not applicable to goal-directed or future-directed instances of human behavior. For example, we might explain an increase in the number of hours that students spend studying by pointing to a future event, examinations, as a cause. Why did a person buy property in a run-down part of town when they could have afforded to buy in a more genteel or picturesque area? A causal account may be put in terms of a proposed development of the area and a consequent increase in property values in the future. Attention is drawn to a future event in such a way as to imply that the event stands in a causal relation to present behavior, that the event functions as an independent variable. But causal accounts of human behavior, even in the case of goal-directed behavior, are more properly given in terms of the present state or the history of the person. A future event, since it has not happened and may never happen, cannot cause present behavior. Examinations may be cancelled, students may become ill and have to abandon their studies, or property values may stay the same or fall. Therefore the future, since it has not happened, cannot be considered a causal influence on the present.

A student whose rate of studying increases before an examination has been introduced to several important antecedent events: she or he will have received verbal instruction or advice relating to forthcoming examinations; an examination timetable will have been made available, perhaps even a written note of examination details has arrived at the student's address; discussions among students of a number of exam-related issues—"how did you do in the previous test?" "what do you think they'll ask about statistics?" "you've covered three topics already!"—often occur. Antecedent events like these affect behavior, usually (but not always) increasing the amount of time a student will spend in study or exam-related activities. The relation between impending examination and increased studying would be unlikely where students had never been informed in any way of an impending exam.

In causal accounts, the relation between antecedent conditions and behavior is sometimes obscured by linguistic conventions. But antecedent causation is as much a part of causal explanation in behavioral sciences as it is in other sciences, even in instances that we ordinarily call goal-directed or future-directed behavior.

Causal determinism in human behavior is not undermined by appealing to individuality, complexity, or purposiveness. Each of these aspects can be accommodated by expressions of antecedent causal conditions without negating the individuality of humans, the complexity of their behavior, or those behaviors that are said to be goal or future-directed. Any continuing tension between determinism and indeterminism in human behavior results from a mistaken understanding of causation or causal laws in science. Causal laws do not presuppose that every feature of a system need be reproduced in order that the law be applicable, and individuality is a common property of the subject matter of all sciences. Causal laws move from complexity toward order, toward understanding common features and expressing relations among those features. The complexity of human behavior does not militate against the discovery of causal laws since the subject matter of other sciences similarly begins with complexity. The complexity argument is an argument from ignorance to indeterminacy. Behavior that is directed toward the future is not exempt from the antecedent causation of other sciences. Rather, it is properly accounted for by antecedent causation; causal relations are between present state (or past) and behavior. Future events that may or may not happen cannot account for present behavior.

Causation in Science

The concept of causation has undergone changes from one historical era to another, following shifts in empirical knowledge, empirical constructs, and fresh philosophical analyses. Causation was conceived differently by early Greek physics and astronomy than by contemporary science. But the first major shift took place relatively recently as a consequence of David Hume's analysis and positivist developments in science and the philosophy of science since that time.

The historical significance of Hume's analysis is seldom alluded to. The analysis tends to be given as the prevailing view of causation in philosophical thinking without reference to the context of ideas in which it was developed. Its historical significance lies in dispensing with the notions of force or agency which, prior to Hume, continued to haunt the concept of causation. Russell (1946), in tracing the rise of science and the development of scientific ideas, does place Hume's analysis in its historical context and in doing so illuminates this aspect and its importance in the overall development of scientific ideas. As well as arguing against appeals to a necessary connection between cause and effect, Hume was also concerned to dispense with the idea, implicit in his era's conception of causation, of a causal force.

Noting that Newton had defined force as the cause of changes of motion, that is to say, of acceleration, Russell wrote, "'Force' in Newton, is the cause of changes of motion, whether in magnitude or direction. The notion of cause is regarded as important, and force is conceived imaginatively as the sort of thing that we experience when we push or pull" (Russell, 1946, p. 524). It gradually became clear, however, that gravitational equations could be worked out without alluding to forces: "What was observable was a certain relation between acceleration and configuration; to say that this relation was brought about by the intermediacy of 'force' was to add nothing to our knowledge" (Russell, 1946, p. 524). Russell described this conception of causal force as "the faint ghost of the vitalist view" of the causes of motion and with the increasing sophistication of scientific equations, "gradually the ghost has been exorcized" (Russell, 1946, p. 524). Science had long been moving away from the notion of an internal life force directing movement, and Hume's influential views on causation moved it still further toward an understanding of causation in terms of constant relations.

Hume pointed out that our perception of causation includes more than simple observations of constant relations. What we observe and learn by experience, he argued, are no more and no less than relations, "the frequent *Conjunction* of objects" (Hume, 1777/1975, p. 70). What we add to our observation is a sense of power or agency on the part of a causal event: "We suppose that there is some connexion between them (cause and effect); some power in the one, by which it infallibly produces the other, and operates with the greatest certainty and the strongest necessity" (Hume, 1777/1975, p. 75). This added supposition, according to Hume, derives from the way *we* feel when *we* move about in the world making changes by pushing, pulling, lifting, dropping, and otherwise manipulating objects, and is merely a thing of thought. Cohen and Nagel (1934) describe this as common-sense causation: "The 'common-sense' notion of cause is an interpretation of nonhuman behavior in terms peculiarly adopted to human behavior. Thus, 'John broke the window,' is supposed to express a causal relation, because there is an agent 'John' who *produced* the breaking of the window" (Cohen & Nagel, 1934, p. 246). Similarly, in a statement like "moist air rusts iron," moist air is said to be the cause and rusted iron the effect where moist air is believed to *produce* the rusting: "In the popular mind, all *changes* require *causes* to explain them, and when found are interpreted as agents producing the change" (Cohen & Nagel, 1934, p. 246). Hume's analysis demonstrated that notions of agency, force, or necessity of connection are superfluous to understanding or describing causal relations.

The modern conception of causation has replaced the notion of force with that of functional relations, and scientific equations refer to events as a function of other events rather than in terms of A exerting a force on B. This is not merely a superficial semantic issue. As noted in Chapter 2, words carry conceptual systems with them in addition to their individual definitions, and these can guide and direct our operations in unnoticed ways. It was suggested above that the notion of agency is especially important in relation to causal thinking and human behavior. That said, because the modern conception of causation is so well established in science, it may be possible today to use the terms cause and effect, causal relation, and the like without invoking force at the same time.

The chain metaphor. Another feature of causal thinking that has undergone revision is the notion of the causal chain. The chain metaphor is perhaps the most popular image of causation, and perhaps the most convenient for certain practical purposes. It embraces the relational nature of causation in that it sets events in a relation of succession to each other without necessarily invoking force on the part of any link in the chain. Thus, the chain metaphor is able to describe a sequence of events between, for example, administration of a drug and the cessation of pain: administration of a drug is followed by a change in the constitution of blood, which is followed by a change in the activity of nerve endings, which is followed by a reduction in pain. Or, as in a much used example, between the cue ball striking the red ball which bounces off the cushion and strikes the black ball which then falls into the pocket. The chain in such examples has an identifiable beginning and end, each link is contiguous in space and time, and the metaphor illustrates causation as a unidirectional linear process. In the above kinds of examples, where the chain is measurable from beginning to end, the metaphor may be useful for practical purposes. One of the unacceptable consequences of the metaphor, however, is that it implies linear causation, traceable backward to a single causal event, as if all causal relations once set in motion proceeded in a straightforward one-to-one fashion.

Causal accounts and theoretical webs. N. R. Hanson (1955) takes the chain metaphor to task. He argues that scientific activity is not concerned with identifying causal chains, that scientists in fact rarely refer to causes, and that in practice there is little in science or in daily life to which the metaphor can be made to apply. Scientists, according to Hanson, do not think in terms of how far along a causal chain they have progressed in their work. Furthermore, and most importantly, the metaphor does not take into account the voluminous background knowledge tacitly involved in causal accounts. It ignores whole systems of constructs and properties included in causal accounts that are not given simply by observation and experience. While the purpose of finding the cause of a given phenomenon is to explain that phenomenon, at the same time there are as many causes as there are explanations.

Consider a scenario in which a person picks up a brick and hurls it toward a window. The brick hits the window and the glass shatters. It would be possible to assemble a team of scientists from several disciplines, including physics, chemistry, mechanics, biology, anthropology, sociology, and psychology (with, it should be emphasized, several different kinds of psychologists present) and to give as many causal accounts of the glass shattering as there were different scientists in the team. Because each account is nested within its own web of constructs, assumptions, and theories, no one of them is comparable to any other. Comparative evaluation would be meaningless. Each account stands or falls not in relation to others but to the methods and background knowledge of its own discipline. The direction in which scientists look for causal relations corresponds roughly to the distinctions among scientific disciplines. All deal with relations among a set of constructs that define each field. Although there may be overlap between some sets of constructs and relations, as in biochemistry for example, each discipline typically deals with its own system of classification, its own set of constructs, and attempts to identify interrelations among those constructs in the form of causal dependencies.

Such distinctions may give the impression that nature itself is composed of these different kinds of elements, the constructs of each discipline. But the distinctions are more properly understood as *human* inventions, convenient ways of dividing nature that have developed in tandem with a growing body of knowledge and, consequently, a growing need for specialization. Romanyshyn (1978) pointed out that knowledge is itself intimately related to its organization, that knowledge does not simply present itself to us as we describe and explain our world. The world does not imprint on us natural distinctions between biology, chemistry, physics, mechanics, and so on. Rather, *we* impose these distinctions upon the world, *we* organize the world in these ways. As Romanyshyn put it, "The organization of knowledge is in one sense the knowledge, and knowledge is in one sense its organization" (Romanyshyn, 1978, p. 18).

Hanson makes the same point when he talks about the theory-laden nature of causal terms and the inability of the chain metaphor to embrace this feature of causality. Drugs, blood, and nerve endings are all conceptual units related within a network of conceptual units. Without the network the words themselves are meaningless as causal explanations. It is the background knowledge, the conceptual network, that gives meaning to causal explanations. The cue ball example, striking in its simplicity, is similarly only meaningful against a conceptual background involving knowledge of the movement of spheroid bodies, angles of deflection, and the properties of billiard tables. Only with this conceptual background is a causal relation thrown into relief. Familiarity, particularly in such simple cases, dissipates or fades background knowledge and leaves a superficial impression of one-to-one causal connections.

The chain account ignores the fact that causal terms are more than observations. It ignores conceptual systems lying behind those terms, giving meaning to them *as causal explanations.* "Genuine causal connexions can be expressed (explicitly or implicitly) only in language that is many-levelled in its generality and its explanatory power. This is why the language of causality is diagnostic and prognostic, and why the simple tick-tock, click-click, links-in-a-chain view of cause and effect is so artificial and inapplicable" (Hanson, 1955, p. 300). Causes and effects are not related as links in a chain, but as webs, as networks, by our theories. Causation is identified within conceptual systems and it is those systems that delineate causal from merely temporal relations. Events may be contiguous in space and time without being causally related. If such events belong to the same conceptual system, the same (or a similar) theoretical web, then they may be causally related. The simple one-to-one implication of the chain metaphor does not properly illustrate the conceptual nature of causal terms.

Links-in-the-chain and mechanistic thinking. Hanson identifies three features of science from which the chain metaphor derives its [illusory] power. One feature is the deductive method of reasoning, which is itself chainlike: "Just as the premises and conclusions of an elegant deduction were chained by a simple series of formal steps, so the causes and effects in a noteworthy natural phenomenon—e.g., the communication of momentum by impact between two elastic bodies—were chained by a simple series of events, links in the causal chain" (Hanson, 1955, pp. 306-307). Another feature is the design of experiments that are set up to work in a chainlike manner. Although superficially an experiment appears sequential or chainlike, beneath the surface lies the intricate theoretical network in which explanations occur. Explanation takes place not at the surface level but at the level of the constructs that define the topic of study in a given experiment.

The third feature is also referred to by Merchant (1982) and Capra (1983) as a fundamental influence on mechanistic causal thinking in science. The simplicity and power of the designed machine, both inside and outside the laboratory, its endurance and stability under changing external conditions, give rise to links-in-the-causal-chain thinking: "Such machines work with considerable indifference to alterations in environment. Clocks, anemometers, windmills, water-wheels, etc. are made *not* to stop for thunderstorms, swarms of bees, the barking of dogs or the crowing of roosters....from this the temptation grew to construe causal explanation as mechanical explanation; that is, explanation of the perseverance of manufactured machines" (Hanson, 1955, p. 309). From this construal it is only a small step to think about natural phenomena in a similar manner, functioning as mechanical systems.

Although, according to Hanson, the chain metaphor is still widespread, causal explanation is better described by terms like causal theories or causal laws. Such terms imply more than the one-to-one relations implied by causal chain and are more indicative of the complexity and web-like nature of causal relations.

Causation in Radical Behaviorism

Several distinctive features of causal thinking within radical behaviorist philosophy feed into the method and interpretation of the science of behavior it informs. The first feature traces back to the philosophy of science of Ernst Mach, a 19th century physicist concerned as much with experimental physics as with the philosophical underpinnings and assumptions of science. Much of Mach's philosophical work aimed at disputing several key assumptions and definitions in Newtonian physics, including the lingering commitment to causal force, the definition of mass, and Newton's absolute space and time. Mach is acknowledged as an important influence on Skinner's early thinking and Skinner appealed directly to Mach's formulation of cause as the formulation from which his own position derived (Skinner, 1931/1972b).

The second feature is the focus of causal influence: where, out of the multiplicity of causes, do radical behaviorists look when trying to identify causal relations? This feature of causal thinking stems from their view of the behaving person as it has been outlined above, and it will be shown in what follows how views on behavior and the person influence causal thinking both within the radical behaviorist tradition and other approaches in psychology.

A third feature distinguishes between the need for mechanistic or contiguous causation as that is implied by the chain metaphor and a causation that accepts causal influences occurring over time; a causation that does not require links-in-the-chain or machine/systems analogies to bridge temporal gaps between dependent and independent variables.

Ernst Mach's "functional relations." The scientific status of causal explanation to a radical behaviorist is directly adopted from the philosophy of science of Ernst Mach, whose *Science of Mechanics* (1893/1960) in particular, and positivist orientation toward science in general, profoundly influenced Skinner in his early years as a graduate student at Harvard (Skinner 1931/1972b, 1938, 1978; Smith 1986). Mach, in his turn, acknowledged Hume's influence on his own view that when we appeal to cause and effect, we do no more than describe observed relations (Mach, 1893/1960).

Mach's biographer, John T. Blackmore (1972), describes Mach's dispute with the concept of residual or resident force to which Newton remained committed. Mach opposed an appeal to forces or agency over and above relations between events and referred to Hume's analysis as his own position on causation. Cause, for Mach, was to be stripped of any implication of agency: "There is no cause nor effect in nature; nature has but an individual existence; nature simply *is*" (Mach, 1893/1960 p. 580). Mach replaced cause (as force or agent) with functional relation. Blackmore notes the same distinction between common-sense causation and the scientific conception of that term described by Cohen and Nagel (1934): "For common sense, forces were causes. For many scientists, laws or functions were causes" (Blackmore, 1972, p. 8). He states that for Mach "Causes did not exist, except insofar as one chose to call constant relations and mathematical functions 'causes'" (Blackmore, 1972, p. 104).

Mach appealed to Hume's analysis in opposing what he considered to be the metaphysical concept of force and replaced the term cause and effect with that of functional relation, arguing that the task of the scientist is a complete description of such relations. In the *Preface* to his *Science of Mechanics*, Mach stated that his aim was to "clear up ideas, expose the real significance of the matter, and get rid of metaphysical obscurities" (Mach, 1893/1960, p. xxii). One of those metaphysical obscurities was precisely the notion of a causal force lingering in Newton's physics.

Skinner in his turn adopted many features of Mach's philosophy of science, among them the replacement of agency, of push-pull causality, with the idea of functional relations: "We may now take that more humble view of explanation and causation which seems to have been first suggested by Mach and is now a common characteristic of scientific thought, wherein, in a word, explanation is reduced to description and the notion of function substituted for that of causation" (Skinner, 1931/ 1972b, pp. 448-449). Distinguishing explanation from description is another important feature of the Machian and Skinnerian philosophy of science which will be discussed in the following chapter. The present point is that causation in science from the time of Hume has moved away from causal forces (the idea of a power inherent in one event to produce or bring about another event) toward causal relations between events. In the Skinnerian system, a cause is replaced with a change in the independent variable, and an effect is replaced with a change in the dependent variable, which in turn replaces the cause-effect connection with functional relation (Skinner, 1953, p. 23).

Especially important with respect to causation and human behavior is the elimination of the concept of agency, because although it is no longer customary to describe relations in other sciences in terms of internal force or agency, these pre-Humean notions persist in descriptions of human behavior, even in contemporary social learning theory (Bandura, 1977, 1989). Skinner's early redefinition of the reflex as a relation between independent and dependent variables was an attempt to apply Machian causation to human behavior: "the notion of a reflex is to be emptied of any connotation of the active 'push' of the stimulus" (Skinner, 1938, p. 21). And in more complex human behavior the same conception of causation, stripped of its older connotation of force or agency, is also applied. Skinner added that the newer terms "do not suggest *how* a cause causes its effect: they merely assert that different events tend to occur together in a certain order" (Skinner, 1953, p. 23). For the purpose of casual discourse, he concedes, the terms cause and effect pose no great difficulty as long as their more precise meaning is understood.

Multiple causation. The term, multiple causation, has a specific meaning in Skinner's analysis of verbal behavior. It is used to refer to the fact that: "(1) the strength of a single response may be, and usually is, a function of more than one variable and (2) a single variable usually affects more than one response" (Skinner, 1957, p. 227). But the term is also useful at a broader level to illustrate that many variables contribute to any situation and that situations can be analyzed according to the way those variables are divided and classified. In the same way that the sciences of physics, chemistry, biology, mechanics, and so on direct themselves differently in the search for causal relations, the various subdisciplines that constitute psychology also look to different aspects in the lives of organisms—human or otherwise—for causal relations. Some areas of psychology search for biological and/or genetic features of organisms that might account for their behavior, or for some combination of biological and social/cultural features that may be construed as causal. Some areas look for stages in the organism's development, either biological, social, or cognitive, that might give a structural account. Others concentrate on developing theoretical internal models, testing those models against real behavior, modifying them as required by evidence from behavior. Still other areas look wholly outside the organism, toward only social factors that might be causally related to behavior. In the example of the person who threw a brick at the window, explanations given by different kinds of psychologists may refer to theoretical terms like aggression, anxiety, motivation, personality, intention, cognitive dissonance, arousal, intelligence, reinforcement history, or consequences. As in all other sciences, each subdiscipline looks to a different place, to a different set of constructs for its causal relations.

Behavior analysts look for causal relations in the interaction between behavior (the person or other organism) and features of its environment. This emphasis does not deny contributions from genetic, biological, biochemical, neurological, and other aspects of the organism. It simply identifies the kinds of causal relations sought by the Skinnerian science of behavior, it is the direction in which behavior analysts look for the relations that explain their subject matter. It would be immodest of any science to assert that their focus, their set of relations, is *the only* or even *the primary* set. Of course a causal account given as relations between person and environment does not ordinarily include statements about biological, chemical, or neurological factors. Although such statements are not precluded, they are not required for the explanation to function *as an explanation.* Similarly, the physicist's explanation of glass shattering does not ordinarily include statements about the behavior of the person who threw the brick, and there is no requirement that it should. If the question to be answered in the case of the brick and the broken window concerns momentum and impact, we turn to a physicist. If we want to know something about the person who threw the brick, we turn to a psychologist. If our concern is primarily about the economic relationship between the person who threw the brick and the person who owns the window, we may consult a sociologist or a political scientist. No science can give a comprehensive list of causal relations for any given circumstance because this would amount to a description derived from most of the sciences now practiced, in effect an impossibly complete account of phenomena that includes all contributory factors.

Selection as a causal mode. The third and perhaps most significant feature of causal thinking in Skinner's philosophy is its departure from the traditional chain metaphor. As Hanson argued, this metaphor derives its illusory power from similarities to the deductive method of reasoning, from surface features of the conduct of experiments, and from the simplicity and predictability of mechanical systems in which a clear linear sequence of events accounts for both the operation and malfunction of the system. In the design of a mechanical system, each required component or function is separately prepared and the system is then assembled into a perfect whole that is the sum of its parts. In the breakdown or malfunction of such a system, it is a relatively simple matter to calculate from the beginning or end of a causal sequence and to identify broken links in the chain.

The chain metaphor requires that, like a machine, causal relations be contiguous in both space and time, that gaps between cause and effect be filled by a sequence of events standing in a relation of succession. If aspirin alleviates headaches it is because from aspirin to headache there is a sequence of events in a relation of succession that culminates in the cessation of pain. If one of the mechanical systems in a car breaks down, it is because one or more components of the chain failed. When the component is restored, the mechanical system proceeds as normal.

The chain metaphor with its requirement of contiguity continues to dominate many areas of contemporary psychology. Cognitive psychology is a particularly good example, where contiguous causality is satisfied by internal systems, machine-like in their organization and predictability. Cognitive psychology considers successive mediating events between the outer world of the organism (environmental input) and the behavior of the organism (response output). Gaps between these two end points are reputed to be filled by various components—for example, a complex memory system comprising several constituent parts, an information processing system also made up of several constituents, a cognitive map, a symbol manipulation system, a semantic network, and so on. These components may be relatively simple in design or may involve complex hierarchically organized structures having multiple functions. Nevertheless, their overall role in the explanatory system is that they satisfy the chain metaphor's requirement of contiguity. Less machine-like and more abstract links are provided by other psychological accounts, with components like expectations, intentions, desires, thoughts, attitudes, motivation, and other mental states. Their common feature is that they act as links, filling spatial and temporal gaps between one event and another and in doing so, giving a machine-like account of the relation between one event and another. And like a machine, a breakdown is attributed to a malfunction in one or more of the components mediating between the two end points.

Radical behaviorists adopt a causal mode that carries no requirement to provide links between one event and another, is not linear, and does not presuppose contiguity in space and time. It encompasses causation over time (life history, experience) and has been compared by Skinner with the Darwinian causal mode of selection on variation. The Darwinian template appeals to the selection of particular biological characteristics of a species over time (selection on variation: phylogenetic). Radical behaviorism appeals to the selection over time of characteristics of behavior out of the wide range of possibilities available to the individual (selection on variation: ontogenetic).

The selective action of the environment was obscured for a long time by theological teaching on creation, on the origin of life, and the variation of species; in some religious groups, Darwinian selection is even today hotly disputed. Additionally, the influence of the chain metaphor in science helped to obscure selection as a causal mode because that metaphor cannot encompass the concept of causation over time or at a distance. Similarly, the causal role of the environment in ontogenetic development has been obscured by the metaphor and by the kind of thinking discussed above that separates self from behavior and ascribes agency to aspects of the self in the same way that agency in biological creation was once ascribed to a Great Creator.

It is true that the gene in natural selection inserts a biological unit into the causal web. But this biological unit does not invalidate selection as a causal mode; it merely adds to the network. So too with behavior—it may be possible to discover biological units that form part of its causal web, but such units would add to the network of causation without invalidating selection as a causal mode. The illusory power of the chain metaphor has drawn much of scientific psychology into machine-like interpretations of the relation between environment and behavior, and has encouraged the creation of contiguous linking events or structures between the two.

Skinner noted, "Selection is a special kind of causality, much less conspicuous than the push-pull causality of nineteenth-century physics, and Darwin's discovery may have appeared so late in the history of human thought for that reason. The selective action of the consequences of behavior was also overlooked for a long time. It was not until the seventeenth century that any important initiating action by the environment was recognized" (Skinner, 1972a, p. 353). Selection on variation, or environmental selection, is a causal mode that does not require contiguity, does not require gaps between independent and dependent variables to be filled by sequences of discrete events. Selection occurs over time, not necessarily in an immediate temporal or spatial relation to the repertoire of interest.

The method of successive approximations, widely used in laboratory and applied settings, illustrates selection in action. An experimenter, social worker, clinician, or teacher, trying to establish a pattern of behavior, waits until the organism, pupil, or client does something that looks like or might lead to the desired behavior. Reinforcing that action will result in its more frequent occurrence, until a point where the experimenter then waits for an instance of behavior that is even closer to the type desired. As the method proceeds, the observed behavior is successively refined, selected by reinforcing consequences, until a reliable relation is produced between behavior and consequence.

A good example is given by Isaacs et al. (1966), who report the successful reinstatement of verbal behavior in the repertoire of a psychiatric patient institutionalized for many years and mute for nineteen years. This patient was described as catatonic schizophrenic, that is to say, he rarely moved. The experimenter discovered that eye movement occurred in the presence of a stick of chewing gum and set up a shaping program using gum as a discriminative stimulus and then giving the gum to the patient immediately after an eye movement. At the end of two weeks (six sessions) reliable relations had been established between the presence of the gum, eye movement, and the patient being given gum:

Setting Condition (S^d)	Behavior (R)	Reinforcer (R^+)
gum	eye movement $\longrightarrow$	receives gum

Having established this relation, the experimenter then created the setting condition but withheld reinforcement until a slight movement of the lips occurred before or along with the eye movement. In this way a reliable relation came to be established between gum, eye and lip movement, and the patient receiving gum:

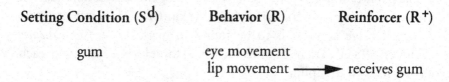

Next, the experimenter withheld the reinforcer until some vocal sound occurred, and at the end of the fourth week (twelve sessions) demonstrated a reliable relation between the setting condition, three discernible responses, and the reinforcer:

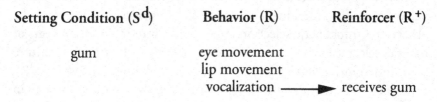

With this pattern established, the experimenter reinforced sounds that increasingly moved closer to the word "gum," and at the end of the sixth week (eighteen sessions) the patient said, "Gum please": "This response was accompanied by reinstatement of other responses of this class, that is, [the patient] answered questions regarding his name and age" (Isaacs et al., 1966, p. 200). At each stage in the shaping process, discrete units of behavior occurred in the presence of a discriminative stimulus and were selected and maintained by reinforcing consequences. As relations were established, the experimenter moved on to another stage, using a reinforcer to select out ever closer approximations to the target. Relations were gradually shaped and demonstrated over a six week period with three sessions each week. No internal event or structures need be appealed to here for explanatory purposes. The experimenter does not have to infer that the reinforcer acted on some internal structure present in each session and carried along in time to mediate relations during following sessions. It is sufficient to demonstrate that the events here were reliably related.

The parallel between phylogenetic and ontogenetic selection was first drawn in *Science and Human Behavior* (Skinner, 1953), but the most comprehensive account is to be found in *Selection by Consequences* (Skinner, 1984a). There, Skinner identified three levels of selection, each having its own discipline:

1) phylogenetic selection, the province of biology;
2) ontogenetic selection, the province of psychology; and
3) the selection of cultural practices, the province of anthropology.

The time span at each level differs, with the second level—selection of behavior in the individual—allowing for selection in progress to be observed. Ontogenetic selection "resembles a hundred million years of natural selection or a thousand years of the evolution of a culture compressed into a very short period of time" (Skinner, 1984*a*, p. 478). Selection of behavior, even of very complex behavior, is demonstrated in the shaping procedures of behavior analytic experiments where behavior is developed, strengthened, maintained, and extinguished by controlling both setting conditions and consequences (contingencies of reinforcement). Thus: "Selection is not a metaphor, model, or concept; it is a fact. Arrange a particular kind of consequence, and behavior changes. Introduce new consequences, and new behavior will appear and survive or disappear" (Skinner, 1984*a*, p. 503). The causal influence of selection is not an assumption; it is empirically validated by the thousands of behavior analytic experiments that demonstrate shaping and maintenance of even complex behavior by complex contingencies.

If causation (selection) occurs over time, then a logical progression is to study its effects over time. Action-over-time is an unusual concept for most of psychology, which tends to see its subject matter episodically. Lee (1988) has argued, "Psychologists neglect personal history. They take an ahistorical strategy, focussing on hypothetical structures inside the organism and thus in the current situation....*history* is not a term frequently used by psychologists" (Lee, 1988, p. 162). Ordinarily, psychological research looks at episodes in the lives of organisms, slices of an ongoing process, and attributes causation to immediate features of the episode. In contrast, research in the radical behaviorist tradition looks at behavioral processes as they occur over time and looks for relations between behavior and environmental events that also occur over time. Causation is not therefore necessarily contiguous, and causal accounts refer to properties not ordinarily included in episodic research. Patterns of behavior, for example, may be established over a long period of time by patterns of consequences (schedules of reinforcement). A one-to-one relation between discrete units of behavior and discrete consequences is not essential to an account of this dynamic interaction because overall patterns can be abstracted and accounted for with reference to events occurring over time in the organism's environment.

In the radical behaviorist formulation, the present organism (that is to say, as of now) consists of an accumulation of past effects but in episodic research, the present organism is divided into behavior and an internal, independent system that is said to account for the behavior. Episodic research, as Lee noted, looks at "selected parts of conduct over limited periods of time, often a few minutes. This research seldom approaches psychological hypotheses by building a history and by studying the effects of this history on subsequent performance. Even when a personal history is built, psychologists seldom attribute the results to the history. Instead they attribute performance to psychological categories such as knowledge, intention, and so forth, with these categories formulated as intervening variables" (Lee, 1988, p. 162). In the case of the patient whose verbal behavior was reinstated after nineteen years, Isaacs et al. (1966) also report that, once reinstated, verbal behavior occurred only in the presence of the experimenter. Whether on the ward, in the dayroom, or in the office, this patient only spoke in the presence of the experimenter. The experimenter had become a discriminative stimulus, setting the occasion for verbal behavior. An observer recently arriving on the ward and not familiar with the patient's history of reinforcement in the presence of the experimenter may easily be drawn into inferences like "the patient obviously likes the experimenter" or "the patient feels secure enough to talk only in the presence of the experimenter." Having access to only an episode of the behavior, an observer may appeal to some internal feature (emotional constructs such as liking or security), temporally contiguous with the behavior, to account for the moment. Episodic observations consider that some feature of the patient's internal state accounts for present behavior but with access to the patient's reinforcement history, it becomes clearer that present behavior is causally related to events at a temporal distance.

Personal history is neglected in the episodic account by a commitment to contiguous causation, but the variation and selection causal mode draws attention to the effects of past experience on current behavior. In the latter mode, the present person is the sum of past effects, and present behavior interacts with both current contingencies and past effects. Personal history (experience) is a necessary part of explanations of present behavior in the variation and selection causal mode.

Beyond Links in the Causal Chain

Causal thinking, in science in general and in the science of behavior in particular, has several features. The present chapter has concentrated on only some of its features as well as on the way culture-specific views of the person inform the direction in which psychology looks for causal relations and the form that those relations take.

Historically, causal thinking in the physical sciences has moved away from the notion of inherent force or agency on the part of the independent variable to a view that causes and effects are no more than functional relations; from "A acts to produce B" to "B is a function of A." Similarly, radical behaviorism dispenses with force or agency, replacing *cause* with *a change in the independent variable* and *effect* with *a change in the dependent variable.* Behavior (the person) stands in a dependent variable relation to environmental events as independent variables.

With its distinctive view of the person and its emphasis on the selective role of the environment, radical behaviorism looks for causal relations in the interaction between behavior (the person) and environmental consequences, a kind of causation that does not require contiguous links between one event and another. Personal history is an important part of causal explanation in this tradition since the present person is the sum of past effects. Behavior analytic experiments that demonstrate the selective action of consequences empirically validate selection as a causal mode.

Another feature of causal thinking is still to be discussed. It has been briefly mentioned as a severe complication for the chain metaphor's ability to account for causation: the theory-laden nature of causal terms. The concepts of causation, explanation, and theory are intimately bound together in the statements we make about how and why things happen in the world. The role of theory and forms of explanation will be considered in the following chapter.

Chapter 6

Interpretive Techniques and Explanatory Theories

Another feature of Mach's philosophy of science that Skinner adopted directly was noted in the previous chapter: "We may now take that more humble view of explanation and causation which seems to have been first suggested by Mach and is now a common characteristic of scientific thought, wherein, in a word, explanation is reduced to description and the notion of function substituted for that of causation" (Skinner, 1931/ 1972b, pp. 448-449). It was pointed out that the distinction between cause and function relates to historical developments in the history of the concept of causation. Similarly, Mach's distinction between explanation and description is historically significant in relation to major theoretical/ philosophical debates of his time and continues to be significant in relation to contemporary experimental psychology.

To the modern reader, accustomed to thinking of science as an enterprise going *beyond* descriptions of phenomena to explanations, the proposal to limit (reduce) explanation to description may seem contradictory to scientific aims. Furthermore, the proposal implies two separate and exclusive activities: that when phenomena are described they are not at the same time explained, and that to explain is in some sense to account for that which is described. In other words, in merely describing events, one is not accounting for those events. Hempel and Oppenheim begin their classic *Studies in the Logic of Explanation* with precisely this assertion, "Scientific research in its various branches strives to go beyond a mere description of its subject matter by providing an explanation of the phenomena it investigates" (Hempel & Oppenheim, 1960, p. 135). If science strives not merely to describe but to go beyond description to explanation, how could such an eminent scientist and philosopher as Ernst Mach propose limiting science to description and thereby exclude the possibility of explaining (accounting for) natural phenomena?

In clarifying Mach's and Skinner's distinction between description and explanation, this chapter adds to the argument that radical behaviorism's accounts (explanations) of its subject matter avoid mechanistic interpretations of the behavior of organisms, human or otherwise.

Description and Functional Relations: Mach

The distinction between description and explanation is a product of two features of Mach's argument:

1) the definition of description, which is related to Mach's views on causation; and

2) Mach's opposition to certain kinds of theories, especially those grounded in a mechanistic view of nature and which draw on the interpretive technique of appealing to hypothetical entities to bridge temporal and spatial gaps between functionally dependent events (causes and effects).

Descriptions, in Mach's terms, are explanatory in the sense that they account for phenomena. The somewhat misleading distinction between description and explanation derives from a major debate of the 19th century concerning appropriate interpretive techniques in physics, and from a dispute over attempts to describe natural phenomena in terms analogous to the workings of a great machine.

Mach asserted that complete descriptions of phenomena suffice as explanations. He wrote of description, "[It] is only possible of events that constantly recur, or of events that are made up of component parts that constantly recur. That only can be described, and conceptually represented, which is uniform and conformable to law; for description presupposes the employment of names by which to designate its elements; and names can acquire meanings only when applied to elements that constantly reappear" (Mach, 1893/1960, p. 6). In this passage, Mach made the point that was also made later by Hanson (1955), referred to in the previous chapter, that the words used to describe phenomena are many-levelled in their generality and explanatory power. When a physicist describes the refraction of light in water, the words, light, refraction, and water, already compact several conceptual properties that, if need be, can be further described by other words compacting conceptual properties. Mach's point (and Hanson's) was that descriptive terms in science imply properties and relations. Unexplained phenomena are those in which the scientist has not yet discovered recurring elements, elements "that amid all multiplicity are ever present" (Mach, 1893/1960, p. 6). Mach added: "When once we have reached the point where we are everywhere able to detect the *same* few simple elements, combining in the ordinary manner, then they appear to us as things that are familiar; we are no longer surprised, there is nothing new or strange to us in the phenomena, we feel at home with them, they no longer perplex us, they are *explained*" (Mach, 1893/1960, p. 7).

Descriptive terms in science, as in other disciplines, are embedded within theoretical frameworks, webs of related constructs and concepts that give them meaning. An explanation of why light refracts in water is contained in another description, a description of the behavior of a general type of wave phenomena (light being a single instance of that general type) that conforms to the law of refraction when travelling through an optical medium that is denser than air (of which water is an instance). In describing the relation between conceptual properties (light and water) in the form of a general law (refraction), the phenomenon is explained.

"Light refracts in water" is a description of a relation between conceptual properties that in itself is not explanatory. It does not satisfy the question, "Why does light refract in water?" That question is satisfied (the phenomenon accounted for) by a further description of the relation between the properties of light, of water, and the law of refraction. In another context the description, light refracts in water, does function as an explanation, as the answer to the question, "Why does this straight rod seem to bend when I put it in the lake?" In this context, "because light refracts in water" (the same description of relations) is an explanation of the phenomenon observed.

"Intermittently reinforced behavior is highly resistent to extinction" is a description of a behavioral regularity that, as it stands, is not explanatory. This regularity is explained by a further description of relations between dynamic properties of operants (a class of behavior), their relation to reinforcing consequences (a class of events), and regularities produced by temporal patterning. The original description functions as an explanation of why behavior continues to occur in some circumstances even after reinforcement has been withdrawn. At each level of questioning, explanations are given by describing relations. Thus, a description of relations given in language that is conceptually many-levelled accounts for the phenomena described. What are described are relations between conceptual properties, Mach's functional relations. Often, the conceptual properties are so compacted, so familiar, that they seem to fade away. Nevertheless, every account of natural phenomena, at whatever level of questioning, amounts to a description of relations. Explanations *are* descriptions.

But if explanations are descriptions, what then necessitated a distinction between the two? If explanation *is* description, why did Mach in the 19th century stand in favor of one and against the other? And why did Skinner in the 20th century maintain this distinction? These questions raise the second feature of Mach's argument and require a brief excursion into one of the major debates of 19th century physics. This debate's relevance to Skinner's views on explanation and theory in contemporary experimental psychology will become clear in the following sections.

Explanation and Theory: Mach

Superficially, the debate centered on the reality of atoms and the explanatory power of atomic theory, with Mach's opposition to certain types and certain treatments of atomic theory widely documented (for example, Cohen & Seeger, 1970; Feyerabend, 1970; Bradley, 1971; Blackmore, 1972). Laudan (1981*e*) and Brush (1968), however, argue that representations of Mach's participation in the 19th century atomic debate tend to ignore the context of that debate as well as the wider implications of his views on physical theory for the philosophy and methodology of science. Laudan, for example, states, "Though the fact of Mach's opposition to atomic/molecular theories is well known and widely cited, Mach's specific argumentative strategies against such theories have been less fully explored and understood" (Laudan, 1981*e*, p. 202). He notes that Mach's opposition to atomism tends to be represented as a "noble espousal of a lost cause." Brush also contends that the modern philosophy of science literature represents Mach as having "bet on the wrong horse," but cautions, "We cannot be content to say that Mach was simply 'right' or 'wrong' on a certain point, judged by accepted modern views" (Brush, 1968, p. 193). Instead, Mach's views should be placed in the context of 19th century physical theory and judged by their relation to that context: "When Mach's statements on atomic theory are put in their historical context, it turns out that Mach's position is much more complex than is generally reported. Moreover, some of the *scientific* questions discussed by Mach are by no means settled even today, to say nothing of the philosophical or methodological ones" (Brush, 1968, p. 193). The atomic debate had wider implications for the philosophy and methodology of science than the simple question of whether atoms did or did not exist, or who was on the right or the wrong side of that debate. Laudan feels that to present the debate at that superficial level is to ignore the subtlety of Mach's argument and that of some of his contemporaries, in addition to ignoring the larger issue of conceptual properties contained in or referred to in explanatory terms (descriptions) and their relation to the phenomena they are said to account for. The atomic debate exemplified a broader 19th century dispute over appropriate interpretive techniques in physical science and the causal mode underlying them.

Mach was deeply troubled by his era's emphasis on atomic explanations for two reasons. First, he was disturbed by the possibility that theories of this sort could distract attention from the phenomena they were invented to account for, that hypothetical constructs within the theory rather than functional relations might become the focus of attention. Second, he saw such theorizing as an attempt to interpret natural phenomena as mechanical systems and to describe the world as though it functioned as a great machine whose whole could be understood by identifying each of its parts. This type of theorizing belonged to a mechanistic world view that Mach did not share with some of his contemporaries.

Continually emphasizing the importance of description, observation, and integration in science, Mach was hostile to interpretations that went beyond descriptions of functional dependencies. He did not entirely rule out unobservable, hypothetical properties or entities such as atoms but saw them as provisional helps rather than ontological realities, as useful heuristics for generating new questions and establishing new relations and laws. Once those new relations had been established, the hypothetical entities themselves were to be abandoned. Temporarily useful props on which to build experimentation and suggest new problems, they were not in the long term to be considered as anything more than "things of thought." Laudan notes, "For Mach, theoretical entities may play an important but intrinsically transitional role in natural science. Once they have suggested those empirical connections that are the warp and woof of scientific understanding, they can be discarded as so much unnecessary scaffolding" (Laudan, 1981e, p. 212). He also notes, "Above all, Mach stresses that we must not confuse the tool with the job by pretending that the model does anything more than establish functional relations between data" (Laudan, 1981e, p. 212).

For Mach, theoretical accounts containing hypothetical entities do not describe anything in the world; they are simply tools of science, provisionally useful, to be discarded when they no longer lead to the discovery of functional dependencies. They are to remain in the realms of the hypothetical and not to be given the status of explanations (descriptions). Laudan notes that Mach did not argue against atomic or molecular theorizing *as long as* its provisional status is understood. That is to say, the theory is provisional for as long as it continues to lead to the discovery of new relations. Such theorizing becomes problematic when elevated to the status of explanation. Mach's distinction between description and explanation, then, is between explanatory systems integrating and describing observed functional dependencies, and explanatory systems invoking hypothetical entities said to come between those dependencies and to account for their relations as links in a causal chain. The atomic debate was less about the question of whether atoms do or do not exist than about interpretive techniques and underlying causal modes.

In his introduction to *The Science of Mechanics* (Mach, 1893/1960), Karl Menger noted that 18th and 19th century physics was suffused with attempts to explain gravitation by appealing to mediating entities: "Physicists hypostasized vortices, or tensions in media, or bombardments of the bodies by particles traversing space at random and driving, for instance, a stone toward the earth because the latter shields the stone against the particles coming from below" (pp. vii-viii). Gravitational attraction or repulsion was attributed in these accounts to action taking place through a particle medium or aether. This medium, hypothetical and unobserved, allowed for contact action, a links-in-the-chain or mechanistic causality. If events at a distance show functional relatedness (so the mechanist's thinking goes), there must be between those events a sequence of other events, some medium, structure, or mechanism, that connects them. And, for the mechanist, it is the *thing-in-between* that explains the relation.

It has already been noted that Mach and several of his contemporaries were deeply disturbed by interpretive modes that went beyond observed relations, that postulated hypothetical media through which action took place and thereby reduced physical phenomena to mechanical systems. Of mechanistic thinking Mach wrote: "The view that makes mechanics the basis of the remaining branches of physics, and explains all physical phenomena by mechanical ideas, is in our judgement a prejudice" (Mach, 1893/1960, p. 596). Specifically in relation to atomic theories, he was critical of the way they so often shifted from the status of scientific tools, tools of thought that assisted the scientist in establishing relations, to the status of explanations, becoming realities in themselves behind the phenomena. He was critical also of scientists who, having created theoretical models involving hypothetical constructs (such as atoms) proceeded to make the constructs themselves into objects of inquiry, relegating to the background the phenomena that the models or constructs were originally developed to connect. He referred to these models as intellectual machinery and cautioned that the machinery of thought should not be mistaken for descriptions of the real world: "A person who knew the world only through the theater, if brought behind the scenes and permitted to view the mechanism of the stage's action, might possibly believe that the real world also was in need of a machine-room, and that if this were once thoroughly explored, we should know all. Similarly, we, too, should beware lest the *intellectual* machinery, employed in the representation of the world on *the stage of thought,* be regarded as the basis of the real world" (Mach, 1893/1960, p. 610).

Mach's emphasis on description versus explanation, a distinction that seems to the modern reader antithetical to the aims of science, is in fact a distinction between different interpretive techniques and causal modes. His position may be summarized as follows: science is descriptive, observational, and integrative; its task is to observe and describe regular functional dependencies and to integrate those dependencies in the form of general laws. Accepting the heuristic value of systems that go beyond the realm of the observed to the hypothetical, Mach opposed the practice of elevating the hypothetical to the status of explanation since nothing is described—hypothetical constructs do not furnish explanations. He also opposed the practice of diverting attention away from functional dependencies toward hypothetical constructs, of turning constructs themselves into ontological realities and into the focus of inquiry. Finally, he opposed a causal mode that requires things-in-between to connect dependent phenomena and that consequently views the workings of the universe as a vast machine, to be understood by breaking it down into its component parts; a world-as-machine view.

For Mach, appropriate explanations consisted of descriptions given in language that is many-levelled, compacting conceptual properties, and relating them in the form of general laws. Inappropriate explanations transform hypothetical entities, the intellectual machinery of science, into ontological realities and attempt to provide links-in-the-causal-chain by means of those entities.

Interpretive Techniques and Explanatory Theories

Description and Functional Relations: Skinner

Skinner's distinction between description and explanation and his objection to particular kinds of interpretive techniques closely follow Mach's arguments. As early as 1938 Skinner described his developing system in the following way: "[The system] is positivistic. It confines itself to description rather than explanation. Its concepts are defined in terms of immediate observations and are not given local or physiological properties. A reflex is not an arc, a drive is not the state of a center, extinction is not the exhaustion of a physiological substance or state. Terms of this sort are used merely to bring together groups of observations, to state uniformities, and to express properties of behavior which transcend single instances" (Skinner, 1938, p. 44). This early passage encapsulates ideas he later elaborated and demonstrates his commitment to a science that is, like Mach's, descriptive, observational, and integrative.

Skinner's descriptions take the same form as Mach's; they are statements of functional dependencies, of regularities in the relation between dependent and independent variables. He was at pains to point out that description in this sense differs from narration, where "The story is simply told of something that has once happened" (Skinner, 1938, p. 9). A narrative statement is not explanatory; it simply states the occurrence of a single event: "In the narrative form, for example, it may be said that 'at such and such a moment the ape picked up a stick.' Here there is no reference to other instances of the same behavior either past or future. It is not asserted that all apes pick up sticks" (Skinner, 1938, p. 9). In the refraction example, a narrative statement would be: "at time X, this beam refracted through this medium," a statement that describes an instance without reference to regularity. "Light refracts in water," however, expresses a uniformity, a regularity in the behavior of light in certain media. "Apes eat bamboo" similarly expresses a regularity, summarizing a uniformity, a relation between conceptual properties.

To be explanatory, a description must relate uniformities between classes or properties. Skinner referred to reflex, drive, extinction, and so forth, terms that in his system simply integrate and summarize relations.

They *do* go beyond single instances to describe uniformities, but *do not* go beyond the relations observed. A reflex, for example, in the Skinnerian system describes a particular kind of correlation between stimulus and response. When Skinner stated that it is "not given local or physiological properties," he was referring to the practice of locating reflex within the organism and ascribing to it physiological properties such as a neurological arc bridging a gap between its two end-terms, stimulus and response. For Skinner, a reflex described no more or less than a relation. The term is an abstraction of a reliable uniformity. If a reflex is located at all, it is located *in the relation* between particular kinds of stimuli and responses and not within the organism. In the expression of these relations, which "amid all multiplicity are ever present" (Mach, 1893/1960, p. 6), lies explanation. Behavior is explained in the description of uniform relations between dependent variables (units of behavior) and independent variables in the context in which it occurs. Explanation, for Skinner as for Mach, *is* description, and again the question of why Skinner sought to confine his system to description is raised. What are the explanations that Skinner ruled out of his scientific system?

In the case of Mach and the atomic debate in 19th century physics, the distinction between explanation and description grew out of disputes over interpretive techniques and causal thinking. Similarly, in 20th century psychology, Skinner's distinction grew out of his opposition to particular kinds of interpretations of human behavior and to a causal thinking that requires temporal gaps between events to be filled by links-in-a-causal-chain.

Explanation and Theory: Skinner

Skinner's views on explanation, description, and theory in a science of behavior are woven into much of his writing from his doctoral dissertation onward, and several papers are given over wholly or mainly to outlining these views, notably; *Current Trends in Experimental Psychology* (1947/1972b), *Are Theories of Learning Necessary?* (1950/1972b),

Critique of Psychoanalytic Concepts and Theories (1956), and *The Flight from the Laboratory* (1972c).

Despite his careful definition of the interpretive technique he regarded as harmful and diversionary in a science of behavior, and his considered outline of a theoretical system he regarded as effective, Skinner's position has often been commented on as if it were an argument that theory is altogether unnecessary in a science of behavior. Westby (1966), for example, described Skinner's approach as a "Grand Anti-Theory." His views have also been read as a claim that his own explanatory system is somehow atheoretical. Scriven (1956), for example, constructed an argument to demonstrate that Skinner's system does in fact amount to a theory: "I shall not be trying to show that Skinner's theories are bad, I wish to show only that he does employ them" (Scriven, 1956, p. 88). Such comments and conclusions are curious caricatures of Skinner's position, but they share a similarity with caricatures of Mach's participation in the atomic debate which, as Laudan noted, addressed more fundamental scientific issues than the ontological status of atoms. Similarly, Skinner's participation in the theory debate goes beyond the question, "Shall we have a theory or not?" to more fundamental issues concerning underlying assumptions of the theories we already have, their usefulness and explanatory power, alternatives to those theories, and the kind of causal mode that underlies traditional interpretive patterns.

Skinner's distinction between description and explanation is, like Mach's, intimately bound to the issues of interpretive techniques and causal modes. Laudan noted that superficial accounts of the atomic debate, presenting it as a dispute over the ontological status of atoms, obscure a more fundamental discomfort with interpretive techniques that adopt a mechanistic causal mode and lead to a mechanistic view of nature. Accounts of Skinner's position that present it as anti-theoretical miss the same important points and obscure the real focus of his analysis.

It is difficult to understand how even the most casual reading of, for example, *Current Trends in Experimental Psychology* (Skinner, 1947/ 1972b) could leave an impression that Skinner opposed theory in a science of behavior; he quite clearly expressed the opposite view. He argued in this paper, "Behavior can only be satisfactorily understood by going beyond the facts themselves. *What is needed is a theory of behavior*" (p. 301, emphasis added) and, "Whether particular experimental psychologists like it or not, experimental psychology is properly and inevitably committed to the construction of a theory of behavior. *A theory is essential to the scientific understanding of behavior as a subject matter*" (p. 302, emphasis added). When Skinner wrote these words, psychology was beginning to doubt the claims of its major theorists that a comprehensive theory of behavior would be forthcoming. Hull's theoretical system had been dominant but was coming under attack, and what has been described as psychology's Age of Theory (Smith, 1986) had begun its decline. Skinner's contribution to the theory debate was to examine the genesis of psychology's dominant interpretive systems and to outline a form of theory construction that would satisfy his (and Mach's) view of science as descriptive, observational, and integrative.

Constructing a Theory

Despite contrary interpretations, it is clear from the above excerpts that Skinner was committed to the development of a theory of behavior. But the term, theory, is somewhat ambiguous since it can carry at least three meanings, two of which involve the notion of speculation and the third, the notion of integration. First, a theory may be simply a guess, a predictive or explanatory guess of the sort, "I have a theory that such and such will happen" or "I have a theory that this is caused by that," where the speaker is guessing an outcome or suggesting a causal relation. Second, "theory" may refer to a model involving one or more hypothetical entities constructed in an attempt to account for mysterious (unexplained) phenomena. This type of theory proposes a speculative explanation which, for scientific purposes, requires experimental testing to establish to what degree the model fits empirical data it attempts to explain.

Interpretive Techniques and Explanatory Theories

Third, theory may also refer to an explanatory system—like Skinner's—that describes regularities, states general principles, and integrates uniformities in a given subject matter. These last kinds of theories do not carry the same requirement of being submitted to experimental check since they are data-driven (derived from observation) and are not constructed prior to experimentation. In this sense, integrative theories are not speculative; they describe without guessing. Theoretical terms in this type of explanatory system do not preempt experimentation; rather, they are derived from it. Speculation does not take place at the level of explanation but at the level of experimentation, when an attempt is made to discover which out of the multiplicity of variables present in a given context may be functionally related. Explanations do not refer to processes or entities beyond observation; rather, the descriptions comprising explanation are statements about observed regularities.

Skinner proposed that a science of behavior may benefit from the construction of the last kind of theory, one that integrates observed regularities. He identified three stages of theory construction. The first and perhaps most important stage is to identify the basic data. The next step involves the development of theoretical terms that express relations among data, integrative terms: "Observed relations of this sort are the facts of a science—or, when a sufficient degree of generality has been reached, its laws" (Skinner, 1947/1972b, p. 307). As further regularities appear, theory construction moves on to a third stage involving the addition of new theoretical terms to describe these new regularities. Third stage concepts (Skinner, 1947/1972b, p. 307) are additions to the regularities expressed at the second stage without being additions to the basic data. They emerge *from* the regularities themselves without invoking unobserved or hypothetical properties.

Skinner gave a simple example from the history of the science of mechanics: "Galileo, with the help of his predecessors, began by restricting himself to a limited set of data. He proposed to deal with the positions of bodies at given times, rather than with their color or hardness or size" (Skinner, 1947/1972b, p. 307). This decision characterizes the first stage of constructing a theory, where data are limited and defined. "Galileo then proceeded to demonstrate a relation between position and time" (Skinner, 1947/1972b, p. 307). At this second stage, theoretical terms are developed to describe lawful regularities in the basic data. To describe the relation between the position of a ball on an inclined plane and the time elapsed since its release, for example, the term, acceleration, is developed. "Later, as other facts were added, other concepts appeared—mass, force, and so on. Third-stage concepts of this sort are something more than the second-stage laws from which they are derived. They are peculiarly the product of theory-making" (Skinner, 1947/1972b, p. 307).

When Skinner first began to construct an explanatory system, he carefully defined his basic data, his subject matter, summarized in the term, behavior: "Behavior is that part of the functioning of an organism which is engaged in acting upon or having commerce with the outside world....by behavior, then, I mean simply the movement of an organism or of its parts in a frame of reference provided by the organism itself or by various external objects or fields of force. It is convenient to speak of this as the action of the organism upon the outside world" (Skinner, 1938, p. 6). Although the definition of behavior has always been a complex matter (for example, see Lee, 1988), the most significant aspect here is *in a frame of reference*, which identified Skinner's data as something other than simple topography (as Galileo's data were something other than intrinsic features of bodies). The data to be explained, the subject matter of Skinner's science of behavior, are not muscle twitches or lever presses; they are relations between behavior and the world that organisms engage with—*behavior and the context in which it occurs.*

Having defined his subject matter, he proceeded to consider terms that might express those relations. It has already been noted that the language in which we ordinarily describe behavior does not always share the accuracy of the descriptive language of other sciences. Vernacular expressions often carry with them hidden conceptual schemes that already imply relations not given by scientific data. An examination of the language of mind, of learning, and of language itself (Chapter 2) demonstrated that although these terms may be adequate for everyday purposes, they imply *a priori* conceptual schemes that may confuse rather than illuminate empirical relations. Skinner did not rule out the use of everyday terms in an explanatory system; he simply cautioned that terms derived from ordinary language should not be adopted uncritically. Behavioral science "must not take over without careful consideration the schemes which underlie popular speech" (Skinner, 1938, p. 7). In line with his view of science as descriptive, observational, and integrative, theoretical terms in the Skinnerian system refer to empirically derived relations within the subject matter. Conditioning and extinction, for example, describe the shaping of behavior as a function of events in the context in which it occurs. *Operant behavior* refers to any act on the part of the organism that produces an effect and *an operant* refers to a class of responses having a particular effect. In experimental situations with rats, for example, lever pressing is a class of responses having the effect of producing food. Topography is not important for experimental purposes. A rat may press a lever with its paw, its foot, its nose, or its tail, but the topography of the operant is of less import than its relation to the context in which it occurs. Human operants may be topographically more diffuse than the single units of the rat's lever presses or the pigeon's key pecks. Depending on the experimental question in hand, an operant can refer to anything from washing dishes to a violent verbal outburst, the common feature being that each is identified as a unit of behavior functionally related to events in its context.

Skinner also designated terms to describe dependencies between the setting conditions and consequences of behavior. *Discriminative stimulus* refers to a discrete aspect of the setting condition in which an operant occurs and which is functionally related to that operant. Similarly, *reinforcer* refers to the effect of a discrete consequence on behavior. Several consequences may follow an operant, but not all of those consequences may be functionally related to it. A reinforcing consequence is one that shapes and/or maintains an operant. In the case of discriminative stimulus and reinforcer, as in the case of operant, intrinsic properties of objects or events are of less import than the functional relations those terms describe. A red light is not a discriminative stimulus because it is red but because it is related to an operant. Candy is described as a reinforcer if and when it shapes and maintains behavior; not because it is sweet, but because it is functionally related to an operant.

At the second stage in the construction of his system, Skinner developed integrative terms to express observed relations in his subject matter. Those terms are derived from the subject matter itself and do not appeal to assumed properties or entities beyond those which are empirically given. Relations between discriminative stimuli, operants, and reinforcers may be expressed as a function of time, of rate of response, of magnitude of reinforcement, of rate of reinforcement, of availability of alternatives, of the presence of verbal behavior, and so on, and it is with the identification of new relations that third stage concepts emerge. For example, early in his experimental career Skinner observed that response rate and rate of reinforcement were related across a broad range of settings. New terms were added to integrate these observations— variable interval, variable ratio, fixed interval, fixed ratio, concurrent, and differential reinforcement of low rate—all describing patterns in rates of reinforcement that are reliably related to patterns of response rates. These third stage concepts emerge out of second stage relations without changing anything in the first stage, the basic data. Basic data are maintained even as theoretical terms are broadened, and those terms always refer to observed regularities in the basic data.

Skinner clearly preferred a Machian approach to explanatory theories; a type of theory that is descriptive, relies on observation, and whose terms integrate relations among basic data. Nothing in the Skinnerian system is conveniently invented or modified to account for data. Behavior is explained by pointing to functional dependencies *within* the data rather than by invoking unobserved properties or entities. When he set out his views on appropriate interpretive techniques he stated, "[A theory] has nothing to do with the presence or absence of experimental confirmation. Facts and theories do not stand in opposition to each other. The relation, rather, is this: theories are based upon facts; they are statements about organizations of facts" (Skinner, 1947/1972b, p. 302). The theoretical terms of his own explanatory system, arrived at inductively rather than deductively, are statements about regularities in the basic data and do not stand or fall on experimental confirmation. Neither does the theoretical system as a whole stand or fall on experimental confirmation since only *observed* regularities form the linguistic basis of the system.

In line with Mach's thinking, and for much the same reasons, Skinner opposed interpretive techniques grounded in mechanistic thinking, which require entities to bridge temporal and/or spatial gaps between dependent and independent variables. The interpretive technique he referred to in posing the question, "Are theories of learning necessary?" is as carefully defined as his own theoretical system. It is: "any explanation of an observed fact which appeals to events taking place somewhere else, at some other level of observation, described in different terms, and measured, if at all, in different dimensions" (Skinner, 1950/1972b, p. 69). This type of interpretive technique he considered to be diversionary for a science of behavior. Perhaps the confusion of his readers would have been spared had Skinner referred to this kind of theory by a different name. Although he did, as always, carefully define his terms, it may be that a term like model or theoretical model would have better served to distinguish this technique from the practices of integration and description. In the same way that the words, description versus explanation, may mislead a reader into assuming that descriptions do not suffice as explanations, arguing in one place *for* a theory of behavior and arguing in another place *against* theory is also likely to lead to confusion. This does not justify gross caricatures and misrepresentations on the part of his readers, but Skinner may have spared at least some of their confusion by referring to different types of interpretive techniques with different labels.

Skinner's disenchantment was obviously not with theory *per se*. But, like Mach, he was concerned with the way particular kinds of explanatory theories can easily divert attention from the controlling effects of manipulable variables in the context in which behavior occurs and toward the structure, function, or activity of hypothetical entities that are given as speculative accounts of behavior. Behavior and the behaving person fade into the background as interest focuses instead on the action of complex, hypothetical structures and mechanisms. Skinner's opposition to the mechanistic thinking underlying these kinds of theories (which will here be referred to as models or theoretical models for the purpose of greater clarity) was based on the Machian view of cause and effect as functional dependency. Like Mach, Skinner found no discomfort in integrating cause and effect (functional relations) *without* a mediating structure or mechanism through which action takes place. To Skinner and other radical behaviorists, behaving organisms, human or otherwise, are not mechanical structures to be likened to telephone exchanges and networks, information processing systems, computer storage banks, and the like. They are biological organisms operating within a context that affects their behavior and that they in turn have an effect upon, organisms that are changed by their experience in that context. As Mach before him refused a view of the world as great machine, Skinner rejected machine analogies in his scientific system and eschewed mechanical principles for describing organisms and their worlds.

Another feature of his opposition to models that include terms not derived from data was a practical argument. Scientific modelling carries a requirement of experimental testing to establish the best fit between competing models and data and as such, Skinner argued, they are wasteful of valuable energy and resources. This argument was raised in Chapter 3, where the methodologies of mainstream experimental psychology and behavior analysis were compared. It was noted there that data obtained in the testing of a model are only considered valuable if they conform to predictions deduced from the model. If results do not conform to predictions, then data so carefully collected in the research process have little meaning or value. The model is either rejected or undergoes modification leading to further experimentation, but the data themselves turn out to be useless except insofar as they demonstrate problems in the model. Since the process of constant experimental check usually leads to the decline of one model and the rise of another (either a modified model or a competing one), a large part of the research associated with the testing of models is discarded: "Research designed with respect to theory is also likely to be wasteful. That a theory generates research does not prove its value unless the research is valuable. Much useless experimentation results from theories, and much energy and skill are absorbed by them. Most theories are eventually overthrown, and the greater part of the associated research is discarded" (Skinner, 1950/1972b, p. 71).

Discussing explanatory systems that appeal to events taking place at some other level will be useful in helping to illuminate Skinner's concerns. This will be done in the following chapter, which will argue that Mach's 19th century views on interpretation and causal modes in his own science remain relevant to 20th century psychology, and that Skinner's views of the 1940s and 1950s remain relevant to psychology today.

Chapter 7

Mechanistic Thinking in Psychology

The two preceding chapters noted that causal thinking in radical behaviorist philosophy does not rely on things-in-between to explain functional relations. Radical behaviorists, following Mach, explain behavior and its frame of reference in integrative theoretical terms derived from observation without offering additional entities, aethers or mediums to bridge spatial and/or temporal gaps between dependent phenomena.

This interpretive technique sets behavior analysis apart from more traditional patterns of explanation that append behavior to some other system or structure that is said to control it, to be its source or cause. The dualistic presumption referred to in Chapter 5 takes behavior to be a secondary feature, a manifestation *of something else*, and any attempt to explain behavior that is guided by this presumption must necessarily appeal to "events taking place somewhere else, at some other level of observation" (Skinner, 1950/1972b, p. 69).

Theoretical accounts referring to some other dimension differ considerably from Skinner's system. They involve a shift away from observation (data) to theoretical concepts not contained in or given by data but which are said to explain it. This interpretive technique involves leaping from the realm of the observed to the realm of the hypothetical and offering the hypothetical as an account of the observed. The leap is not necessitated by data but by prescientific assumptions about behavior and the behaving person (assumptions that are not part of radical behaviorism's philosophy of the person). Where Skinner insisted on relying on observation to describe uniform relations in integrative theoretical terms, other systems insist on explanations in additional theoretical terms not derived from observation.

For example, Skinner referred to "two great explanatory systems which have held the psychological field for a hundred years" (Skinner, 1947/ 1972b, p. 302):

(1) explanations couched in theoretical terms referring to a controlling mind or to subdivisions of mind (memory, desires, intention, purpose, attitudes, will, and so on), and

(2) explanations couched in theoretical terms referring to physiological properties of organisms.

The theoretical terms composing these explanatory systems are additions to data. When one observes learning in a pigeon or a human, for example, one does not observe the storage of information in mind or any other mental process, nor does one observe the formation of synaptic connections. Learning is observed in the graphs and curves that form experimental data, in records of behavior. Accounts of learning that leap from records of behavior to some other system, mental or physiological, rely on the traditional view of behavior as an appendage to another system and give priority to that other system. The data in hand give no indication of another realm in which learning takes place, but terms that appeal to another realm form the linguistic basis of theoretical models as they were referred to in Chapter 6.

Given that psychology as a whole is made up of many subdisciplines and theoretical systems, it is not feasible to attempt a comprehensive review of the entire discipline. To illuminate Skinner's concerns about the diversionary and mechanistic nature of theoretical models, the present chapter focuses on three influential explanatory systems in contemporary psychology. This is not intended to be an exhaustive analysis of all or any one of the models. Rather, these examples are chosen as illustrations of the underlying issues.

Skinner's concerns about psychodynamic accounts of behavior will be illustrated by a discussion of the Freudian theoretical model. It is doubtful whether anyone would claim the Freudian model as an example of experimental psychology, and it may seem inappropriate to include it here. Psychodynamic accounts of behavior, however, especially Freudian accounts, continue to be widely drawn on in the applied contexts of clinical psychology, psychiatry, and social work (Sheldon, 1982). It is therefore appropriate that their merit as explanatory accounts should be considered. Working memory is a good example of an explanatory account in cognitive psychology, and the concept of motivation helps to illustrate confusions that can result from including ordinary language concepts in scientific systems. Before moving on to these models, however, there are some important points to make about types of physiological accounts and their explanatory status from the viewpoint of radical behaviorism.

The Physiology of Behavior

Physiological accounts have a long history and follow the traditional pattern of appealing to internal characteristics of the organism to explain behavior. In the fifth century B.C., Hippocrates theorized that four basic fluids within the body (blood, phlegm, black bile, and yellow bile) were each associated with a personality type or temperament (sanguine, phlegmatic, melancholic and choleric). The Victorian science of phrenology vigorously attempted to correlate the size and configuration of the skull with personality types or characteristics (de Giustino, 1975), and in this century it was suggested that physical patterns such as endomorph, ectomorph, and mesomorph underpinned behavioral patterns (Sheldon, 1942). Nowadays, the brain and nervous system are often taken to be the underlying location of certain activities. Skinner (1953, pp. 27-28) noted that in everyday settings people are frequently described as nervous, as suffering from nervous exhaustion or nerve strain, or in terms that otherwise refer to the nervous system as causal. And another contemporary causal determinant is said to be found in a person's genetic makeup. Invoking biological/physiological characteristics of organisms as explanations of behavior has almost as long a history as explanations couched in terms of a creative mind or will.

Some physiological accounts conform to theoretical models while others do not. The type which refers to a person suffering nervous exhaustion or nerve strain, for example, is theoretical in the sense that it is speculative, that no direct observation of the nervous system is involved. A physiological account that differs from theoretical models is given by Miller (1980). This account involves direct observation of neurological or other biological deficit in organisms and relates those deficits to behavior. Miller describes the process of examining the behavior of organisms that have suffered damage to some part of the nervous system (for example, brain damage or neural lesions) and comparing their behavior to that of intact organisms. Since damage to the nervous system is here directly observed, the theoretical terms of the account are not hypothetical. And since a relation can be demonstrated between neural deficit and behavioral deficit in contrast to the behavior of intact organisms, the relation is not purely speculative. Causal dependencies, although not directly observed, are inferred by comparison with the behavior of intact organisms. This type of account is based partly on observation and partly on comparison. It is not strictly speculative in the sense of appealing to the nervous system without any direct observation, nor is it strictly causal because dependent relations are not directly demonstrated.

Although the reasoning seems straightforward, physiological accounts can also suffer from confusion at the interpretive level. Efron (1990) considers the interpretive language of hemispheric specialization and the scientific issues involved. He notes that neuropsychologists use the term, specialization, to mean that a particular region of the brain is crucially responsible for the performance of a specific cognitive function on the basis of observing a relation between neurological damage and, for example, visual or linguistic deficit. Visual neurophysiologists know that if the striate cortex is damaged bilaterally, primates become essentially blind (Efron, 1990). They also know that 95% of humans experience serious disturbances in language functions if the left fronto-temporal lobe is damaged (Efron, 1990). From these observations, neuropsychologists draw the conclusion that part x of the brain is specialized for function y. According to Efron, this conclusion ignores the fact that collections of brain cells are only parts of anatomically extensive systems and that damage to the cells affects the system rather than simply the function: "Over time, [neuropsychologists] have come to believe that a function called vision is 'located' in the striate cortex, when it is no more 'located' there than in the retina, optic nerve, or parastriate cortex, and that the function called language is 'located' in the left fronto-temporal area. Expressed in another way, this scientifically empty restatement of the facts has predisposed [neuropsychologists] to forget that the striate cortex and left fronto-temporal cortex are only *components* of anatomically extensive visual and linguistic *systems*" (Efron, 1990, p. 8).

With reference to the philosophy of science issues involved, physiological accounts based on direct observation of the system pose no problem to the Skinnerian theoretical system. They do not, however, override the account given by behavior analytic theory and are not an essential part of a behavioral analysis. Physiological and behavioral accounts may complement and inform each other, but neither one is dependent on or takes precedence over the other. Each account involves its own definition of the subject matter, its own theoretical terms, and its own web of causal constructs: "New methods and instruments have brought the nervous system and other mechanisms under direct observation. The new data have their own dimensions and require their own formulations" (Skinner, 1984*b*, p. 514). A physiological account of behavior requires a different definition of its subject matter than that of Skinner's system—behavior and the context in which it occurs. It may one day be possible to give a physiological account of *how* a reinforcer reinforces, but that account will not identify *which* events out of the context of behavior act as reinforcers. Each definition, each set of theoretical terms, and each causal web is of equal importance: "Both sets of facts, and their appropriate concepts, are important—but they are *equally* important, not dependent one upon the other" (Skinner, 1984*b*, p. 514). Any claim that a physiological account is somehow more fundamental than a behavioral account simply subscribes to "a contrary philosophy of explanation, which insists upon the reductive priority of the inner event" (Skinner, 1984*b*, p. 515).

The Psychodynamic Model

The psychodynamic model, founded and developed by Freud, follows the traditional pattern of accounting for behavior by appealing to processes within the individual and adopts the mechanistic causal mode of providing internal mediating links between behavior and the context in which it occurs. Skinner considered some aspects of Freud's contribution to psychology praiseworthy. One of Freud's great contributions to the analysis of human behavior was to draw attention to the fact that events in the life history of the individual (experience) may be causally related to present behavior. Freud's work also contradicted the traditional view of human behavior as inherently rational and self-generated by arguing that causal influences may be unsuspected by individuals, that individuals are not necessarily aware of the causes of their behavior. Skinner also noted Freud's ability to carry his arguments without the usual experimental testing characteristic of science: "His achievement in this respect appears all the more impressive when we recall that he was never able to appeal to the quantitative proofs characteristic of other sciences. He carried the day with sheer persuasion—with the massing of instances and the delineation of surprising parallels and analogies among seemingly diverse materials" (Skinner, 1956, p. 77).

The psychodynamic model is particularly interesting in relation to present arguments. Although Freud followed the traditional pattern of locating causes of behavior inside the organism and invented three discrete inner agents—id, ego, and superego—whose conflicting needs gave rise to behavior, he also went beyond those inner agents to explain their behavior in turn in terms of environmental variables in the history of the person. One of Skinner's arguments against traditional interpretive patterns was that internal determiners of behavior seem to bring inquiry to an end, giving the impression of having solved the problem of accounting for behavior by pointing to some presumed event, process, or entity that is said to give rise to behavior. What is often forgotten is that the internal determiner itself has still to be accounted for, otherwise the relation has not been demonstrated empirically but merely stated verbally: "We do not really explain 'disturbed behavior' by attributing it to 'anxiety' until we have also explained the anxiety. The extra step required is in the spirit of an experimental science: it is a search for a manipulable variable rather than a verbal explanation" (Skinner, 1972c, p. 316). Skinner pointed out that as "a thoroughgoing determinist" (Skinner, 1956, p. 79), Freud accepted the responsibility of explaining his internal entities by looking for past environmental influences and that his model therefore consists of three steps in a causal sequence from past to present: "Some environmental condition, very often in the early life of the individual, leaves an effect upon the inner mental apparatus, and this in turn produces the behavioral manifestation or symptom. Environmental event, mental state or process, behavioral symptom— these are the three links in Freud's causal chain" (Skinner, 1956, pp. 78-80). This sequence differs from other internal accounts in that it links the person's past and present. It is, however, similar to other internal accounts in that it strives to fill the temporal gap between cause and effect by providing a structure through which action takes place. In the same way that some 18th and 19th century physicists could not accept observed gravitational attraction and repulsion without postulating a mediating aether through which action takes place, Freud proposed a mediating structure to account for the influence of the past on present behavior. Like 18th and 19th century aether theorists, Freud used his three-component model "to bridge the gap in space and time between events he had proved to be causally related" (Skinner, 1956, p. 80). And like 18th and 19th century aether theories, his three internal links in the chain were not derived from data but were additions to it.

Such additions to data are problematic on two counts. In the first place, as Skinner noted, rather than clarifying relations between dependent and independent variables, they multiply the variables to be explained. For example, a psychodynamic account of phobic behavior takes a relation between some object/event and behavior and multiplies it into relations between event/object, intrapsychic conflict, and behavior, with intrapsychic conflict mediating between past and present.

Second, such additions to data quickly become a focus of interest in their own right, diverting attention from observable functional relations in the context in which phobic behavior occurs and toward conflicting relations said to be taking place among components of the model. As with other theoretical models, Freud's emphasis on the intrapsychic life of the individual diverts attention away from the context of behavior and careful definitions of the properties of behavior. Skinner noted Freud's suggestion that sibling rivalry played an important part in his early relationship with a boy who was older than himself but who was in the subordinate family position of being Freud's nephew. To classify their relationship as one of sibling rivalry diverts attention from the specific properties of the circumstances and obscures the functional relations that would describe what actually took place between Freud and his older rival. As Skinner put it, "An emphasis upon behavior would lead us to inquire into the specific acts plausibly assumed to be engendered by these childhood episodes" (Skinner, 1956, p. 83). What did Freud do to or with his nephew, in what context did the behavior occur, and what were the consequences of his actions? How was the behavior of the young Freud shaped by his encounters with his nephew and what patterns of behavior survived into adulthood? Skinner noted, "What has survived through the years is not aggression and guilt, later to be manifested in behavior, but rather patterns of behavior themselves. It is not enough to say that this is 'all that is meant' by sibling rivalry or by its effects upon the mental apparatus. Such an expression obscures, rather than illumi-nates, the nature of the behavioral changes taking place in the childhood learning process" (Skinner, 1956, p. 84). The intrapsychic life of aggression, guilt, repression, fixation, and so forth diverts attention from careful descriptions of the properties of behavior and the context in which it occurs. As a result, the specific relations operating in that context are lost and replaced by relations assumed to be taking place in some other dimension.

Skinner matched Mach's criticism of models that become the focus of interest in their own right. But whereas Mach was prepared to accept that models could be provisionally useful in suggesting new functional relations, Skinner was not convinced. Given the dominance of interpretations guided by prescientific views of human behavior, which *require* another system or dimension to explain behavior, it may be that any theoretical model of this subject matter is doomed to relegate behavior to secondary status and give primacy to the model because, in this view, behavior *begins* as an expression of something else. Had physicists in Mach's day viewed the relative movement of bodies as merely the manifestation of an internally located system, it is plausible to suggest that Mach would have been less amenable to models in his own science for the same reason that Skinner opposed them in a science of behavior. When one set of events is viewed as the manifestation of a more fundamental (if unobserved) set of events, then it is likely that the more fundamental system will assume primacy over the data which it is said to explain. Where Mach in his physics had one traditional pattern to contend with—mechanistic causal thinking—Skinner in his behavioral science had to contend with two—mechanistic causal thinking and the practice of interpreting behavior as a manifestation of a more fundamental, internal, system.

The psychodynamic system is traditional in both of these senses. Important relations in a psychodynamic interpretation take place not between behavior and context or behavior and experience, but between behavior and some inner world of conflict that provides a mediating structure between a person's past and their present. The model diverts attention from specific properties of behavior and the context in which it occurs, obscuring relations *actually* taking place by focusing on relations *assumed* to be taking place.

Modelling Memory

Contemporary models of memory fall into the broad category of cognitive psychology, along with information processing, artificial intelligence, semantic networks, cognitive mapping, and so on. Like psychodynamic systems, the cognitive system follows the traditional pattern of accounting for behavior by appealing to processes taking place within the individual, in some other dimension, and by providing links in a causal chain between behavior and the context in which it occurs.

Models of memory rely on two metaphors, the metaphor of storage and retrieval and the spatial metaphor. Chapter 2 noted Skinner's views on the metaphor of storage and retrieval. He argued that although humans have for centuries stored information on tablets of stone, on papyrus and vellum, in filing systems, on magnetic tape, and more latterly in computer banks for later retrieval, this metaphor in the case of learning or remembering is not necessarily the most appropriate. He suggested that the storage battery metaphor was perhaps more appropriate, arguing that living organisms are changed by their experience as a storage battery is changed when electricity is put into it; as it is a changed battery which puts out electricity, so it is a changed organism which behaves at a later date in its environment. Models of memory assume that representations of the world are somehow stored inside the organism in much the same way that information is stored, neatly filed for access, in computer banks and filing cabinets, awaiting retrieval by some similar process of scanning through the system.

The spatial metaphor likens memory to a physical space and implies that memories, thoughts, ideas, dreams, words, and so on, are held somewhere within that space. Michael Eysenck describes it thus: "The basic assumptions of this metaphor are that memories are treated as objects stored in specific locations within the mind, and the retrieval process involves a search through the mind in order to find specific memories" (Eysenck, 1984, pp. 79-80). The conceptual system inherent in the language of mind has been dealt with in Chapter 2 and those arguments remain relevant to any explanatory system purporting to account for behavior by appealing to mental processes. The issue of primary interest here is Skinner's objections to particular kinds of interpretive techniques in a science of behavior.

Morris (1986) reviewed a decade of research on the working memory model (Baddeley & Hitch, 1974). Working memory is a term used to refer to "a store that engages in processing information in real time" (Morris, 1986, p. 281) or, as it is perhaps better understood, short-term memory. Working memory is conceptualized as a complex system comprised of at least three major components: a Central Executive and two slave systems—an Articulatory Loop and a Visuo-spatial Scratchpad. This complex system was developed because an older and simpler memory model—Atkinson and Shiffrin's (1968) two-component model—could not account for "the plethora of information-processing capabilities of complex organisms, especially humans" (Morris, 1986, p. 281). Since its original formulation the model has been updated on a number of occasions (Morris, 1986).

The components, like the behavior they are said to account for, are extremely complex in both their form and function, and the model is summarized in the following way: "The central executive which formed the control center of the system was assumed to select and operate various control processes. It was assumed to have a limited amount of processing capacity, some of which could be devoted to the short-term storage of information. It was able to offload some of the storage demands onto subsidiary slave systems of which two were initially specified, namely the Articulatory Loop, which was able to maintain verbal material by subvocal rehearsal, and the Visuo-Spatial Scratch Pad, which performed a similar function through the visualization of spatial material" (Baddeley, 1981; quoted in Morris, 1986, p. 281).

What is of interest here is not so much the form or function of components of the model as the development and function of the model itself. Note that a two-component model (Atkinson & Shiffrin, 1968) has developed into a more complex model comprising *at least* three components as the data on remembering have become more complex. Note also that working memory's three components elaborate on only one aspect of the older model—short term memory. Here is a good example of a practice opposed by 18th and 19th century inductive scientists in the dispute over methodology and interpretation referred to in Chapter 3. A feature of the induction/hypothetico-deduction dispute was the inductive scientists contention that hypothetical entities could be modified or multiplied at will depending on the needs of the scientist. The development of one aspect of a two-component model into a three-component model exemplifies the inductivists' concern in that it now seems to require yet further expansion to accommodate complex data.

Toward the end of his review, Morris states, "The slave systems have proved to be more complex entities than was at first imagined, and their number is proliferating" (Morris, 1986, p. 293), and "The future of working memory seems to be heading toward further fractionation of the system" (Morris, 1986, p. 293). Note that the author does not refer to behavior having proved more complex than first imagined, but to unimagined complexity of aspects of the model. The model has taken on characteristics of the behavior it was invented to explain, relegating the behaving person to secondary status. Further, since all of the constructs of the model are hypothetical, they may take on whatever features or properties the scientist decides.

The model, hypothetical in nature, is modified and multiplied, and whether this is done in an effort to account for data or in an effort to save the metaphors on which the model is based is a debatable issue. As more of the complexities of human remembering become evident, existing structures are conveniently modified or more structures added to reflect that complexity. As in other theoretical models, terms referring to those structures are additional to the behavior observed and the causal mode is essentially mechanistic. A hypothetical system provides one or more links in a chain between behavior and the context in which it occurs.

Working memory with its Central Executive, its Articulatory Loop and its Visuo-spatial Scratchpad may well function as one of Mach's tools of thought, a useful heuristic for establishing previously unknown functional relations but to be dispensed with when it no longer generates new relations: "I hope to demonstrate that such a [theoretical] concept provides a useful background for a very wide range of both pure and applied research" (Baddeley, 1982, p. 414). The model does appear to help experimentally establish functional relations, four of which are outlined here (Baddeley, 1982, P. 415):

1) The phonological similarity effect: a relation between phonological properties of letter sequences and people's ability to reproduce them— "The more phonologically similar the sequence is, the harder the subject will find it to reproduce the sequence."

2) The word-length effect: a relation between the length of words in a sequence and people's ability to reproduce the sequence—"Memory span for words is a simple function of the spoken duration of the constituent words."

3) The unattended speech effect: a relation between visual and aural material presented simultaneously and people's ability to recall the visually presented material—"If a subject is required to remember a sequence of visually presented items, then his performance will be markedly impaired if irrelevant material is spoken at the same time."

4) Articulatory suppression: a relation between material presented to a subject at the same time as s/he is required to speak and people's ability to report the material presented—"If subjects are prevented from subvocally rehearsing material by requiring the subject to utter some irrelevant speech sounds such as the word 'the' then their immediate memory span is impaired." (References to subvocal rehearsal and memory span may be dispensed with without altering the empirical relation).

These four experimentally demonstrated functional relations can be described in the following way:

1) phonological similarity affects remembering;
2) word length affects remembering;
3) simultaneous presentation of visual and aural material affects remembering; and
4) simultaneous presentation of material and speaking affects remembering.

Additional theoretical terms like Central Executive, Visuo-spatial Scratchpad, and Articulatory Loop are irrelevant in describing these relations since what or how much a person remembers is shown to be a direct function of aspects of the context in which behavior occurs—word lengths, list lengths, phonemic similarities, acoustic similarities, and so on—and no amount of additional, internal, theoretical references alters those relations. If the terms of the model are omitted from the expression of functional relations, then Mach would not dispute its usefulness but would applaud its ability to lead to the establishment of new relations. If, however, the model becomes an object of interest in its own right, Mach would be as critical of this practice in psychology as he was critical of it in physics.

The developmental history of this model suggests that a focus on functional relations gives way to intense concern over the structure of the model. Titles such as *"Disruption of Short-Term Memory by Unattended Speech: Implications for the Structure of Working Memory"* (Salame & Baddeley, 1982) imply that the focus of interest is not so much functional relations between remembering and features of its context as it is the structure of the model. Further, it has been noted above that Morris's (1986) review was concerned with assessing the structure of working memory's components and with suggesting ways those components may be altered to accommodate new and unimagined complexities in the structure of the model. The model does indeed appear to take precedence over the behavior it is intended to account for.

Although such models *may* be heuristically useful in basic research settings, in applied settings (in contexts where behavior has somehow "gone wrong" or where efforts are made to strengthen or weaken desirable or undesirable behavior respectively) the transitory function of their additional theoretical terms is even more apparent. For example (Baddeley, 1982), where poor readers appear to be less influenced by phonemic similarity than normal readers, the suggestion is made that they are "not fully utilizing the articulatory loop" (p. 416). And in circumstances where the behavior of a group of dyslexic boys demonstrated the phonological similarity effect, the word length effect and articulatory suppression (all of which can be described without reference to additional theoretical terms), this is taken to be an indication that "they were indeed *using the articulatory loop*, but does not mean that the system was functioning as efficiently as in normals" (p. 416, emphasis added). Instead of being dispensed with, the theoretical concept develops a new status, an ontological status, becoming a system that is malfunctioning or that the individual is not using to the full.

Two strategies are suggested for improving reading. First, a poor reader should be encouraged to scan words before trying to pronounce and, second, a poor reader should be discouraged from breaking down words into individual consonants. Both strategies are derived from observing the behavior of dyslexic children attempting to read and if the strategies work, reading should improve. However, rather than reasoning from behavioral strategy to improved reading, common practice with such a model is to reason from strategy to structure to outcome: "Both of these [strategies] *should enhance the memory component substantially* and...lead to better reading in both normal and dyslexic children" (p. 417, emphasis added). The theoretical concept is not dispensed with; it is ontologized, inserted between dependent relations and attributed characteristics of the behavior it was invented to explain. Where behavior goes wrong, the hypothetical construct is said to have gone wrong. Where behavior improves, the hypothetical construct is said to be enhanced.

Quite apart from the philosophical difficulties involved in granting ontological status to hypothetical components, such components are simply irrelevant in applied settings. How can a social worker, or an educational or clinical psychologist expect to restore or enhance a hypothetical construct? Retaining such constructs after the establishment of functional relations merely satisfies the requirements of a mechanistic causality by filling spatial and temporal gaps between the stimulating environment and behavior.

Motivation and Behavior

Other types of mediating entities, less clearly delineated than models of memory, also divert attention from careful definition or description of behavior and the context in which it occurs and are also modified or multiplied at will.

The concept of motivation provides another good example of some of Skinner's scientific as well as philosophical concerns. In most instances the concept is poorly defined, and throughout the experimental and theoretical literature vacillates between mediating entity status and quite simply a replacement term for behavior as a dependent variable. Unlike models of memory and information processing, motivation cannot be given dimension. Models of memory have in the computer a powerful real-life machine operating on the encoding-storage-retrieval principle that lends a certain natural plausibility to the metaphors. Motivation and other less machine-like psychological constructs have no such real-life structure to support them, so a picture of what the concept might look like is less easily drawn, its dimensions more nebulous. Models of memory can literally be drawn on paper, their dimensions and relations between components given form. What would motivation look like if we tried to draw it? Motivation has only linguistic convention as its base and is another example of an ordinary language concept entering the scientific domain and complicating scientific relations by carrying with it other terms from the conceptual scheme to which it belongs. Dickinson (1989) and Bernstein (1990) note also that the concept derives from the philosophical presupposition that at least some aspects of behavior are internally self-generated—the person-as-agent assumption.

As a topic, motivation occasionally comes under the cognitive psychology heading (for example, in the literature of self-perception and attribution theory, Bem, 1972; Lepper et al., 1973, Deci & Ryan, 1980). More often, however, it is assigned a heading of its own (for example, Evans, 1975; Deci, 1975; Zimbardo, 1992) or combined in titles and text book chapter headings with studies of emotion (for example, Stein & Rosen, 1974; Atkinson et al., 1993), giving in each instance a clear impression of being a distinct field of scientific inquiry. Like many other current explanatory entities in psychology, motivation defies straightforward definition as well as being difficult to pin down at the level of experimentation. Occasionally, when causal variables are identified in the context in which behavior occurs, the term motivation or motivator will be applied to those variables. Otherwise, motivation is considered to be a mediating construct internal to the behaving organism.

In everyday language motivation belongs to a conceptual scheme including words such as impulse, force, incentive, inducement, spur, goad, drive, energy, and the like (Webster's, 1986), and is not separated out from this scheme in its scientific usage. It is particularly related to notions of drive and force, as if organisms are driven or compelled to behave in particular ways at particular times by motive powers. The concept of drive is explicitly related to motivation in the behavioral tradition of Hull (1951) and drive and tension reduction form an important part of the accounts of Freud and the field theorists Murray and Lewin (Bolles, 1975). The concept of force (in the sense of internal, personal causation or agency) is woven into the conceptualization of motivation in accounts such as Deci (1975), Deci and Ryan (1980) and McClelland (1987).

Bolles (1975) traces the development of the concepts of drive and force and their relation to the study of motivation in experimental psychology. According to Bolles, drive was introduced into scientific psychology in 1918 by R. S. Woodworth who sought an alternative to nebulous terms like impulse and desire to account for the energizing of behavior. Drive, for Woodworth, conveyed precisely the mechanistic flavor he sought: "Woodworth was primarily concerned with showing that a large part of behavior could be thought of as the product of the psychophysical machinery, machinery that revealed itself in innate and habitual dispositions to action. Like any other machine, Woodworth contended, it will not operate without fuel, without some source of motive power or force. Woodworth sought a word to denote this psychological force and, disliking the mentalistic connotations of impulse and desire, he suggested drive, which he felt conveyed the proper mechanistic connotation. Subsequently, drives have always been assumed to have the ability to goad an organism into action" (Bolles, 1975, p. 48).

Drive and force retain their relation in the conceptual scheme of physiological motivation, and force, in the sense of personal agency, the self-generation of behavior, is unequivocally related to motivation in social psychological studies. In addition, Bolles (1975) has noted the relation between the psychological conception of force and mechanistic causal thinking: "In psychology the concept of force has sometimes been used as though it were nothing but an analogy from the modern physicist's use of the term, that is, as a term that describes changes in behavior. More often, however, force is given surplus meaning; it is used to imply some sort of internal agency or mechanical causation. Perhaps the same promise of an effective reductionism in psychology that maintains our faith in physical causes also leads us to perpetuate the idea that the motivating agents (motives, tensions, drives, etc.) goad or force or drive the organism into action" (p. 48).

In order to consider the status of motivation as a scientific concept or a legitimately discrete subject matter, two areas will be examined here; both are identified as discrete fields of inquiry within the broad discipline of Psychology and carry the heading, Motivation. Physiological studies provide the clearest picture of motivation's status as a mediating concept between functionally related events, but they are complicated by terminology that frequently confuses motivation as a mediating variable with behavioral measures themselves (dependent variables). The second area examined involves a distinction between extrinsic and intrinsic motivation. This area also fails to differentiate between intrinsic motivation and measures of behavior.

Physiological motivation. In the physiological tradition, the empirical data in motivation experiments combine physiological and behavioral variables. Typically, some part of the brain is interfered with and some previously unseen pattern of behavior occurs. For example, a lesion in the ventromedial nucleus near its midline is followed by tremendous overeating, but animals with lesions 1.5 to 2 millimeters off the midline stop eating altogether (Stellar, 1974, p. 8). These experiments demonstrate functional relations between damage to some part of the brain (independent variable) and different kinds of observable, measurable behavior (dependent variable), either overeating or cessation. Another example notes that when an area of the posterior hypothalamus is removed, organisms sleep excessively while, conversely, removal of an area of the anterior hypothalamus results in animals remaining constantly awake (Stellar, 1974, p. 9). Again, independent variables (specified brain lesions) and dependent variables (time spent asleep or awake) are functionally related. At the level of experimentation, data derived from these studies are clear. At the level of explanation, the theoretical level, scientific and conceptual confusions proliferate.

To say that the independent variable affects motivation, which in turn affects behavior:

1) is not a statement of what was observed (the mediating concept is a theoretical term additional to the data);
2) cannot be given the status of a scientific explanation since motivation is not described except by reference to measures of behavior (the dependent variable), and
3) is scientifically inelegant in that it multiplies rather than simplifies empirical relations.

The empirical data in physiological studies demonstrate the following functional relation:

Independent Variable (lesion or deficit)

↓

Dependent Variable (measure of behavior)

But these data become complicated at the theoretical level by the addition of a mediating variable:

Independent Variable (lesion or deficit)

↓

Motivation/Motive

↓

Dependent Variable (measure of behavior)

Furthermore, the theoretical term, motivation, often functions simply as a replacement for measures of behavior and can be discarded without losing sight of the scientific relation. For example:

1) "No lesion of the hypothalamus has ever been reported that has resulted in an exaggeration of sexual motivation" (Stellar, 1974, p. 9).

2) "No lesion of the hypothalamus has ever been reported that has resulted in an exaggeration of sexual behavior."

The second statement has the advantage of elegance in that it does not allude to additional processes or entities and does not confuse the data by referring to a relation that has not been demonstrated.

At the experimental level, physiological psychology makes an important contribution to the search for causal relations between biology and behavior. At the theoretical level, however, motivation as a mediating concept tends more to cloud and confuse the empirical relations than to illuminate them. Indeed, "The Physiology of Motivation" may be translated comfortably and without scientific loss into "The Physiology of Behavior."

Intrinsic motivation. The literature and experimental study of motivation also considers the concept in a manner that is not physiological and yet is somehow internal to the organism. This literature has a heading of its own, although it was noted above that the data and theoretical terms are occasionally considered to belong to the cognitive approach, especially to self-perception and/or attribution theory (Bem, 1972; Lepper et al., 1973; Deci & Ryan, 1980).

In one type of nonphysiological research, a distinction is drawn between behavior motivated by external variables, extrinsic motivation, and behavior that is not apparently dependent upon external variables—intrinsically motivated behavior (for example, Deci, 1975; Deci & Ryan, 1980). Again, the scientific data from this research count as important contributions in the ongoing attempt to unravel complex relations between behavior and its causal variables. But the theoretical language in which conclusions are drawn and behavior explained confuses the empirical relations and, in this case especially, diverts attention from careful definition of the contexts in which behavior occurs.

Before examining the available scientific data, we should not overlook some logical and linguistic problems involved in the definition of intrinsic motivation. First, it is asserted that intrinsic motivation is an independent event or process: "[This book] reviews an enormous amount of research which establishes unequivocally that intrinsic motivation exists" (Deci, 1975, p. v). But when defined, intrinsic motivation slips from being a unitary event to being a more complex process involving three new concepts: "Intrinsically motivated behaviors are those behaviors that are motivated by the underlying need for competence and self-determination" (Deci & Ryan, 1980, p. 42). The relations contained in this definition are as follows:

(1) some behaviors are motivated by an underlying *need* for *competence* and *self-determination*;
(2) those behaviors are called intrinsically motivated behaviors.

Intrinsic motivation is thus defined as an underlying need for competence and self determination. Moving on to an operational definition creates another difficulty in that it refers to an absence of something without allowing for the demonstration of a need for competence and self determination: "We operationally define intrinsically motivated behaviors as those that are performed in the absence of any apparent external contingency" (Deci & Ryan, 1980, p. 42). This definition asserts that behavior that an observer cannot account for by appeal to historical or current causal variables is to be accounted for by the concept of intrinsic motivation. The absence of causal variables, however, is not equivalent to a demonstration of the concepts of need, competence, and self-determination. Those concepts are merely *assumed* by the original definition. The causal relation between need, competence, self-determination, and behavior is asserted without being demonstrated.

Data in this field are generated for the most part by a standard experimental procedure in which baseline measures are compared with measures recorded after intervention. At the baseline stage, activities like puzzle solving, drawing, writing newspaper headlines, and so on are freely available and the time spent by individuals in these activities is recorded.

Subsequent interventions take several forms: some groups of subjects are instructed that the activity will be followed by a reward or payment of money; some are rewarded or paid after the activity but not instructed beforehand that this will be done; other subjects simply continue to engage in the activity without any mention or presentation of reward or payment.

When the activities become freely available again some time after intervention, measures of involvement by the subjects reveal that under certain circumstances, groups whose behavior was followed by some kind of reward in the intervention stage subsequently engage in the activity at reduced levels. The circumstances are identified as: the initial attractiveness of the task in comparison to alternatives; preintervention instructions on the relation between behavior and reward; the material value of the reward; and a contingent relation between activity and reward but not between quality or magnitude of the activity and reward (Deci & Ryan, 1980; Dickinson, 1989; Bernstein, 1990).

The first measure, the baseline, is considered to be a measure of intrinsic motivation insofar as it conforms to the operational definition of that concept: subjects engage in an activity in the absence of any apparent external contingency. The final measure, postintervention, is also taken to be a measure of intrinsic motivation for the same reason. Thus, the conclusion is drawn that paying or otherwise rewarding people for engaging in activities (within the limited circumstances described above) reduces their intrinsic motivation for those activities (Deci, 1975; Lepper et al., 1973; Deci & Ryan, 1980; Deci & Ryan, 1985).

In this area, as in the area of physiological research, data themselves are not problematic and results have been replicated with different types of behavior and different interventions. Again, it is at the conceptual, explanatory level that the account becomes confused by the addition of a hypothetical mediating entity—intrinsic motivation.

The term, intrinsically motivated behaviors, describes situations where some kind of behavior occurs without the experimenter being able to point to controlling variables. Measures before and after intervention are measures of the frequency or duration of some aspect of behavior. The conclusion that "paid subjects evidenced a significant decrease in intrinsic motivation relative to the nonpaid subjects" (Deci & Ryan, 1980, p. 44) implies that payment had a decremental effect on the entity, intrinsic motivation, which in turn reduced the behavior:

Mechanistic Thinking in Psychology

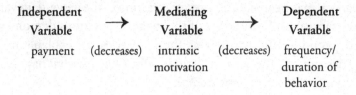

Independent Variable	→	Mediating Variable	→	Dependent Variable
payment	(decreases)	intrinsic motivation	(decreases)	frequency/ duration of behavior

Experiments in this field repeatedly demonstrate a relation between aspects of the context in which behavior occurs and a later reduction in frequency or duration of behavior. They do not demonstrate a reduction in intrinsic motivation nor do they demonstrate a relation between interventions and an underlying need for competence and self-determination. Again, the mediating concept, the additional theoretical term, can be replaced with behavior (the dependent variable) without any loss to the scientific relations observed: "paid subjects evidenced a significant decrease in behavior (frequency/duration) relative to the nonpaid subjects."

The clarity of the data is unquestioned here, and the serious social implications of the repeated finding in this type of research have been noted by Deci and Ryan (1985) and Bernstein (1990). At issue here is the scientific status of the concept, intrinsic motivation. First, it is invoked in the absence of identifiable current or historical causal variables and as such is similar to the concepts of spontaneity or volition. Second, at the level of explanation, the theoretical level, it is additional to the relations observed and included as a hypothetical mediating entity or process between those relations. Third, it is a superfluous addition at the theoretical as well as the practical level since it may be simply replaced by behavior (the dependent variable) without any scientific loss. And fourth, demonstrating an increase or decrease in intrinsic motivation (operationally defined as activities without identifiable external contingencies) is not equivalent to a demonstration that those activities are causally related to a need for competence and self-determination. That causal relation is merely asserted in another definition of intrinsically motivated behaviors.

The language of motivation. It has been argued above that in both physiological and social psychological research, the mediating entity, motivation, may be replaced by terms referring to the dependent variable (behavior) without losing sight of the scientific relations demonstrated. Indeed, retaining the concept at the theoretical or explanatory level multiplies and confuses those relations. Dispensing with it has the effect of clarifying functional dependencies.

Like other hypothetical entities, motivation can also be modified and multiplied at will. This practice is evident especially in social psychological studies where different descriptive labels are added to the basic concept so that considerable research energy and expertise is devoted to areas such as: the achievement motive; the power motive; affiliative motives; avoidance motives, and so on (McClelland, 1987). Relations are further confused when causal constructs are multiplied yet again, for example when the concept of incentive is added: "What is the incentive for the achievement motive?" (McClelland, 1987, p. 226). As noted above, incentive and motive (or motivation) are included in the same ordinary language conceptual scheme as impulse, force, drive, goad, spur, inducement, and so on (Webster's, 1986), a scheme that implies a propelling or driving energy. So in tackling questions about behavior and its causal relations, motivation (a propelling energy) is inserted between functional dependencies.

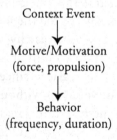

Context Event
↓
Motive/Motivation
(force, propulsion)
↓
Behavior
(frequency, duration)

Questions then begin to be raised about the origins and strength of the mediating entity and when this happens, another force or drive is called upon—what is it that drives the motives that drive behavior?

Mechanistic Thinking in Psychology

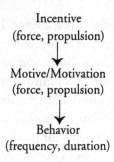

Incentive
(force, propulsion)

↓

Motive/Motivation
(force, propulsion)

↓

Behavior
(frequency, duration)

Hypothetical mediating concepts here, as in other areas of psychology, continue to multiply and have the effect of removing interest further and further from behavior and the context in which it occurs to questions about the hypothetical concepts themselves.

Because concepts like achievement, affiliation, power, and avoidance can readily be added to motivation, and given the linguistic structure of assertions such as "this person is motivated by a need for achievement (or a need for competence, self-determination, affiliation, and the like)," it is possible that the concept could expand as far as ordinary language would allow. Many other ordinary language expressions could similarly be attached to motivation: "this person is motivated by a need for punctuality or by a need for laughter"; "this person is motivated by aggression or by vanity." These statements all assert causal status for ordinary language concepts but those concepts simply describe characteristic patterns of behavior. We describe people as punctual when they typically arrive at meetings at an agreed time. We describe as aggressive a person whose behavior is in our opinion brutal, angry, loud, violent, and so on. Vain people typically preen and talk about their own merits without praising or applauding others. And we refer to someone who works hard, gets good marks in examinations, is rapidly promoted, and so on as a high achiever or highly motivated. Using these descriptions as if they were causal entities, drives, forces, or motivators is merely circular.

Why does the rat press the lever? Consider how the concept of motivation might be invoked in the simplest behavior analytic preparation, a rat in an operant chamber trained to press a lever. In this situation a behavior analyst demonstrates the origins of behavior; a rat comes to press a lever at a rate that depends on the shaping and maintenance procedure. An observer without access to the rat's reinforcement history may well want to conclude that lever pressing is motivated by hunger (since food deprivation is normally part of this procedure) or by rewarding it with food pellets. Where the rat's behavior has been discriminatively conditioned so that it presses the lever in the presence of a red light but not in the presence of a green light, what now "motivates" the behavior—hunger, food pellets, or the red light? The observer could justifiably maintain that all three events act as motivators simply in the sense that they are all causally related. But the situation becomes more complicated for the observer when two rats are trained to press levers on different schedules of reinforcement. One rat, for example, is trained on a fixed-ratio schedule that generates a high rate of pressing and a second rat is trained on a DRL (differential reinforcement of low rate) schedule to press at a lower rate. Both rats enter the chamber at 80% of their free-feeding weight (equally hungry) and emit, respectively, high and low rates of lever pressing. What explanatory options are available now to the observer concerned with the concept of motivation?

Both rats are equally food-deprived, so hunger might still be invoked to account for lever pressing but cannot account for the clearly different rates of response. What is more likely is that the observer will retreat to the notion of levels of motivation, arguing that one rat is highly motivated to press while the other rat's level of motivation is significantly lower. Throughout all these attempts to appeal to internal or external motivation, however, the behavior analyst will point to the animals' history of reinforcement, to shaping by successive approximations, and to the schedules on which reinforcers were delivered to explain both the behavior itself and the rate at which it occurs. The concept of motivation would add no explanatory weight to this account.

Situations have been reported where rats continue pressing a lever without consuming the food pellets that become available, and where rats continue to press the lever and consume the consequent food pellets even when a dish of freely available food is in the chamber (see Morgan,

1974). Although these situations satisfy the operational definition of intrinsically motivated behaviors, it is difficult to imagine that lever pressing satisfies in the rat a need for competence and self determination.

Causes of behavior. By making a distinction between behavior motivated by external events and behavior for which no external motivator can be identified, the operational definition of intrinsic motivation recognizes that behavior can be functionally related to events in the context in which it occurs. Therefore, there is no scientific merit in alluding to motivation as though it meant something other than cause.

Behavior analysts occasionally refer to motivation without embarrassment. Ayllon and Azrin (1968), for example, refer to the concept when outlining therapeutic techniques in *The Token Economy: A Motivational System for Therapy and Rehabilitation.* Since every attempt at experimental analysis is an attempt to uncover the motivation (the causes) of behavior, independent variables may be referred to comfortably as sources of motivation and therapeutic programs as systems for motivation. Behavior analysts do not confuse the concept by referring to it as a mediating entity between an independent variable and behavior, by substituting it for measures of behavior, or by treating it as an internal system of propulsion or driving force. The motivator, for a behavior analyst, *is* the independent variable.

Motivation is a complex concept with a varied and confusing literature. Physiological and social experiments sometimes refer to motivation as a mediating variable and sometimes as a dependent variable. The ordinary language system to which it belongs implies an energy or driving force internal to the organism, so the concept relies on the philosophical presupposition of internal agency in behavior.

The word, motivation, seems to refer to nothing other than the causes of behavior; it is misleading to continue with separate chapter and field headings in textbooks because scientific psychology throughout concerns itself with causes. Furthermore, given the conceptual confusion generated by motivation as a descriptive or explanatory construct or as a topic heading, there are strong arguments for abandoning the concept altogether.

19th Century Physics and 20th Century Psychology

The previous chapter quoted Brush's comment on the ongoing relevance of Mach's scientific arguments: "Some of the *scientific* questions discussed by Mach are by no means settled even today, to say nothing of the philosophical and methodological ones" (Brush, 1968, p. 193). Mach's participation in the 19th century dispute over interpretive techniques and causal modes in physics was echoed by Skinner's arguments in 20th century psychology, and the above discussion illustrates that Skinner's arguments of the 1940s and 1950s are as relevant today as at the time of the decline of Hull's theoretical system. Contemporary psychology remains grounded in a dualistic view of the person that guides psychological theory away from behavior and into unobserved dimensions said to account for behavior. Psychodynamic accounts, models of memory, and ordinary language concepts such as motivation are evidence that mechanistic thinking also characterizes much of contemporary psychology. In each of these models mediating structures are appealed to as links in a causal chain, as though without them behavior is not properly accounted for. Mechanistic thinking in psychology requires things-in-between, as the 19th century aether theorists required some medium through which they could envisage action taking place. Mechanistic thinkers cannot visualize relations between events occurring at temporal or spatial distances because their concept of causation is sequential or chainlike. Causal accounts are only satisfactory for such thinkers when they involve mediating entities between causes and effects.

Chapter 8

Behaviorism and Radical Behaviorism

Chapter 1 argued that contemporary psychology is best thought of as a set of subdisciplines, each with its own view of the subject matter, its own questions, its own methods for tackling those questions, and its own set of theoretical constructs by which to describe and explain its subject matter. As a whole, the discipline is given its most basic organization in the same place as other academic and scientific disciplines, in introductory texts. With little variation from text to text, authors divide psychology into six major approaches: Biological, Ethological, Behavioral, Cognitive, Psychodynamic, and Humanistic. This organization implies that each approach is unified around some of the crucial paradigmatic issues that ordinarily delineate disciplines, the sorts of issues described above. By comparing Skinner's work with that of four other key figures in the history of behaviorism—Pavlov, Watson, Tolman, and Hull—this chapter challenges the implication that Behaviorism is now, or ever was, unified on important scientific issues such as subject matter, methods, and explanatory constructs. It also exposes the fact that much of contemporary psychology continues to operate within a scientific framework that Skinner abandoned at an early stage in his career, a mechanistic, S-O-R framework appealing to mediating constructs between stimulus input and response output. Behaviorism marks a point in the history of psychology's development when an attempt was made to develop methods more consonant with those of the natural sciences. As such, it is a useful historical marker. The implication that it describes a unified approach is neither consistent with history nor with the current fact that much of contemporary psychology belongs to a behavioral tradition.

Like the examination of theoretical models in the previous chapter, this presentation is not intended to be an exhaustive analysis of the history of behaviorism or of psychology. It is selective, and intended only to illustrate fundamental differences between systems ordinarily classified under one heading. Pavlov and Watson are selected because they are usually cited as precursors to Skinner's work under the general headings *Conditioning* or *Behaviorism*. The choice of Tolman and Hull is not quite as clear since many authors also cite Perry, Holt, Spence, Mowrer, and Guthrie as examples of behaviorism or neobehaviorism. Smith (1986) used Tolman and Hull to illustrate the differences between behaviorism and logical positivism. Similarly, this analysis uses them to illustrate differences between the Skinnerian tradition and other branches of psychology that are usually included under the heading, Behaviorism.

Introducing Behaviorism

The student of psychology is commonly introduced to the work of B. F. Skinner in one of two ways: a) either under the heading, Behaviorism or Behavioral Perspective, after an exposition of the position of John B. Watson or b) under the heading, Conditioning, after a detailed description of Pavlov's research. A typical introductory text outlines different approaches such as Biological, Behavioral, Cognitive, Psychoanalytic, and Phenomenological (Atkinson et al., 1993). Under the heading, Behavioral Approach, the student learns that "*Behaviorism*, as Watson's position came to be called, helped shape the course of psychology during the first half of this century. One offshoot of behaviorism, *stimulus-response psychology*, is still influential. Stimulus-response psychology (S-R psychology) studies the relevant stimuli in the environment, the responses that are elicited by these stimuli, and the rewards or punishments that follow these responses" (Atkinson et al., p. 9). The authors note that behavioral psychologists do not infer mental activity from behavioral data and do not propose variables to mediate between stimulus input and response output. The section concludes with the assertion that: "Today, few psychologists would regard themselves as strict behaviorists" (Atkinson et al., 1993, p. 10). The same text later deals with Learning and Conditioning, detailing experiments with rats and pigeons in Skinner boxes under the heading, Operant Conditioning. It immediately follows a section on Pavlov's classical conditioning experiments. In this way, lines of development are traced from Watson and Pavlov to Skinner.

More sophisticated treatments of psychology's development present behaviorism in several ways. Sometimes, a short history of the shift from introspection to behaviorism is presented, emphasizing the momentum given to that shift by Watson, followed by an outline of the principles of classical and operant conditioning. In this way, Watson's ideas provide a background and the line is traced from there via Pavlov to Skinner (for example, Hirschorn, 1979). At other times, a distinction is drawn between behaviorists and neobehaviorists, the former category consisting of Watson, Holt, Tolman and Kuo, and the latter of Spence, Hull, Guthrie, and Skinner, with Pavlov's work classified under Associationism (for example, Hillix & Marx, 1974). The work of Watson, Perry and Holt, Tolman, Hull, Spence, Skinner, and Mowrer has been discussed under the heading, Behaviorist Interpretations of Purpose, with Hull, Spence, Skinner, and Mowrer labelled Later Behaviorists and Pavlov given only occasional mention in relation to Watson and Mowrer (Boden, 1978). Occasionally, Skinner is singled out from general discussions of behaviorism, as when Mackenzie (1977) devotes a final section of his work, *Behaviorism and the Limits of Scientific Method*, to "The Principal Unsystematic Contribution of Behaviorism as Exemplified by Certain Features of Skinner's Psychology." And, as the Introduction noted, Smith (1986) compares and contrasts the work of Tolman, Hull, and Skinner with the logical positivist view of science.

Clearly, tracing behaviorism's line of development is not an easy task. Some authors attempt to draw a continuous line from Pavlov through Watson to Skinner. Others present Skinner's operant psychology as a development of Pavlov's work on classical conditioning. Still others suggest a discontinuity between early and later behaviorists (or behaviorists and neobehaviorists). All presentations share a common feature in the sense that they are treatments of behaviorism, and it is in this sense that the Skinnerian behaviorist faces a problem.

To the new student, Behaviorism is often presented as a stimulus-response or black box view of the person, a psychology concerned only with what goes into and what comes out of the organism, ignoring the private world of the organism. Skinner's contribution may be presented purely from a technical perspective, as no more than a world of experimental techniques and data describing the behavior of rats or pigeons in Skinner boxes, thus divorced from its broader philosophy. Even at a more advanced level, the Skinnerian system, considered under the heading Behaviorism, is presented as a continuation of the systems developed and promoted by Watson, Hull, Tolman, and others, as founded on the same philosophy of science or holding the same view of the subject matter of psychology and/or the same view of the person. In practice, however, radical behaviorism has little in common with other systems sharing the Behaviorism heading. It is sufficiently dissimilar to warrant use of a different term to characterize it; for example, behavior analysis, operant psychology, or functional analysis, which all help to express both the uniqueness of the position and the wholeness of its philosophy.

Ivan P. Pavlov

The details of Pavlov's work on conditioned reflexes are widely published. Virtually every introductory psychology text contains a section on Pavlov's dogs and an account of conditioning, extinction, generalization, and discrimination. The historical/philosophical importance of Pavlov's work is not often mentioned. These aspects are dealt with here, rather than the fine details of experimental procedure.

Before Pavlov, reflex physiology concerned itself with the movement of organisms that had been operated on in some way, perhaps by decapitation or a cut made through the spinal cord to separate off the higher centers of the nervous system. Although the field gradually came to study live rather than dead animals, the nervous system of the organism was always interfered with in some way. Pavlov and his students concerned themselves with live and intact organisms (the extent of interference being to insert tubes for collecting salivary secretions) and in doing so, experimentally established the important principle that the behavior of organisms with *intact* nervous systems is susceptible to scientific treatment. They demonstrated orderly functional relations between behavior and features of the context in which it occurred. Keller notes that until then, "Most physiologists were apparently sure that any higher animal, with a normally functioning brain, would defy the procedures of natural science. Something 'mental' or 'psychic' might enter the picture to distort the lawful cause-effect relations on which a science must depend" (Keller, 1973, p. 29). Pavlov demonstrated that mental or psychic concepts need not be invoked in the description of conditioned reflexes because these limited responses could be shown to be functionally related to aspects of the organism's environment. "For a consistent investigator," he wrote, "there is in the higher animals only one thing to be considered—namely, the response of the animal to external impressions" (Hillix & Marx, 1974, p. 99: Pavlov, 1906). Of the task of natural science he wrote, "Strictly speaking, natural science is under an obligation to determine only the precise connection which exists between the given natural phenomenon and the responsive faculty of the living organism with respect to this phenomenon" (Hillix & Marx, 1974, p. 99: Pavlov, 1906).

These quotations show that Pavlov's concern lay with the action of the stimulating environment. It is this emphasis, as well as the demonstration that lawful relations could be seen in the behavior of intact organisms without recourse to concepts from the tradition of introspection, that chiefly endeared him to behaviorists. The budding behaviorist movement was ready to embrace a position centered on the action of the environment, demonstrating its effects through a high degree of experimental control.

As a graduate student at Harvard, Skinner took a course in the Department of General Physiology covering conditioned reflexes and looking at the earlier work of Magnus and Sherrington on reflexes in organisms that had undergone surgical preparation (Skinner, 1978, p. 113). Skinner had his own copy of Pavlov's *Conditioned Reflexes* (1927) and his early research was, in his own words, "pretty much in the tradition of reflex physiology" (Skinner, 1978, p. 114). It was at this early stage that "quite by accident" something changed the direction of his research. He began to time delays between a rat's being fed at the end of his apparatus and then returning down a back alley to begin its run again. He found that the delays changed in an orderly way: "Here was a *process*, something like the process of conditioning and extinction in Pavlov's work, where the details of the act of running, like those of salivation, were not the important thing" (Skinner, 1978, p. 115). Like Pavlov, Skinner was already dedicated to "the organism as a whole," and concerned not with details of the act of running (or in Pavlov's case, salivation), but with orderly relations between that act and other observable variables. In these respects—an interest in lawful relations and an emphasis on relations between environment and behavior—Skinner and Pavlov are alike.

Skinner referred to Pavlov's work as historically fundamental (Skinner, 1931/1972b, p. 441) in that it dispensed with two concepts previously ascribed to the behavior of intact organisms—volition and spontaneity. In tracing the development of the concept of the reflex, Skinner (1931/1972b) noted that an irrelevant and unsupported assumption had been made—that the reflex is involuntary. This definition of the reflex lent credence to the concepts of spontaneity and volition. For if the reflex could be said to be involuntary behavior, then other kinds of behavior could be said to be voluntary or spontaneous and therefore not susceptible to scientific treatment. The study of reflexes in surgically prepared organisms had identified relations between specific external stimuli and specific muscular responses. Prior to Pavlov, reflex physiologists had been unable to similarly identify stimuli for the behavior of intact organisms and had concluded that some aspects of behavior are spontaneous. Pavlov contributed to the process of undermining volition and spontaneity by demonstrating lawful relations in the behavior of intact organisms.

Skinner (1931/1972b) argued that we habitually invoke nonphysical concepts such as volition, mind, or spontaneity when the behavior observed cannot be seen to be related in physical terms (intrinsic motivation, referred to in the previous chapter, belongs in this category of concepts). He further argued that the experimental justification for these concepts is nothing more than "the absence of demonstrable necessity" (Skinner, 1931/1972b, p. 440). Throughout his career Skinner, was consistently critical of the inclusion of such concepts in a scientific account, arguing (as Chapter 4 noted), "Spontaneity is negative evidence; it points to the weakness of a current scientific explanation, but does not in itself prove an alternative version. By its very nature, spontaneity must yield ground as a scientific analysis is able to advance" (Skinner, 1953, p. 48). Pavlov had given the lead in demonstrating lawful relations in the behavior of intact organisms, and Skinner followed when he argued that a science of behavior must, like other natural sciences, assume lawfulness in its subject matter. It is contradictory to claim to be a behavioral scientist and at the same time allow concepts such as volition or spontaneity as part of a scientific account.

The Skinnerian system follows Pavlov in the following important respects: a) it is dedicated to "the organism as a whole"; b) both systems emphasize behavior as a function of environmental events; c) both systems are dedicated to describing the behavior of intact organisms in scientific (lawful) terms; and d) in demonstrating lawful processes, both systems undermine concepts such as volition and spontaneity and dispense with these concepts in their accounts.

These similarities are historically important because Pavlov's work helped to create a shift in both physiology and psychology. In the former discipline, the shift was from a "parts" view of the organism to consideration of the organism as a whole, and in the latter, the shift was from introspection to an emphasis on the control of behavior by features of the context in which it occurs.

Two fundamental dissimilarities between the Skinnerian and Pavlovian systems are important in a philosophical rather than a historical sense, involving different philosophical positions on both the nature of scientific inference and on the explanation of complex behavior. With forty three references to Pavlov and copious quotations from his *Conditioned Reflexes* (Pavlov, 1927), Skinner's first major work, *The Behavior of Organisms* (1938), may be viewed as a scholarly critique of the Pavlovian system, marking a development in thinking and practice that distances the Skinnerian system from Pavlov's account in two crucial ways. First, it argues against explanations of behavior given in terms of the activity of the nervous system and for the investigation of behavior as a subject matter in its own right. Second, it moves beyond a stimulus-response psychology by developing an analysis of operant (emitted) behavior rather than focusing on responses that are built in.

Behavior and the nervous system. Although Pavlov is noted for encouraging an account of behavior free from mental or psychic concepts, he was nevertheless making inferences that were removed from the data themselves. The subtitle of his *Conditioned Reflexes* attests to this in claiming to be *An Investigation of the Physiological Activity of the Cerebral Cortex* (Pavlov, 1927). Chapter 6 discussed in detail Skinner's views on accounts that relegate behavior to secondary status in relation to a presumed underlying system, and it is useful to place those views in the context of his critique of the Pavlovian explanatory system.

In *The Behavior of Organisms*, Skinner (1938) argued that accounts seeking to explain behavior in terms of the nervous system stem from an inability to conceive of behavior as a lawful subject matter in its own right. If behavior is considered to be too complex to be comprehensible, it might be made comprehensible by pointing to an underlying system, a physiological system, that can more easily be conceived of as lawful: "The more sophisticated neurological views generally agree with the popular view in contending that behavior is in itself incomprehensible but may be reduced to law if it can be shown to be controlled by an internal system susceptible to scientific treatment. Facts about behavior are not treated in their own right, but are regarded as something to be explained or even explained away by the prior facts of the nervous system" (Skinner, 1938, p. 4).

Paradoxically, while Pavlov had demonstrated that the behavior of intact organisms was lawful in certain respects, he maintained a commitment to explaining behavior by an appeal to the nervous system. "What is it that the nervous system of the dog recognizes as individual phenomena of external origin?" he asked (Hillix & Marx, 1974, p. 103: Pavlov, 1906), and on the contribution of his field of research he wrote, "The investigation of the conditioned reflexes is of very great importance for the physiology of the higher parts of the nervous system" (Hillix & Marx, 1974, p. 105: Pavlov 1906). It is paradoxical also that Pavlov thought he was liberating physiology from the evil influences of psychology while at the same time his work in physiology was creating profound changes in psychology. As Hillix and Marx summarized, "Ironically, after he became famous for his work on the conditioned reflex, the Russians set about Pavlovinizing psychology and the Americans set about psychologizing Pavlov. It was a fate Pavlov deserved, for his empirical work was really behavioral and thus psychological, despite the fact that his hypotheses were about presumed cortical events" (Hillix & Marx, 1974, p. 99).

As a physiologist, Pavlov considered himself to be studying the cortical functioning of dogs. This is an important point of departure for Skinner, and he used Pavlov to illustrate his contention that behavioral data are frequently translated from the form in which they are observed into evidence of some underlying system or structure, requiring a conceptual leap from the data into another system of explanation. Crucially, Skinner argued that this need not be the case. Behavior can be treated as a subject matter in its own right, as the experiments reported in *The Behavior of Organisms* demonstrate. He argued further that in making this translation from behavioral data to neurological concepts, both the sciences of behavior and neurology are hampered by a confusion of subject matter.

Neurologists are hampered by a lack of behavioral data, having to confine their research to relatively simple cases, or to cases in which the absence of complete behavioral function and some neurological deficiency present themselves together. It is simpler to demonstrate the relation between the inability to speak, for example, and some malfunction in the higher nervous system than to demonstrate the relation between an intact nervous system and the complete behavioral function of speaking. The latter difficulty arises in part because an adequate behavioral account or analysis of the complete function is lacking. A science of behavior may provide the account that could inform neurology's research into normal cortical functioning and normal behavior.

The behavioral scientist is hampered by constant reference to neurological concepts, diverted from examining behavioral data as it presents itself to hypothesizing internal, neurological structures as explanations of those data. Examining the data at the level at which they present themselves, validating the relations contained in the data, and proceeding to other questions and problems about behavior would more rapidly advance the science of behavior than would the confusion of behavioral data with theoretical terms referring to neurological structures. Both would benefit from independent development: "The current fashion in proceeding from a behavioral fact to its neurological correlates instead of validating the fact as such and then proceeding to deal with other problems in behavior hampers seriously the development of a science of behavior" (Skinner, 1938, p. 428). Likewise, the lack of a complete behavioral account of the normal functioning of an intact organism relegates the science of neurology to dealing with simple or with negative cases.

Behavior as a subject matter in its own right, without the neurological concepts appealed to by Pavlov, is the essence of Skinner's *The Behavior of Organisms*. In this sense the Skinnerian system, while owing much to moves initiated by Pavlov, is entirely divorced from the Pavlovian tradition. Its subject matter, behavior and the context in which it occurs, is different from Pavlov's, which gave center stage to the nervous system. Its form of inferring from the data is also different. Pavlov, as a physiologist, used behavioral data to make inferences about events taking place in another dimension. Skinner stayed close to his data, asking questions *of* the data without invoking concepts from another dimension or another system said to underlie behavior.

Stimulus-response psychology. Another important departure from the Pavlovian system is the distinction Skinner drew between respondent and operant behavior and the consequently differing view of the genesis of complex behavior. When behaviorism emerged, it was widely thought that acquired reflexes could form the basis of explanations of complex behavior. Skinner took issue with this view on the grounds that a large part of the behavior of organisms cannot be shown to be under the control of simple eliciting stimuli. In the case of acquired reflexes, conditioned responses develop from the process of repeatedly pairing neutral events with simple, unconditioned stimuli. Skinner was not convinced that complex behavior could be traced to an initial unconditioned stimulus: "I do not believe that the 'stimulus' leading to the elaborate responses of singing a song or of painting a picture can be regarded as the mere substitute for a stimulus or a group of stimuli which originally elicited these responses or their component parts" (Skinner, 1938, p. 20). Complex behavior, in the radical behaviorist view, is not a composite of acquired reflexes.

The shaping of complex behavior is a different process in behavior analysis than the conditioning of built-in responses, which involves pairing a neutral event with one that reliably elicits a response. In the Skinnerian system, complex behavior comes into being through the process of selection on variation, the shaping of novel (emitted) behavior by its consequences. In the radical behaviorist account, complex contingencies rather than acquired reflexes give rise to complex behavior. In the sense that the Skinnerian system does not deal with built-in or elicited behavior, it is far removed from Pavlov's stimulus-response psychology.

In summary, the Skinnerian system differs from Pavlov's in these important respects: first, as a physiologist, Pavlov thought he was investigating the physiological activity of the cerebral cortex and appealed to behavioral data as evidence of an underlying system. Skinner's philosophy of science rejects such inferences, and behavior analysis continues to demonstrate that behavior may be treated lawfully as a subject matter in its own right. The Pavlovian and Skinnerian systems offer explanatory accounts in different theoretical terms. Second, the Pavlovian tradition is concerned with responses that are built into organisms and elicited by specifiable stimuli. Pavlov's work involved pairing neutral stimuli with unconditioned stimuli and transferring built-in responses to those neutral stimuli. The Skinnerian system is concerned with behavior emitted by the organism and with functional relations between behavior and the context in which it occurs. In this view, complex behavior is not a composite of acquired reflexes; it is a product of complex contingencies.

John B. Watson

If a single figure can be held to be the founder of behaviorism, it must be John B. Watson. The historians Hillix and Marx have summarized him thus: "Watson hated introspecting in experiments or trying to do it for the animals he loved, and he finally made a clean break with the functionalist tradition that demanded these things of him. He made this clear in a famous 1912 lecture at Columbia University, and in his even more famous paper of 1913. By 1914 he was catapulted into the leading position in American psychology!" (Hillix & Marx, 1974, p. 200).

Watson, naturally closer to American psychology than Pavlov, felt it had failed signally to create itself as an undisputed natural science due to its concern with consciousness, sensation, imagery, and mental life. Failure to reproduce findings in the natural sciences is followed by a questioning of experimental procedures, whereas in introspectionist psychology such problems were attributed to the failure of subjects to properly introspect, a failure in the training of subjects. The natural sciences do not concern themselves with consciousness or introspection, and neither should psychology, he argued.

Watson initially advocated abandoning introspection in his short paper *Psychology as the Behaviorist Views It* (Watson, 1913), arguing that the study of mental life, consciousness, sensations, and so on was leading psychology nowhere and should be provisionally abandoned in favor of concentration on behavioral research until the development of methods better able to shed some light on these processes. Principles of behavior should be applied in a scientific way, without reference to mental states, in order to advance psychology as a natural science. If at some point in methodological development psychologists find a way of introducing mentalistic concepts that can be practically studied, so be it. They can study inner life at that time using new formulations and new methods. When Watson wrote, methodology was insufficient for such study and the focus of psychology diversionary: "The introspective method has reached a cul-de-sac with respect to [imagination, judgement, reasoning, and conception]. The topics have become so threadbare from much handling that they may well be put away for a time. As our methods become better developed it will be possible to undertake investigations of more and more complex forms of behavior. Problems which are now laid aside will again become imperative, but they can be viewed as they arise from a new angle and in more concrete settings" (Hillix & Marx, 1974, p. 212: Watson, 1913). Watson proposed a practical program aimed at lifting psychology out of the mire of introspection and bringing it closer to the natural sciences. The definitional status of mind and mentalistic concepts was in doubt, and attempts to study quantitatively concepts that could not even be defined seemed to him nonsense. He felt such deeply flawed premises should be dispensed with. If the questions asked by introspectionist psychology were getting nowhere, then ask other kinds of questions in other ways. Watson's suggestion that psychology should ignore internal events until better methods for describing and studying them had been found was a practical development for psychology, and his position was wholeheartedly embraced by psychologists attempting to develop methods with a degree of experimental control characteristic of those of the natural sciences.

Along with Pavlov's *Conditioned Reflexes*, Skinner took with him to graduate school a copy of Watson's *Behaviorism* (1924). His interest in Watson was fuelled less by his studies in psychology than by an interest in epistemology. Skinner had been introduced to Watson's behaviorism via the work of Bertrand Russell. Russell had drawn on it as a basis for an empirical epistemology by extrapolating Watson's formulation to problems of knowledge, and it was the epistemological implications of Watson's behaviorism that chiefly endeared him to Skinner. According to Smith: "Russell's application of behavioral psychology to the problem of knowledge provided a model that Skinner has followed ever since. The details of Russell's account were soon thereafter rejected by Skinner, but the general notion of developing an empirical epistemology from a behaviorist basis has been a continuing theme throughout Skinner's career" (Smith, 1986, p. 263). Skinner was impressed by the epistemological possibilities initially suggested by Watson's behaviorism, but took issue with Watson's formulation on substantive experimental issues.

Watson's program used the same unit of analysis as Pavlov's program, the same built in stimulus-response relation. Like Pavlov, Watson was also concerned with the way acquired reflexes are built by pairing unconditioned and conditioned stimuli. Skinner's departure from stimulus-response as a unit of analysis needs no further elaboration.

The goal of psychology as conceived by Watson—"the ascertaining of such data and laws that, given the stimulus, psychology can predict what the response will be; or, given the response, it can specify the nature of the effective stimulus" (Watson, 1919, p. 10)—was considered impractical by Skinner. A program seeking to pursue this goal would result in a catalogue of acquired reflexes referring to the behavior of an individual organism which would undergo constant review and revision throughout the lifetime of that individual as new reflexes were conditioned and others extinguished. Skinner referred to this as the "botanizing of reflexes": "The number of stimuli to which a typical organism may respond originally is very great. The number of stimuli to which it may come to respond...is indefinitely large, and to each of them it may be made to respond in many ways. It follows that the number of possible reflexes is for all practical purposes infinite and that what one might call the botanizing of reflexes will be a thankless task" (Skinner, 1938, p. 10). Skinner was greatly impressed by the epistemological possibilities of Watson's behaviorism but was critical of both its subject matter (stimulus-response relations) and its program for psychology.

Dispensing with dualism. In another (and perhaps more fundamental) respect, the Skinnerian system rejects a philosophy that is central to the early behaviorist program; a dualistic view of the person. Watson proposed that mind and body be thoroughly separated in a pragmatic research program. What takes place inside the organism was for the time being necessarily denied, a separate system with no relevance to the study of behavior. Psychology swung from the study of inner life, feelings, states, and so on to its opposite pole, the objective measurement of observable behavior.

Skinner identified Watson's behaviorism (methodological behaviorism) as a kind of "psychological version of logical positivism or operationism" (Skinner, 1974, p. 14) in that it required: a) truth by agreement (as logical positivism) and b) the reduction of concepts (for example, sensation, perception, and so on) to the operation of discrimination. In these respects Skinner felt that it was a move forward for psychology, freeing it from philosophical digressions and encouraging it to explore similarities between human and other species. The Skinnerian system, however, is distinguished from Watson's program primarily because it dispenses with the dualistic view of the person inherited in Western philosophy from Descartes.

Dualism solved the problem of voluntary and involuntary behavior for Descartes, allowing him to distinguish mechanical behavior from behavior generated by free will and thus to satisfy important religious concerns of his time. For Watson, it solved the practical problem of how to free psychology to take its place as a natural science. Watson advocated putting aside mental events until methods had become better developed, when they could possibly be reviewed in the light of these developments. But, as was argued in Chapters 2 and 5, methodology alone is not enough because a system grounded in dualism will inevitably be concerned with questions informed by that view. Watson was quite correct when he wrote, "Something is wrong with our premises and the types of problems which develop from them" (Hillix & Marx, 1974, p. 205: Watson, 1913). His solution was to ignore the more troublesome half of the dichotomy. Skinner also felt there was something wrong with the premises, but instead of accepting the dichotomy and ignoring events taking place within the organism, the troublesome half, Skinner dispensed with the dichotomy itself on the grounds that no one would seriously deny the importance of what we think and what we feel. Each individual is a world of thoughts, feelings, networks of relations that bear on those feelings, and vice versa. What was needed was a new philosophy, a new way of thinking about the person that could embrace private events, thinking and feeling, without setting those things apart as though belonging to another dimension.

Skinner's solution was to reexamine the premise that there are two systems, two worlds, the physical and the mental, and as a result, to move beyond a dualistic view of the person: "Methodological behaviorism and some versions of logical positivism ruled private events out of bounds because there could be no public agreement about their validity. Introspection could not be accepted as a scientific practice, and the psychology of people like Wilhelm Wundt and Edward B. Titchener was attacked accordingly. Radical behaviorism, however, takes a different line. It does not deny the possibility of self-observation or self-knowledge or its possible usefulness but it questions the nature of what is felt or observed and hence known. It restores introspection but not what philosophers and introspective psychologists believed they were 'specting,' and it raises the question of how much of one's body one can actually observe" (Skinner, 1974, p. 16).

About Behaviorism (Skinner, 1974) outlines a philosophy involving a different way of conceptualizing the person and of incorporating private events within the system as a whole. When Watson proposed rephrasing mentalistic concepts to incorporate them into refined scientific methods, he offered only a partial solution to difficulties stemming largely from psychology's dualistic view of the person. Until a philosophy that separates voluntary behavior from involuntary and private events from behavior is replaced by one encompassing private experience as part of a unified system, then the same difficulties that Watson attempted to tackle will remain unresolved.

Self-knowledge and the verbal community. Radical behaviorism directs attention to the way verbal behavior, like other kinds of behavior, is shaped by events in the context in which it occurs and thus directs attention to the social origins of consciousness, awareness, and self-knowledge (see Blackman, 1991). The community shapes verbal behavior to correspond to external, observable objects and events, and it attempts to do the same thing where events are private. The extent to which we know or are aware of our private world in the sense of being able to describe it verbally depends on the extent to which our community has been able to establish relations between our private world and linguistic terms. In the radical behaviorist formulation, there is nothing mental or psychic about our private world: "A small part of the universe is contained within the skin of each of us. There is no reason why it should have any special physical status because it lies within this boundary" (Skinner, 1974, p. 21). Neither is our private world excluded from the realm of scientific analysis: "Private events are observable, even if only by an audience of one....Mental [fictional] events, in contrast are unobservable because they are nonphysical; no one can ever observe belief itself or intelligence itself, regardless of claims that they can be inferred from their physical manifestations, public and private." (Baum & Heath, 1992, p. 1313). The verbal community can solve the problem of privacy to the extent that it can establish a best fit in its shaping of verbal terms for private events. In this formulation the need for parallel systems, for dichotomous worlds, evaporates. "Self-knowledge is of social origin" (Skinner, 1974, p. 31); we come to know ourselves through social interaction to the extent of the sensitivity and skill of our verbal community.

Watson in his methodological behaviorism accepted dualistic presumptions about behavior and the behaving person, but Skinner in his radical behaviorism moved beyond dualistic formulations, giving no special status to private events and allowing for their inclusion in a scientific analysis. Radical behaviorism's account of self-knowledge, consciousness, awareness, and so on is philosophically closer to George Herbert Mead's (1934) symbolic interactionism and to the position of Lev S. Vygotsky (1962) on the relation between language, thinking, and consciousness than it is to Watson's formulation (Blackman, 1991).

Edward C. Tolman

Edward C. Tolman is variously classed under the headings, behaviorism (Hillix & Marx, 1974), neobehaviorism (as in Smith, 1986), and cognitive-organizational theories (Bower & Hilgard, 1981). He was awarded his Ph.D at Harvard in 1915, two years after the publication of Watson's *Psychology as the Behaviorist Views It* (1913). Tolman was first introduced to Watson's behaviorism in 1914 and was, in his own words, sold on the approach (Tolman, 1959, p. 94). In addition to this stated commitment to behaviorism, Tolman's experimental work was mostly carried out with rats in maze learning situations and so his subject matter appeared closely linked with the early behavioral tradition. His classification under the heading, cognitive-organizational theories, is explained below, as is the gulf between his system and radical behaviorism.

S-O-R psychology. Watson created a swing in psychology from introspection to the measurement of observable stimulus-response relations. Tolman was concerned to swing back again at least a little and to try to put the organism between those relations. From a stimulus-response psychology, Tolman moved to a stimulus-organism-response psychology, arguing that stimulus-response relations could not account for the behavior of rats in his maze learning experiments. In 1922 he proposed a new behaviorism that would come between the older introspectionist school and the newly dominant stimulus-response psychology. It would be a nonphysiological behaviorism, unconcerned with synaptic connections and nervous impulses, which would still find a place for some aspects of introspective psychology. "This new behaviorism," he wrote, "will be found capable of covering not merely the results of mental tests, objective measurements of memory, and animal psychology as such, but also all that was valid in the results of the older introspective psychology. And this new formula for behaviorism which we would propose is intended as a formula for *all* of psychology—a formula to bring formal peace, not merely to the animal worker, but also to the addict of imagery and feeling tone" (Hillix & Marx, 1974, pp. 221-222: Tolman, 1922). Rather than accept the mutual exclusiveness of behaviorism and introspection as Watson would have preferred, Tolman attempted to bring them closer together and to preserve the objective tone of behaviorism without rejecting the role of internal mediators between stimulus and response. Behaviorism, in Tolman's system, moved from an S-R to an S-O-R framework.

A simple illustration of his mediational behaviorism is to be found in *Cognitive Maps in Rats and Men* (Tolman, 1948) where he took issue with S-R psychologists who contended that maze learning in rats is a simple matter of the strengthening of stimulus-response connections. He summarized the S-R position thus: "Learning, according to this view, consists in the respective strengthening and weakening of various of these [synaptic] connections; those connections which result in the animal's going down the true path become relatively more open to the passage of nervous impulses, whereas those which lead him into the blinds become relatively less open" (Tolman, 1948, p. 190). Tolman felt that this was an inadequate view, that brain processes occurring during maze learning are considerably more complex than this account allows. He classed himself among a group whom he called field theorists, who viewed maze learning as the development of a "cognitive map." This cognitive map is said to direct the rat toward its goal. Tolman contrasted the analogies of a map control room and a telephone exchange. In the S-R account, synaptic connections seem similar to the connections of a telephone exchange, with incoming information (stimuli) connected in a one-to-one manner with outgoing responses. In the S-O-R or field account, the central office (the S-R account's telephone exchange) is more like a map control room. When faced with a novel situation (perhaps some previously learned route has been blocked off) the rat scans its cognitive map and draws up a picture of another route by which it might reach its goal.

The cognitive map is an elaborate theoretical construction, an explanatory device located inside the organism. It is given a complex structure of its own, and one of the intriguing tasks of research is to discover more and more precisely the nature of that structure. Tolman became interested in discovering "how far these maps are relatively narrow and strip-like or relatively broad and comprehensive" (Tolman, 1948, p. 193) and felt that his experiments gave a clue to the conditions favoring development of the narrow strip map. He discussed the implications of this for clinical psychology, suggesting that certain human/social problems can result from the development of narrow strip maps. One of the conditions he believed can lead to the development of these kinds of narrower cognitive maps is "the presence of too strongly motivational or of too strongly frustrating conditions" (Tolman, 1948, p. 207). He suggested that "at least the three dynamisms called, respectively, 'regression', 'fixation', and 'displacement of aggression onto outgroups' are expressions of cognitive maps which are too narrow and which develop as a result of too violent motivation or of too intense frustration" (Tolman,

1948, p. 207). If the conditions leading to the development of these narrow strip maps can be discovered, then they can be controlled for the purpose of alleviating regression, fixation, and displacement of aggression.

Tolman's paper exemplifies a kind of reasoning referred to in Chapter 2, where it was argued that referring to nouns in psychological research guides the scientist to ask questions about the structure of the thing referred to. It was argued in the same chapter that referring to nouns also encourages the scientist to assume that the noun is a causal rather than a descriptive construct. Tolman faced the problem of accounting for latent learning, which involved rats being placed in a maze with no reward and allowed to run free; subsequently, the same rats were placed in the same maze with food available at a goal box. Very shortly after this the rats ran from the start of the maze to the goal box with few errors. In Tolman's words, "They demonstrated that during these preceding non-rewarded trials they had learned where many of the blinds were. They had been building up a 'map' and could utilize the latter as soon as they were motivated to do so" (Tolman, 1948, p. 195). This is the first step in the reasoning process: a cognitive map is constructed and placed inside the organism to explain latent learning. The next step consists of identifying the structure of the map—is the map narrow and strip-like, or is it relatively broad and comprehensive? The structure of the map begins to be of interest in its own right, quite apart from the behavior of the organism. The final step is taken in the concluding section of Tolman's paper when the map shifts from being an explanatory construct to being the cause of certain kinds of behavior. At all levels in the process, behavior is initiated by an internal (and hypothetical) construct which both *explains* latent learning and *causes* other kinds of behavior, for example, the behavior of a person who is regressive, fixated, or who displaces aggression onto outgroups.

Cognitive psychology past and present. Although by 1959 Tolman himself had to some extent lost faith in his system, or "so-called system" as he put it (Tolman, 1959, p. 152), the final words of Bower and Hilgard's section on Tolman suggest that his impact has been greater than he anticipated: "The sort of program Tolman envisioned seems now to be coming to fruition in modern cognitive psychology" (Bower & Hilgard, 1981, p. 351). This claim is given additional weight in *An Introduction to Animal Cognition* (Pearce, 1987), which deals carefully with Tolman's general approach and with some of his specific claims, such as the existence of cognitive maps. The author notes that Tolman was unhappy with S-R relations as explanations of learning and preferred explanations in terms of expectations and anticipation: "Thus animals can be regarded as acquiring knowledge rather than responses, and it is this that marks Tolman's approach as cognitive rather than behavioral" (Pearce, 1987, p. 30). In a historical context, as a psychologist attempting to develop methods more in line with the natural sciences, Tolman belongs to the "behavioral" tradition. But in the context of contemporary psychology his S-O-R approach is soundly cognitive.

Cognitive psychology and its consequences. Skinner was critical of Pavlov's claim to be studying cortical functioning in his work on the conditioned reflex, arguing that Pavlov's data were not about the nervous system but about behavior-environment relations, and that theoretical interpretation should refer only to those relations. Similarly, cognitive psychology claims its data are about processes taking place inside the organism and is subject to the same criticism. The data of cognitive psychology are behavioral, and according to Skinner's descriptive, observational, and integrative philosophy of science should equally be interpreted at that level. He argued that the concepts of cognitive psychology are "internal surrogates" of contingencies of reinforcement: "Take, for example, the so-called process of association. In Pavlov's experiment a hungry dog hears a bell and is then fed. If this happens many times, the dog begins to salivate when it hears the bell. The standard mentalistic explanation is that the dog 'associates' the bell with the food. But it was Pavlov who associated them! 'Associate' means to join or unite. The dog merely begins to salivate upon hearing the bell. We have no evidence that it does so because of an internal surrogate of the contingencies" (Skinner, 1978, p. 97). According to Skinner, associations take place in the real world, not in some other inferred world of mental processes. "Word association" is another example: "If we say 'home' when someone says 'house', it is not because we associate the two words but because they are associated in daily English usage. Cognitive association is an invention" (Skinner, 1978, p. 98).

Cognitive psychology implants the real world inside the head of the organism, and this form of reasoning, Skinner maintained, contributes to our inability to solve many of our pressing social problems. If the world exists in some internal representation of mind, associations, ideas, and attitudes then the problems of the world also exist in that same place and change must be effected in that place. If, however, behavior is interpreted in relation to environmental contingencies, in mutual inter-action between environment and behaving organism, in the real world inhabited by the behaving organism, then change can be effected in the real world. Skinner was deeply concerned with the fate of the human species, with human, social problems. This concern can be noted throughout *Reflections on Behaviorism and Society*, which deals with, among other topics, Human Behavior and Democracy, Are We Free to Have a Future? The Ethics of Helping People, and Humanism and Behaviorism (Skinner, 1978). An earlier work, *Science and Human Behavior* (1953), discusses the role of controlling agencies like govern-ment and law, religion, psychotherapy, and education, dealing with The Individual as a Whole, The Behavior of People in Groups, and the question, Can Science Help? *Upon Further Reflection* (1987) tackles issues such as: Why We Are Not Acting to Save the World, What Is Wrong with Daily Life in the Western World? The Shame of American Education, Intellectual Self-Management in Old Age, and Some Thoughts about the Future.

Skinner's criticisms of cognitive psychology are rooted partly in his philosophy of science, which rejects inferences from observation to dimensions not given in data, and partly in his deep concern with human/social problems: "The appeal to cognitive states and processes is a diversion which could well be responsible for much of our failure to solve our problems. We need to change our behavior and we can do so only by changing our physical and social environments. We choose the wrong path at the very start when we suppose that our goal is to change the 'minds and hearts of men and women' rather than the world in which they live" (Skinner, 1978, p. 112).

To place Tolman and Skinner under one Behaviorism heading may be accurate in a historical context, but is wholly inaccurate in a philosophical context. Tolman sought to identify processes that mediate between input and output, an S-O-R framework, and gave the lead to contemporary cognitive psychology. Radical behaviorism, in contrast, seeks to identify relations between the behavior of organisms, human or otherwise, and the context in which it occurs. Skinner's philosophy of science rejects inferences from behavioral data to hypothetical inner processes, and his concern for human well-being draws him toward interpretations of behavior that carry with them a potential for change.

Clark L. Hull

Hull's *Principles of Behavior* (1943) appeared five years after the publication of Skinner's *The Behavior of Organisms* (1938). In it, Hull attempted to prescribe a strictly mathematical system based in the postulate-deductive method. His college training had been in engineering and philosophy, and his system for psychology seems to have brought together concerns from each of these disciplines: philosophical issues relating to the nature of psychology as a science, along with an attempt at the mathematical precision characteristic of engineering. The two main points of divergence between Hull's approach and Skinner's are first, their view of the nature of the scientific process, and second, their view of mechanistic causal sequences that mediate between stimuli and responses. The gulf between Hull and Skinner will require comparatively little elaboration, since it is largely illustrated by previous sections.

Hull saw science as a strictly formal/logical process: "The body of a scientific system consists of the mathematical derivations of the theorems which correspond to the empirical facts of the science" (Hull, 1952, p. 3). A scientific system, in Hull's view, begins with a set of postulates from which theorems are deduced, and the important relations of the subject matter of the system are expressed mathematically. He viewed scientific practice as a rigorously deductive process characterized by the formal methodology of hypothetico-deduction and the logic of falsification: "The typical procedure in science is to adopt a postulate tentatively, deduce one or more of its logical implications concerning observable phenomena, and then check the validity of the deductions by observation. If the deduction is in genuine disagreement with observation, the postulate must be either abandoned or so modified that it implies no such conflicting statement. If, however, the deductions and the observations agree, the postulate gains in dependability. By successive agreements under a very wide variety of conditions it may attain a high degree of justified credibility, but never certainty" (Hull, 1943, p. 15).

This view of the scientific process contains the methodological ingredients of contemporary experimental psychology as described in Chapter 3. Skinner's less formal and inductive approach to science was also described in that chapter. Radical behaviorists attempt to derive general principles *from* data and do not concern themselves with testing speculative hypotheses or falsifying theoretical statements. Their theoretical statements integrate observed regularities in their subject matter (behavior and the context in which it occurs); a type of theoretical system that also differs from Hull's. Acknowledging that the term, theory, may have several meanings, Hull described "the deductive nature of scientific theory and explanation" (Hull, 1943, p. 2) and defined the meaning of theory for the purpose of his own system: "As understood in the present work, a theory is a systematic deductive derivation of the secondary principles of observable phenomena from a relatively small number of primary principles or postulates, much as the secondary principles or theorems of geometry are all ultimately derived as a logical hierarchy from a few original definitions and primary principles called axioms" (Hull, 1943, p. 2). On a deductive-inductive continuum, Hull's view of the scientific process and Skinner's are at opposite extremes.

Hull's was a system more rigid and formal than those of Pavlov, Watson, and Tolman. Its formality—sixteen postulates, each with an equation describing the main characteristics of the postulate and stating the relations between those characteristics from which theorems should be derived—does not lend itself to simple exposition. It was a cumbersome system; a feature which, according to Smith (1986), is chiefly responsible for Hull's loss of prominence in psychology during the 1950s. Bower and Hilgard found it necessary to "paraphrase and recast [the postulates] in order to make them more comprehensible" (Bower & Hilgard, 1981, p. 96) and their exposition of Hull's system will mainly be drawn on here.

According to Bower and Hilgard, "Hull's basic goal was to break down the stimulus-response link of a learned response into a series of intervening variables that mediate the causal influence of the conditioned stimulus upon the response performed" (Bower & Hilgard, 1981, p. 96). Hull's system belongs in the category of mediational, S-O-R approaches, with mediating constructs referred to in theoretical terms such as habit strength, drive, conditioned inhibition, and reaction fatigue. In some cases Hull, like Pavlov, appealed to features of the nervous system as links in a causal chain between input and output: "It is clear that the immediate determinant of action in organisms is not the stimulating energy, but the neural impulse as finally routed to the muscles. A presumably critical neural determinant intermediate between these two extremes of stimulus (S) and response (R) is the afferent neural impulse (s) at about the time it enters the central ganglia of the nervous system" (Hull, 1943, p. 41). In the Hullian system, it was the relation between stimulus, some internal aspect of the organism, and response that accounted for stimulus-response relations. Hull did not invoke cognitive concepts like consciousness, purpose, expectation, and so on. His mediating constructs were of a different character than Tolman's, a character he hoped would render them capable of mathematical expression. But the system as a whole was, like Tolman's, concerned with constructs that mediate between the action of the stimulating environment (input) and the behavior of organisms (output).

By now, the differences between Hull's system and the Skinnerian system should be clear, since they are mostly dealt with in preceding sections. Hull's was an S-O-R psychology, concerned with the chain of events taking place between stimulus input and response output. Although his mediating constructs differed from Tolman's, the causal mode is the same in that theoretical terms in both systems refer to hypothetical events occurring between stimulus and response. The

Skinnerian system differs from Hull's in the following important respects: a) Hull's system was concerned with the causal chain between stimulus input and response output. It was similar in that respect to Tolman's S-O-R formulation and was unlike Skinner's system, which considers functional relations between behavior and the context in which it occurs; b) where Hull appealed to neurological constructs as mediators between input and output, Skinner was equally critical of this form of inference in the work of Hull and Pavlov; c) where Hull viewed science as a formal/logical process and prescribed hypothetico-deduction and the principle of falsification for testing theories, Skinner's system attempts to describe uniformities in integrative theoretical terms and to formulate principles derived *from* data.

Behaviorism as a Historical Marker

Bower and Hilgard describe the Skinnerian system as "a thoroughgoing behaviorism" (Bower & Hilgard, 1981, p. 169), implying both a unitary definition of behaviorism and a continuum extending from strong behaviorism at one pole to weak behaviorism at the other. Skinner appears at the strong end of this continuum according to Bower and Hilgard's description, although it is not made clear which characteristics of his system render it a thoroughgoing behaviorism.

This chapter has drawn attention to fundamental differences between radical behaviorism and some of the theorists whose work traditionally comes under a "major approach" heading called Behaviorism. Pavlov and Watson concerned themselves with eliciting stimuli and built-in responses and are correctly characterized as S-R psychologists. Tolman and Hull shared an interest in chains of causal events linking input and output (although their mediating events were of a different character) and are correctly regarded as S-O-R psychologists. Tolman stands apart from Pavlov, Watson, Hull, and Skinner in appealing to cognitive concepts such as expectation and cognitive maps and thus in giving the lead to contemporary cognitive psychology. In a sense, Pavlov's system is also mediational in that he was convinced his work shed some light on cortical functioning in intact organisms, and this appeal to the nervous system is a feature shared with Hull's system (although this point should not be pressed too forcefully since the extent to which they each appealed to the nervous system differs greatly). Watson's approach was firmly anchored in the view that complex behavior could be explained as a composite of acquired reflexes, a simple S-R approach unconcerned with mediation between stimulus and response, and in this sense quite distinct from Pavlov, Tolman, and Hull. It was distinct also from Skinner's approach in both its admission of dualism and its concern with reflexes rather than operants. Pavlov and Skinner shared the tradition of reflex physiology, as well as a dedication to the organism as a whole, but they differ in that Pavlov's work addressed reflexes, conditioned and unconditioned, whereas Skinner's system addresses operant behavior.

The Skinnerian system is distinct from other behavioral traditions in the following ways: a) its subject matter is the mutual relation between behavior and environment, emphasizing the role of environmental events in shaping and maintaining behavior; b) the system is not mechanistic and does not appeal to mediating events such as cognitions or the nervous system; c) complex behavior is a function of complex contingencies rather than a function of either acquired reflexes or internal states of the organism; d) the system dispenses with dualistic interpretations of private events, arguing that our awareness of private events is a product of social interaction, the shaping of linguistic terms by the verbal community. Especially in relation to the last point, Blackman (1991) argues that radical behaviorism has much in common with some aspects of social psychology and that its combination of social and biological concerns bridges the gap that has traditionally divided these two disciplines.

Placing Pavlov, Watson, Tolman, Hull, and Skinner under the same heading misrepresents their relationship because some kind of continuum or common thread is implied. The heading, Behaviorism, is only useful in a historical context, to identify an overall methodological shift in psychology that took place in the early part of this century. It should not be used to imply continuity in the thinking of major theorists of the time because when their work is closely examined it becomes clear that they were concerned with different kinds of problems and offered different kinds of explanations of their subject matter. The traditional division of psychology into six major approaches—Biological, Ethological, Behavioral, Cognitive, Psychodynamic and Humanistic—obscures the fact that a great many explanatory accounts in contemporary psychology are grounded in the scientific framework of Tolman and Hull, the S-O-R framework, where an environmental event is said to impact upon some system internal to the organism (articulatory loop, superego, attitude, attribution, self, personality, motivation, and so on) which in its turn generates behavior. For all its admitted vagaries, Tolman and Hull's S-O-R formulation continues to provide the framework for mainstream scientific psychology, even though radical behaviorism and contemporary scientific thinking in other fields has moved well beyond the interpretive (mechanistic) metaphor that this framework takes as fundamental.

Chapter 9

Concluding Remarks

Radical behaviorism's explanatory system focuses on relations between behaving persons (or other organisms), the setting conditions of behavior, and its consequences: behavior in its context. It rejects a dualistic view of the person that divides the person into behavior and something else and which consequently treats behavior as the superficial manifestation of processes taking place at some other, inaccessible, unobservable, and usually hypothetical level. Behavior is a naturally occurring phenomenon, amenable to scientific analysis without recourse to conceptually confusing metaphysical concepts or philosophical presumptions inherent in Western philosophy. The approach is empirically validated in laboratory settings and in clinical, educational, and social work contexts by behavior analysts' demonstrations of orderly relations between behavior and the context in which it occurs. The person in radical behaviorism is conceived of as a unique individual, a conception that is worked into behavior analytic research strategies and consequently into its scientific assertions. Persons in this system are indivisible wholes, active in and interactive with their environments, changing and changed by the context and consequences of their behavior—a concept identical to Capra's network of dynamic relationships (Capra, 1983, p. 32) in the world of contemporary physics. Relations between organisms and their world comprise the focus of causal accounts, expressed in integrative theoretical terms that explain behavior over time without the need for mechanistic links between functionally dependent events.

A commitment to scientific method continues to distinguish psychology from philosophy, a view from which few psychologists would dissent. Clearly, however, psychologists are not all committed to the same kind of science. Skinner's commitment was to a descriptive,

201

observational, and integrative science not requiring mediating structures or mechanisms to account for cause-effect relations; a science informed by a relational view of its subject matter (contained in its definition) and a philosophy that does not separate persons into behavior and internal systems. It seeks to describe (explain) how persons and environments interact, the effect persons have in producing consequences in their environment, and the effect the environment has in shaping and maintaining behavioral repertoires. Few psychologists are committed to this kind of science, the majority conceiving of causation as contiguous and sequential, demanding links in the chain to account for behavior.

Mach's participation in the 19th century dispute over interpretation and causal modes in physics is echoed by Skinner's natural science concerns in 20th century psychology. Mach's concerns relating to mechanistic explanatory systems were not so much over the ontological status of hypothetical constructs (such as atoms, vortices, particles, and other mediating entities postulated by physicists of his time) but broader scientific, philosophical, and methodological concerns (Brush, 1968). Similarly, debates over psychological structures or events are often mistaken today for ontological disputes—do memory, mind, and mental states in general exist? These debates take on a new form when viewed from a philosophy of science perspective. They become debates about the meaning of explanation, the conception of causation employed, and the pragmatic value of theories and theoretical models. To paraphrase Brush (1968): "Some of the scientific questions discussed by Skinner are by no means settled even today, to say nothing of the philosophical or methodological ones." Behaviorism as a historical movement concentrated on scientific and methodological concerns and created a shift in the direction of methods more consonant with those of the natural sciences. Some behaviorists, however, found it impossible to move beyond the 19th century mechanistic framework. Contemporary psychology continues to rely on the input-system-output (S-O-R) framework of those early behaviorists.

Radical behaviorism belongs to a philosophy of science tradition that explicitly rejects mechanistic interpretations of natural phenomena and refuses to describe the behavior of organisms, human or otherwise, by mechanical principles. Its relation to other traditions sharing the heading, Behaviorism, is historical rather than philosophical; it is concerned neither with the S-R connections of conditioned reflexes as Pavlov and Watson were, nor with mediating structures between environmental input and behavioral output as were the S-O-R psychologies of Tolman and Hull. Eysenck's comment, "There is no doubt that contemporary research in the field of cognition represents a strong reaction against the facile approach of Behaviorism" (Eysenck, 1984, p. 20) now seems curious in the light of the acknowledged relation between the S-O-R tradition of Edward C. Tolman and contemporary cognitive psychology. The assertion that Skinner was concerned with input-output functions and the implication that a critique of the Pavlovian system functions as a critique of the Skinnerian system also seem curious given that Skinner diverged from the Pavlovian tradition so early in his research career. Mahoney and others who equate radical behaviorism with the behaviorism of Pavlov, Watson, Tolman or Hull, rely on the error that presents Behaviorism as a philosophical/methodological unity rather than a historical marker. Mahoney also wrongly ascribed billiard ball causation to radical behaviorism and, consequently, his assertion that radical behaviorism has "isolated itself and [come] to lag behind changing perspectives on the nature and practice of optimal scientific inquiry" (Mahoney, 1989, p. 1373) is unfounded. Much of contemporary psychology *is* grounded in mechanistic thinking, a conception of causation that is linear and contiguous, and is therefore subject to this criticism. Ironically, radical behaviorism is not.

Macleod (1970) equated the Skinnerian system with a Newtonian doctrine of man, implying that Skinnerian accounts of human behavior are analogous to accounts of physical phenomena couched in terms of interacting physical particles. In light of the arguments presented in this book, such a description bears no resemblance to Skinnerian accounts. There are no "interacting particles" in behavior analytic interpretations of behavior. Capra's summary—"behaviorists still adhere to the mechanistic paradigm and often defend it as the only scientific approach to psychology, thus clearly limiting science to the classical Newtonian framework" (Capra, 1983, p. 181)—although directed at Skinner, clearly applies to other behavioral traditions and to much of contemporary psychology, but not to radical behaviorism. Of Newtonian science, Skinner explicitly stated, "A science of human behavior cannot be closely patterned after geometry or Newtonian mechanics because its problems are not necessarily of the same sort" (Skinner, 1938, p. 437).

It is unfortunate that the recurring errors of behaviorism, mechanism, and dualism have been repeated in descriptions of radical behaviorism by participants in the new world view debate; unfortunate because radical behaviorism and behavior analysis have much to contribute to this debate. Important as it is for scientific thinking and practice, and with interest reaching far beyond the walls of academia, the debate has implications for the way we relate to our global environment and for the problems created and suffered by people. Participants in this debate have cited the wrong branch of contemporary psychology as an example of the old world view of mechanistic, dualistic, Newtonian/Cartesian science. In addition, they have failed to recognize the similarities between their own concerns and those of B. F. Skinner and, by dismissing radical behaviorism as an example of an outmoded world view, have failed to recognize the importance of Skinner's philosophy for their own argument. These concluding remarks will suggest an outcome to the new world view debate that may surprise some of its participants.

Facing a Global Crisis

There is an essential similarity in the arguments of Skinner and Capra (1983) concerning the immediacy of modern global problems and the need for a new way of thinking to overcome them. Skinner argued, "Most thoughtful people agree that the world is in serious trouble. A nuclear war could mean a nuclear winter that would destroy all living things; fossil fuels will not last forever, and many other critical resources are nearing exhaustion; the earth grows steadily less habitable; and all this is exacerbated by a burgeoning population that resists control. The timetable may not be clear, but the threat is real" (Skinner, 1987a, p. 1).

Concluding Remarks

Capra begins *The Turning Point: Science, Society, and the Rising Culture* (1983) by juxtaposing the cost of the United States' nuclear weapons program with a statistical breakdown of the malnourishment, starvation, and poor access to health care that are features of life in many of the world's poorest nations. The threat of nuclear catastrophe, industrial pollution, overpopulation, and disruption of the planet's ecological balance are all cited as a modern global crisis: "a crisis of a scale and urgency unprecedented in recorded human history" (Capra, 1983, p. 1).

Skinner and Capra agree that the world is threatened in a great many ways by aspects of human behavior. Both address themselves to identifying sources of this global crisis and to offering a broad solution. At this point their reasoning diverges, but their conclusions may be closer than the new-world-view argument would have anticipated.

Capra traces the root cause to a misplaced emphasis on science: "Our culture takes pride in being scientific; our time is referred to as the Scientific Age. It is dominated by rational thought, and scientific knowledge is often considered the only acceptable kind of knowledge. That there can be intuitive knowledge, or awareness, which is just as valid and reliable, is generally not recognized. This attitude, known as scientism, is widespread, pervading our educational system and all other social and political institutions" (Capra, 1983, pp. 22-23). He argues that our understanding and control of nature has been greatly improved by science, but our understanding and control of social affairs has not improved in a similar manner: "Scientific and technological knowledge has grown enormously since the Greeks embarked on the scientific venture in the sixth century B. C. But during these twenty-five centuries there has been hardly any progress in the conduct of social affairs" (Capra, 1983, pp. 25-26). Since the seventeenth century, he argues, physics has given the lead to other sciences—biology, medical science, psychology, economics, and so on—and these have modelled themselves on the conceptual framework and the methodology of classical physics. Capra defines this framework as a "mechanistic view of the world" and argues that a mechanistic conception of reality dominated the seventeenth, eighteenth, and nineteenth centuries when "Matter was thought to be the basis of all existence, and the material world seen as a multitude of separate objects assembled into a huge machine. Like human-made machines, the cosmic machine was thought to consist of elementary parts. Consequently it was believed that complex phenomena could always be understood by reducing them to their basic building blocks and by looking for the mechanisms through which these interacted" (Capra, 1983, pp. 31-32). This mechanistic vision of natural phenomena, he argues, is now deeply ingrained in our culture and informs the methodology and theoretical interpretation of branches of science that have modelled themselves in accordance with the Newtonian world view: "Whenever psychologists, sociologists, or economists wanted to be scientific, they naturally turned toward the basic concepts of Newtonian physics" (Capra, 1983, p. 32).

Modern physics, he argues, has overthrown the vision of natural phenomena as mechanical and the universe as a great machine and it is time for other scientific disciplines to take their cue from the new vision of the universe—the organic or relational conception of nature. Natural phenomena in modern physics are not made up of separable and discrete parts, but of interrelations: "In the twentieth century…physics has gone through several conceptual revolutions that clearly reveal the limitations of the mechanistic world view and lead to an organic, ecological view of the world.…The universe is no longer seen as a machine, made up of a multitude of separate objects, but appears as a harmonious indivisible whole; a network of dynamic relations that include the human observer" (Capra, 1983, p. 32). Capra suggests that we may go some way toward alleviating features of the global crisis if the organic conception of nature revealed in modern physics were adopted by other sciences, if other sciences were to give up mechanistic interpretations of their subject matter and recognize its harmonious, indivisible, wholeness. By mistakenly ascribing the wrong historical tradition and the wrong philosophy of science to radical behaviorism, Capra and others have missed the opportunity of suggesting that radical behaviorism may well be the nonmechanistic, nondualistic, organic/relational approach that will free psychology to pursue its science within the new world view offered by modern physics.

Concluding Remarks

Science and Human Behavior

Skinner agreed with Capra on the issue of global crises, and likewise argued that science has progressed immeasurably since the time of Plato and Aristotle but that our understanding of human/social issues has not equally improved: "Greek physics and biology are now of historical interest only (no modern physicist or biologist would turn to Aristotle for help), but the dialogues of Plato are still assigned to students and cited as if they threw light on human behavior. Aristotle could not have understood a page of modern physics or biology, but Socrates and his friends would have little trouble in following most current discussions of human affairs. And as to technology, we have made immense strides in controlling the physical and biological worlds, but our practices in government, education, and much of economics, though adapted to very different conditions, have not greatly improved" (Skinner, 1971, p. 11).

Skinner argued that science is our strength. He also recognized, like Capra, that it can be and has been abused. He took issue with calls to turn away from science on grounds of its abuse, arguing instead that science is not the problem, but the behavior of those who deal with science and who apply it. It is true that some of the problems described by Skinner and Capra as factors in today's global crises are products of science, but science itself is not at fault. The other side of science is that it has also led to the alleviation of much suffering, famine, and illness. The problem Skinner identified is the behavior of those who use and abuse science, and he advocated applying the power of scientific analysis to this field as it is applied to others.

To dispense with science would be a regressive step with disastrous results: "Unfortunately we cannot stand still; to bring scientific research to an end now would mean a return to famine and pestilence and the exhausting labors of a slave culture" (Skinner, 1953, p. 5). Rejecting a scientific analysis of human behavior is no advance on the position we find ourselves in now. And continuing the mechanistic approach characteristic of much of contemporary psychology, the framework that separates persons into behavior and some other, more fundamental system, adds no new insight into the ways people interact with their environment. Explanations in this framework occur in theoretical webs involving hypothetical constructs—self, motivation, attitude, articulatory loop, attribution, semantic network, theory of mind, and so on. The constructs are said to generate and account for behavior, including, therefore, the behavior that concerns Capra and Skinner, behavior that results in war, pollution, famine, rising birth rates, weapons development and construction, and so on. Relying on these constructs for explanation dictates that if behavior is to be altered, then the constructs must be altered—but there is no logical way of altering hypothetical constructs. The framework offers no way forward, no solution. A scientific analysis of how people interact in their worlds, how setting conditions and consequences affect behavior, presents the possibility of altering behavior. Since behavior is functionally related to events in the context in which it occurs, then change can be achieved by analyzing those relations and altering aspects of the context. Turning away from science is no solution; examining science as it is practiced in psychology reveals that the relational framework of radical behaviorism offers possibilities for change unmatched by the mechanistic approach.

Throughout his lifetime, Skinner continually confronted the task of developing empirically valid methods and terms to explain behavior. He consistently advocated a relational framework for the subject matter of psychology, patiently working out how this might be achieved within a scientific tradition. The success of behavior analytic methods across a broad range of applied settings encourages the view that this descriptive, observational, and integrative framework is appropriate to dealing with problems of human behavior. Radical behaviorism provides a stable and coherent philosophical position within psychology today.

References

American Psychological Association. (1983). *Publication manual of the American Psychological Association* (3rd ed.). Washington, DC: Author.

Atkinson, R. C., & Shiffrin, R. M. (1968). Human memory: A proposed system and its control processes. In K. W. Spence & J. T. Spence (Eds.), *The psychology of learning and motivation: Advances in research and theory* (Vol. 2). New York: Academic Press.

Atkinson, R. L., Atkinson, R. C., Smith, E. E., & Bem, D. J. (1993). *Introduction to psychology* (11th ed.). Orlando, FL: Harcourt Brace Jovanovich.

Ayllon, T., & Azrin, N. (1968). *The token economy: A motivational system for therapy and rehabilitation.* New York: Appleton-Century-Crofts.

Baddeley, A. D. (1981). The concept of working memory: A view of its current state and probable future development. *Cognition, 10*, 17-23.

Baddeley, A. D. (1982). Reading and working memory. *Bulletin of the British Psychological Society, 35*, 414-417.

Baddeley, A. D., & Hitch, G. J. (1974). Working memory. In G. H. Bower (Ed.). *Recent advances in learning and motivation* (pp. 47-89). London: Academic Press.

Bakan, D. (1967). *On method: Toward a reconstruction of psychological investigation.* San Francisco: Jossey-Bass.

Bandura, A. (1977). Self-efficacy: Toward a unifying theory of behavioral change. *Psychological Review, 84*, 191-215.

Bandura, A. (1989). Human agency in social cognitive theory. *American Psychologist, 44*, 1175-1184.

Baum, W. M., & Heath, J. L. (1992). Behavioral explanations and intentional explanations in psychology. *American Psychologist*, 47, 1312-1317.

Bem, D. J. (1972). Self-perception theory. In L. Berkowitz (Ed.), *Advances in experimental social psychology* (Vol. 6, pp. 1-62). New York: Academic Press.

Bernstein, D. J. (1990). Of carrots and sticks: A review of Deci and Ryan's *Intrinsic Motivation and Self-Determination in Human Behavior. Journal of the Experimental Analysis of Behavior*, 54, 323-332.

Binyon, M. (1977). Rats! It's a prophet crying 'destiny-control this way.' *The Times Higher Education Supplement*, 4, 3, 77, pp. 7 and 9. London: Times Newspapers Limited.

Blackman, D. E. (1991). B. F. Skinner and G. H. Mead: On biological science and social science. *Journal of the Experimental Analysis of Behavior*, 55, 251-265.

Blackmore, J. T. (1972). *Ernst Mach: His work, life, and influence.* Berkeley: University of California Press.

Boden, M. A. (1978). *Purposive explanation in psychology.* Sussex: Harvester Press Ltd.

Bolles, R. C.(1975). *Theory of motivation* (2nd ed.). New York: Harper & Row.

Bower, G. H., & Hilgard, E. R. (1981). *Theories of learning* (5th ed.). Englewood Cliffs, NJ: Prentice-Hall.

Bradley, J. (1971). *Mach's philosophy of science.* London: The Athlone Press of the University of London.

Brownstein, A. J., & Shull, R. L. (1985). A rule for the use of the term, 'Rule-Governed Behavior.' *The Behavior Analyst*, 8, 265-267.

Brush, S. G. (1968). Mach and atomism. *Synthese*, 18, 192-215.

Capra, F. (1975). *The tao of physics: An exploration of the parallels between modern physics and Eastern mysticism.* London: Wildwood House.

Capra, F. (1983). *The turning point: Science, society and the rising culture.* London: Fontana.

Catania, A. C. (1992). *Learning* (3rd ed.). Englewood Cliffs, NJ: Prentice-Hall.

References

Chomsky, N. (1959). *Verbal Behavior*, by B. F. Skinner. *Language*, 35, 26-58.

Clegg, F. (1982). *Simple statistics: A course book for the social sciences.* Cambridge, England: Cambridge University Press.

Cohen, M. R., & Nagel, E. (1934). *An introduction to logic and scientific method.* London: Routledge & Kegan Paul.

Cohen, R. S., & Seeger, R. J. (Eds.). (1970). *Ernst Mach: Physicist and philosopher.* Boston Studies in the Philosophy of Science (Vol. VI). Dordrecht, Holland: D. Reidel.

Cooke, N. L. (1984). Misrepresentation of the behavioral model in preservice teacher education textbooks. In W. L. Heward, T. E. Heron, D. S. Hill, & J. Trap-Porter (Eds.), *Focus on behavior analysis in education* (pp. 197-217). Columbus, Ohio: Merrill.

Czubaroff, J. (1988). Criticism and response in the Skinner controversies. *Journal of the Experimental Analysis of Behavior*, 49, 321-329.

Davies, P. (1987). *The cosmic blueprint.* London: William Heinemann Ltd.

de Giustino, D. (1975). *The conquest of mind: Phrenology and Victorian social thought.* London: Croom Helm.

Deci, E. L. (1975). *Intrinsic motivation.* New York: Plenum Press.

Deci, E. L., & Ryan, R. M. (1980). The empirical exploration of intrinsic motivational processes. In L. Berkowitz (Ed.), *Advances in experimental social psychology* (Vol. 13, pp. 39-80). New York: Academic Press.

Deci, E. L., & Ryan, R. M. (1985). *Intrinsic motivation and self-determination in human behavior.* New York: Plenum.

Deese, J. (1972). *Psychology as science and art.* New York: Harcourt Brace Jovanovich.

Deitz, S. M., & Malone, L. W. (1985). Stimulus control terminology. *The Behavior Analyst*, 8, 259-264.

Dickinson, A. M. (1989). The detrimental effects of extrinsic reinforcement on 'intrinsic motivation.' *The Behavior Analyst*, 12, 1-15.

Efron, R. (1990). *The decline and fall of hemispheric specialization.* Hillsdale, NJ: Lawrence Erlbaum.

Estes, W. K., Newell, A., Anderson, J. R., Brown, J. S., Feigenbaum, E. A., Greeno, J., Hayes, P. J., Hunt, E., Kosslyn, S. M., Marcus, M., & Ullman, S. (1983). Report of the Research Briefing Panel on Cognitive Science and Artificial Intelligence. *Research briefings 1983.* Washington, DC: National Academy Press.

Evans, P. (1975). *Motivation.* London: Methuen.

Eysenck, H. (1980). The bio-social model of man. In A. J. Chapman & D. Jones (Eds.), *Models of man* (pp. 49-60). Leicester: The British Psychological Society.

Eysenck, M. (1984). *A handbook of cognitive psychology.* London: Lawrence Erlbaum.

Fashing, J., & Goertzel, T. (1981). The myth of the normal curve. *Humanity and Society,* 5, 14-31.

Ferster, C. B., & Skinner, B. F. (1957). *Schedules of reinforcement.* New York: Appleton-Century-Crofts.

Feyerabend, P. K. (1970). Philosophy of science: A subject with a great past. In R. H. Stuewer (Ed.), *Historical and philosophical perspectives of science.* Minnesota Studies in the Philosophy of Science (Vol. V, pp. 172-183). Minneapolis: University of Minnesota Press.

Fisher, R. A. (1947). *The design of experiments.* Edinburgh: Oliver and Boyd.

Glanzer, M., & Cunitz, A. R. (1966). Two storage mechanisms in free recall. *Journal of Verbal Learning and Verbal Behavior,* 5, 351-360.

Gleeson, S., & Lattal, K. A. (1987). Misdescribing the Carneau: A perplexing plurality. *The Behavior Analyst,* 10, 111-112.

Gleick, J. (1988). *Chaos: Making a new science.* London: William Heinemann Ltd.

Green, J., & D'Oliveira, M. (1982). *Learning to use statistical tests in psychology: A student's guide.* Milton Keynes: Open University Press.

Grünbaum, A. (1953). Causality and the science of human behavior. In H. Fiegl & M. Brodbeck (Eds.), *Readings in the philosophy of science* (pp. 766-778). New York: Appleton-Century-Crofts.

Guilford, J. P. (1950). *Fundamental statistics in psychology and education* (2nd ed.). New York: McGraw-Hill.

References

Hacking, I. (1990). *The taming of chance.* Cambridge, England: Cambridge University Press.

Hanson, N. R. (1955). Causal chains. *Mind, 64,* 289-311.

Hanson, N. R. (1958). *Patterns of discovery: An inquiry into the conceptual foundations of science.* Cambridge, England: Cambridge University Press.

Hawking, S. W. (1988). *A brief history of time: From the big bang to black holes.* London: Bantam Press.

Hempel, G., & Oppenheim, P. (1960). Studies in the logic of explanation. In E. H. Madden (Ed.), *The structure of scientific thought* (pp. 19-29). Boston: Houghton Mifflin.

Hersen, M., & Barlow, D. H. (1976). *Single case experimental design: Strategies for studying behavior change.* New York: Pergamon Press.

Hilgard, E. R., Atkinson, R. L., & Atkinson, R. C. (1979). *Introduction to psychology* (7th ed.). New York: Harcourt Brace Jovanovich.

Hillix, W. A., & Marx, M. H. (Eds.). (1974). *Systems and theories in psychology: A reader.* St. Paul, MN: West.

Hineline, P. N. (1980). The language of behavior analysis: Its community, its functions, and its limitations. *Behaviorism, 8,* 67-86.

Hineline, P. N. (1983). When we speak of knowing. *The Behavior Analyst, 6,* 183-186.

Hineline, P. N. (1990). The origins of environment-based psychological theory. *Journal of the Experimental Analysis of Behavior, 53,* 305-320.

Hineline, P. N. (1992). A self-interpretive behavior analysis. *American Psychologist, 47,* 1127-1286.

Hirschorn, P. (1979). The behaviorist approach. In J. Medcof & J. Roth (Eds.), *Approaches to psychology* (pp. 105-142). Milton Keynes: Open University Press.

Hospers, J. (1956). *An introduction to philosophical analysis.* London: Routledge and Kegan Paul.

Hull, C. L. (1943). *Principles of behavior: An introduction to behavior theory.* New York: Appleton-Century-Crofts.

Hull, C. L. (1951). *Essentials of behavior.* New Haven, CT: Yale University Press..

Hull, C. L. (1952). *A behavior system.* New Haven, CT: Yale University Press.

Hume, D. (1777/1975). *Enquiries concerning human understanding and concerning the principles of morals* (3rd ed., with text revised and notes by P. H. Nidditch). Oxford: Clarendon Press.

Isaacs, W., Thomas, J., & Goldiamond, I. (1966) Application of operant conditioning to reinstate verbal behavior in psychotics. In R. Ulrich, T. Stachnik, J. Mabry (Eds.), *Control of human behavior* (Vol. 1, pp. 199-202). Illinois: Scott Foresman.

Johnston, J. M., & Pennypacker, H. S. (1980). *Strategies and tactics of human behavioral research.* Hillsdale, NJ: Lawrence Erlbaum.

Jones, E. E., & Nisbett, R. E. (1971). *The actor and the observer: Divergent perceptions of the causes of behavior.* Morristown, NJ: General Learning Press.

Keller, F. S. (1973). *The definition of psychology.* New York: Appleton-Century-Crofts.

Kline, M. (1980). *Mathematics: The loss of certainty.* New York: Oxford University Press.

Kline, M. (1985). *Mathematics and the search for knowledge.* New York and Oxford: Oxford University Press.

Koch, S. (Ed.). (1959). *Psychology: A study of a science* (Vol. 2). New York: McGraw-Hill.

Koch, S. (1961). Psychological science versus the science-humanism antinomy: Intimations of a significant science of man. *American Psychologist,* 16, 629-639.

Koch, S. (1964). Psychology and emerging conceptions of knowledge as unitary. In T. W. Wann (Ed.), *Behaviorism and phenomenology: Contrasting bases for modern psychology* (pp. 1-38). Chicago: University of Chicago Press.

Kuhn, T. S. (1962). *The structure of scientific revolutions* (2nd ed.). Chicago: University of Chicago Press.

Lakatos, I., & Musgrave, A. (Eds.). (1970). *Criticism and the growth of knowledge.* Cambridge: Cambridge University Press.

Laudan, L. (1977). *Progress and its problems: Towards a theory of scientific growth.* London: Routledge and Kegan Paul.

References

Laudan, L. (1981). *Science and hypothesis.* Dordrecht, Holland: D. Reidel.

Laudan, L. (1981*a*). Hume (and Hacking) on induction. In L. Laudan, *Science and hypothesis* (pp. 72-85). Dordrecht, Holland: D. Reidel.

Laudan, L. (1981*b*). Why was the logic of discovery abandoned? In L. Laudan, *Science and hypothesis* (pp. 181-191). Dordrecht, Holland: D. Reidel.

Laudan, L. (1981*c*). The sources of modern methodology: Two models of change. In L. Laudan, *Science and hypothesis* (pp. 6-19). Dordrecht, Holland: D. Reidel.

Laudan, L. (1981*d*). The epistemology of light: Some methodological issues in the subtle fluids debate. In L. Laudan, *Science and hypothesis* (pp. 111-140). Dordrecht, Holland: D. Reidel.

Laudan, L. (1981*e*). Ernst Mach's opposition to atomism. In L. Laudan, *Science and hypothesis* (pp. 202-225). Dordrecht, Holland: D. Reidel.

Laudan, L. (1984). *Science and values: The aims of science and their role in scientific debate.* Berkeley: University of California Press.

Leahey, T. J. (1980). *A History of psychology: Main currents in psychological thought.* Englewood Cliffs, NJ: Prentice Hall.

Lee, V. L. (1981). Terminological and conceptual revision in the experimental analysis of language development: Why. *Behaviorism, 9,* 25-53.

Lee, V. (1988). *Beyond behaviorism.* Hillsdale, NJ: Lawrence Erlbaum.

Lepper, M. R., Greene, D., & Nisbett, R. E. (1973). Undermining children's intrinsic interest with extrinsic reward: A test of the 'overjustification' hypothesis. *Journal of Personality and Social Psychology, 28,* 129-137.

Loftus, E. F., Miller, D. G., & Burns, H. J. (1978). Semantic integration of verbal information into a visual memory. *Journal of Experimental Psychology: Human Learning and Memory, 4,* 19-31.

Loftus, E. F., & Palmer, J. (1974). Reconstruction of automobile destruction. *Journal of Verbal Learning and Verbal Behavior, 13,* 585-589.

MacCorquodale, K. (1969). B. F. Skinner's *Verbal Behavior.* A retrospective appreciation. *Journal of the Experimental Analysis of Behavior, 12,* 831-841.

Mach, E. (1893/1960). *The science of mechanics: A critical and historical account of its development.* Illinois: Open Court.

Mackenzie, B. D. (1977). *Behaviorism and the limits of scientific method.* London: Routledge & Kegan Paul.

Macleod, R. B. (1970). Newtonian and Darwinian conceptions of man, and some alternatives. *Journal of the History of the Behavioral Sciences,* 6, 207-218.

Mahoney, M. J. (1989). Scientific psychology and radical behaviorism. *American Psychologist,* 44, 1372-1377.

Malcolm, N. (1964). Behaviorism as a philosophy of psychology. In T. W. Wann (Ed.), *Behaviorism and phenomenology: Contrasting bases for modern psychology* (pp. 141-155). Chicago and London: University of Chicago Press.

Martin, G., & Pear, J. (1983). *Behavior modification: What it is and how to do it* (2nd ed.). Englewood Cliffs, NJ: Prentice-Hall.

Matthijs, W. (1988). The development of complex equivalence relations in a schizophrenic subject. Paper (*unpublished*) presented at the Second European Meeting on the Experimental Analysis of Behavior (EMEAB II). Liege: Belgium, July 1988.

McClelland, D. C. (1987). *Human motivation.* Cambridge: Cambridge University Press.

Mead, G. H. (1934). *Mind, self, and society: From the standpoint of a social behaviorist.* Edited with an Introduction by C. W. Morris. Chicago: University of Chicago Press.

Merchant, C. (1982). *The Death of Nature: Women, ecology and the scientific revolution.* London: Wildwood House Ltd.

Miller, E. (1980). Neuropsychology and the relationship between brain and behavior. In A. J. Chapman & D. Jones (Eds.), *Models of man* (pp. 75-83). Leicester, England: The British Psychological Society.

Morgan, M. J. (1974). Resistance to satiation. *Animal Behavior,* 22, 449-466.

Morris, E. K. (1985). Public information, dissemination, and behavior analysis. *The Behavior Analyst,* 8, 95-110.

References

Morris, N. (1986). Working memory, 1974-1984: A review of a decade of research. *Current Psychological Research & Reviews*, 5, 281-295.

Oppenheimer, R. (1956). Analogy in science. *American Psychologist*, 11, 127-135.

Pavlov, I. P. (1906). The scientific investigation of the psychical faculties or processes in the higher animals. *Science*, 24, 613-619.

Pavlov, I. P. (1927). *Conditioned reflexes: An investigation of the physiological activity of the cerebral cortex.* London: Oxford University Press.

Pearce, J. M. (1987). *An introduction to animal cognition.* Sussex, England: Lawrence Erlbaum.

Popper, K. (1965). *Conjectures and refutations: The growth of scientific knowledge.* New York: Basic Books.

Prigogine, I., & Stengers, I. (1985). *Order out of chaos: Man's new dialogue with nature.* London: Fontana.

Quetelet, L. A. J. (1969). *A treatise on man.* Gainesville, FL: Scholar's Facsimilies and Reprints.

Rachlin, H. (1970). *Introduction to modern behaviorism.* San Franscisco: W. H. Freeman.

Rescorla, R. A. (1988). Pavlovian conditioning: It's not what you think it is. *American Psychologist*, 43, 151-160.

Rogers, C. R. (1967). *On becoming a person.* London: Constable.

Romanyshyn, R. (1978). Psychology and the attitude of science. In R. S. Valle & M. King (Eds.). *Existential-phenomenological alternatives for psychology* (pp. 18-47). New York: Oxford University Press.

Ross, L. (1977). The intuitive psychologist and his shortcomings: Distortions in the attribution process. In L. Berkowitz (Ed.), *Advances in experimental social psychology.* (Vol. 10, pp. 173-220). San Diego: Academic Press.

Russell, B. (1946). *A history of western philosophy.* London: Allen & Unwin.

Salame, P., & Baddeley, A. (1982). Disruption of short-term memory by unattended speech: Implications for the structure of working memory. *Journal of Verbal Learning and Verbal Behavior*, 21, 150-164.

Scriven, M. (1956). A study of radical behaviorism. In H. Feigl & M. Scriven (Eds.), *The foundations of science and the concepts of psychology and psychoanalysis.* Minnesota Studies in the Philosophy of Science (Vol. I, pp. 88-130). Minneapolis: University of Minnesota Press.

Sheldon, B. (1982). *Behavior modification: Theory, practice, and philosophy.* London: Tavistock.

Sheldon, W. (1942). *The varieties of temperament: A psychology of constitutional differences.* New York: Harper.

Sherrard, C. (1988). Rhetorical weapons: Chomsky's attack on Skinner. *Educational Psychology, 8,* 197-206.

Sidman, M. (1960). *Tactics of scientific research.* New York: Basic Books. (Reprinted, 1988. Boston: Authors Cooperative.)

Skinner, B. F. (1931). The concept of the reflex in the description of behavior. *The Journal of General Psychology, 5,* 427-458.

Skinner, B. F. (1931/1972b). The concept of the reflex in the description of behavior. In B. F. Skinner, *Cumulative record: A selection of papers* (3rd ed., pp. 429-457). New York: Appleton-Century-Crofts.

Skinner, B. F. (1938). *The behavior of organisms.* New York: Appleton-Century-Crofts.

Skinner, B. F. (1945). The operational analysis of psychological terms. *Psychological Review, 52,* 270-277.

Skinner, B. F. (1945/1972b). The operational analysis of psychological terms. In B. F. Skinner, *Cumulative record: A selection of papers* (3rd ed., pp. 370-384). New York: Appleton-Century-Crofts.

Skinner, B. F. (1947). Experimental psychology. In W. Dennis et al. (Eds.), *Current trends in psychology.* Pittsburgh: University of Pittsburgh Press.

Skinner, B. F. (1947/1972b). Current trends in experimental psychology. In B. F. Skinner, *Cumulative record: A selection of papers* (3rd ed., pp. 295-313). New York: Appleton-Century-Crofts.

Skinner, B. F. (1950). Are theories of learning necessary? *Psychological Review, 57,* 193-216.

References

Skinner, B. F. (1950/1972b). Are theories of learning necessary? In B. F. Skinner, *Cumulative record: A selection of papers* (3rd ed., pp. 69-100). New York: Appleton-Century-Crofts.

Skinner, B. F. (1953). *Science and human behavior.* New York: Macmillan.

Skinner, B. F. (1956). Critique of psychoanalytic concepts and theories. In H. Feigl & M. Scriven (Eds.), *The foundations of science and the concepts of psychology and psychoanalysis.* Minnesota Studies in the Philosophy of Science (Vol. I, pp. 77-87). Minneapolis: University of Minnesota Press.

Skinner, B. F. (1957). *Verbal behavior.* Englewood Cliffs, NJ: Prentice-Hall.

Skinner, B. F. (1959). A case history in scientific method. In S. Koch (Ed.), *Psychology: A study of a science* (Vol. 2, pp. 359-379). New York: McGraw-Hill.

Skinner, B. F. (1961). The flight from the laboratory. *Current Trends in Psychological Theory.* Pittsburgh: University of Pittsburgh Press.

Skinner, B. F. (1966). Operant behavior. In W. K. Honig (Ed.), *Operant behavior: Areas of research and application* (pp. 12-32). New York: Appleton-Century-Crofts.

Skinner, B. F. (1969). *Contingencies of reinforcement: A theoretical analysis.* New York: Appleton-Century-Crofts.

Skinner, B. F. (1971). *Beyond freedom and dignity.* New York: Knopf.

Skinner, B. F. (1972*a*). A lecture on "having" a poem. In B. F. Skinner, *Cumulative record: A selection of papers* (3rd ed., pp. 345-355). New York: Appleton-Century-Crofts.

Skinner, B. F. (1972b). *Cumulative record: A selection of papers* (3rd ed.). New York: Appleton-Century-Crofts.

Skinner, B. F. (1972c). The Flight from the Laboratory. In B. F. Skinner, *Cumulative record: A selection of papers* (3rd ed., pp. 314-330). New York: Appleton-Century-Crofts.Skinner, B. F. (1974). *About behaviorism.* New York: Knopf.

Skinner, B. F. (1978). *Reflections on behaviorism and society.* Englewood Cliffs, NJ: Prentice-Hall.

Skinner, B. F. (1980). *Notebooks.* Englewood Cliffs, NJ: Prentice-Hall.

Skinner, B. F. (1984*a*). Selection by consequences. *The Behavioral and Brain Sciences*, 7, 477-481 and 502-510.

Skinner, B. F. (1984*b*). Methods and theories in the experimental analysis of behavior. *The Behavioral and Brain Sciences*, 7, 511-546 and 541-546.

Skinner, B. F. (1985). Cognitive science and behaviorism. *British Journal of Psychology*, 76, 291-301.

Skinner, B. F. (1987). *Upon further reflection.* Englewood Cliffs, NJ: Prentice-Hall.

Skinner, B. F. (1987*a*). Why we are not acting to save the world. In B. F. Skinner, *Upon further reflection* (pp. 1-14). Englewood Cliffs, NJ: Prentice-Hall.

Skinner, B. F. (1988). Preface to *The Behavior of Organisms. Journal of the Experimental Analysis of Behavior*, 50, 355-358.

Skinner, B. F. (1989). The origins of cognitive thought. *American Psychologist*, 44, 13-18.

Smith, G. A. (1986). Observer drift: A drifting definition. *The Behavior Analyst*, 9, 127-128.

Smith, L. D. (1986). *Behaviorism and logical positivism: A reassessment of the alliance.* Stanford, CA: Stanford University Press.

Stein, D. G., & Rosen, J. J. (1974). *Motivation and emotion.* New York: Macmillan.

Stellar, E. (1974). The physiology of motivation. In D. G. Stein & J. J. Rosen (Eds.). *Motivation and emotion* (pp. 5-25). New York: Macmillan.

Stewart, I. (1989). *Does God play dice?.* Oxford: Basil Blackwell.

Storms, M. D. (1973). Videotape and the attribution process: Reversing actors' and observers' points of view. *Journal of Personality and Social Psychology*, 27, 165-175.

Todd, J. T., & Morris, E. K. (1983). Misconception and miseducation: Presentations of radical behaviorism in psychology textbooks. *The Behavior Analyst*, 6, 153-160.

Tolman, E. C. (1922). A new formula for behaviorism. *Psychological Review*, 29, 44-53.

References

Tolman, E. C. (1948). Cognitive maps in rats and men. *Psychological Review*, 55, 189-208.

Tolman, E. C. (1959). Principles of purposive behavior. In S. Koch (Ed.), *Psychology: A study of a science* (Vol. 2, pp. 92-157). New York: McGraw Hill.

Vygotsky, L. S. (1962). *Thought and language.* Cambridge, MA: MIT Press.

Watkins, M. J. (1990). Mediationism and the obfuscation of memory. *American Psychologist*, 45, 328-335.

Watson, J. B. (1913). Psychology as the behaviorist views it. *Psychological Review*, 20, 158-177.

Watson, J. B. (1919). *Psychology from the standpoint of a behaviorist.* Philadelphia: J. B. Lippincott Company.

Watson, J. B. (1924). *Behaviorism.* New York: Norton.

Webster's third new international dictionary of the English Language, unabridged. (1986). Chicago: Encyclopaedia Britannica.

Westby, G. (1966). Psychology today: problems and directions. *Bulletin of the British Psychological Society*, 19, 1-19.

Whorf, B. L. (1956). *Language, thought, and reality.* Cambridge, MA: MIT Press.

Wolfle, D. (1959). Preface. In S. Koch (Ed.), *Psychology: A study of a science* (Vol. 2, pp. v-vii). New York: McGraw-Hill.

Woolgar, S. (1988). *Science: The very idea.* Sussex, England: Ellis Horwood.

Zimbardo, P. G. (1992). *Psychology and life* (13th ed.). New York: Harper Collins.

Index

Index

Clinical psychology, 147, 191
Clinician, 118
Clocks, 14, 102, 110
Cognitions, 4, 8, 39, 193, 199, 203
Cognitive psychology, 116, 147, 153, 160, 192-195, 198, 203
Cognitive science, 26
Cohen, M. R., 106-107, 112
Cohen, R. S., 128
Columbia, 184
Commerce, 138
Common-sense, 106, 112
Communication, 23, 110
Communicators, 36
Community, 8, 18, 23, 46-48, 58, 80, 188-189, 199
Competence, 165, 167, 169, 171
Complexities, 13, 101, 103-105, 111, 156, 158
Computer, 142, 154, 160
Computing, 96
Concepts, 1, 6-7, 13, 19-20, 25, 29, 36-37, 59, 67, 69-72, 74-75, 80-82, 95-96, 98, 100, 105, 112-113, 117, 120, 123, 125, 127, 133, 135, 137-138, 140, 145, 147, 149, 156, 158-172, 177-182, 184-185, 187-188, 193, 197-198, 201, 206
Conception, 13, 16, 38-39, 76, 92, 98, 105-107, 112-113, 161, 184, 201-203, 205-206
Conceptualization, 19, 44, 75, 161
Conditioned responses, 15, 182
Conditioning, 11-12, 68, 139, 174-176, 178, 183
Conditions, 40, 46, 50, 63, 88, 99, 102, 104, 110, 120, 139, 191-192, 196, 201, 207-208
Conduct, 6-7, 46, 115, 121, 205
Confidence, 19, 47, 78-79, 81, 90, 92, 100
Confirmation, 56, 61-62, 140-141
Conflicts 97-98, 152-153
Confrontation, 5
Connections 11, 105, 107, 109, 113, 130, 146, 177, 190-191, 203
Consciousness, 15-16, 184, 188-189, 197
Consequences, 19, 38, 47, 49-51, 55-56, 58, 59, 64-65, 78-80, 98-100, 105, 108, 114, 117-123, 128, 139, 152, 183, 193, 201-202, 208
Consistencies, 26
Construction, 67, 136-137, 140, 191, 208
Constructs, 7, 20-21, 105, 108-110, 114, 121, 127, 129, 131-132, 149, 156, 159-160, 168, 171, 173, 192, 197-198, 202, 208
Context, 8-9, 17, 22, 26, 32-33, 41, 57, 65, 67, 69, 86, 90-91, 105, 127, 129, 134, 137-139, 141-142, 147, 149-150, 152-154, 156-160, 164, 167-169, 171, 177, 179-180, 182-183, 188, 193, 195-196, 198-199, 201, 208
Contiguity, 116, 118
Contingencies, 18, 30-31, 66, 69, 84-85, 99, 120, 122, 165-167, 183, 193-194, 199
Continuity, 10, 199
Continuum, 196, 198-199
Control, 19, 26, 40, 46, 48, 52, 82-84, 86-89, 92, 145, 155, 177, 179, 182, 185, 191, 204-205
Controlled, 84, 90, 101, 180, 192
Controlling variables, 17, 33, 39, 41, 82, 166
Convention, 36, 38, 43, 48, 77, 79-80, 104, 160
Conventional, 19, 96

Index

Index

Index

Index

May, R., 8
Mead, G. H., 189
Meanings, 23, 29, 31-32, 52, 79, 81, 109, 114, 127, 136, 142, 162, 196, 202
Measure, 1, 24, 47, 73, 84, 87, 163, 166
Measurement, 3, 51, 73-74, 83, 186, 190
Measurer, 74
Mechanics, 9, 3, 12, 23, 108-109, 112, 114, 131, 137, 204
Mechanisms, 11, 19, 49, 57-58, 69-70, 96, 99, 131-132, 141-142, 149, 202, 204, 206
Mechanist, 131
Mechanistic theories, 17, 20
Mechanistic thinking, 16, 18, 20, 96, 110, 131, 141-142, 145, 172, 203
Media, 131, 133
Mediate, 15, 20, 64, 119, 174, 195, 197
Mediating entities, 19, 58, 131, 159-160, 166-168, 171-172, 202
Mediating processes, 65
Mediating variable, 162-163, 171
Mediation, 199
Mediators, 190, 198
Mediums, 28, 127, 131, 133, 145, 172
Memory, 4, 35, 39, 50-51, 57, 98, 116, 146-147, 153-160, 172, 190, 202
Men, 190, 195
Menger, K., 131
Mental elements, operations, processes, states, 13-14, 26, 96, 116, 146, 151, 154, 184, 193, 202
Mental life, 28, 184
Mentalistic statements, 29
Mentality, 13
Merchant, C., 2, 14-16, 110

Mesomorph, 147
Metals, 55, 57, 85-86
Metaphors, 14-16, 20, 30-32, 33, 37-39, 107-112, 115-117, 120, 123, 154, 156, 160, 200
Metaphysics, 1, 26
Meteor, 34
Methodological behaviorism, 186-187, 189, 202
Methodological package, 18, 48, 71, 76
Methodologists, 45, 67
Methodology, 3, 45, 59, 65-66, 68-69, 129, 142, 155, 184, 187, 196, 205-206
Methods, 6-7, 1, 3-7, 18-19, 21, 31, 45-46, 48, 52-53, 61-62, 67-69, 71-72, 83, 87, 91-92, 100, 108, 149, 173, 184-185, 187-188, 193, 202, 208
Mill, J. S., 63-64
Miller, E., 148
Mind, 5, 13-14, 16-17, 26, 28-29, 31-33, 44, 60, 97, 107, 138, 146, 148, 154, 178, 185-186, 194-195, 202, 208
Misrepresentations, 9, 141
Modes, 12, 15-16, 20-21, 27, 41-44, 70, 96, 115-117, 122-123, 129, 131-132, 135, 143, 150, 156, 1272, 197, 202
Models, 6, 14, 16, 19, 30, 78, 86, 88, 92, 98, 114, 120, 130-132, 136, 141-142, 146-148, 150-160, 172, 174, 185, 202
Momentum, 110, 115, 175
Money, 86, 165
Morgan, M. J., 170
Morris, E. K., 9
Morris, N., 154-156, 158
Motion, 82, 106, 108

Index

Index

Index

Index